I0803127

IMAGES
of America

GALAX

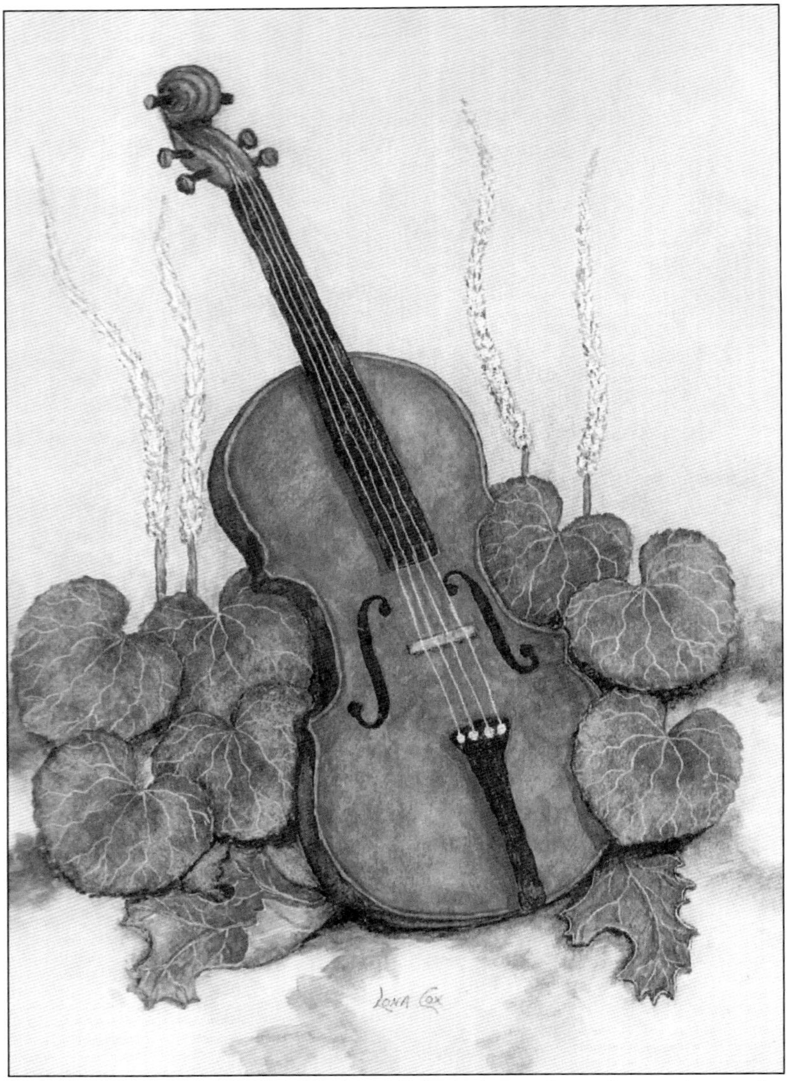

The city of Galax derives its name from the broad, shiny, heart-shaped green leaves that flourished on the hillsides above Chestnut Creek. The plants thrive in the cool, moist soil of the shady mountains and are ready for picking any time of the year except mid-March through May. Entire mountain families, known as "galackers," would take to the woods to pick the Galax leaves. During the early years, a good picker could pick 10,000 leaves in a day and received 25¢ for each 1,000 leaves tied in bundles of 25. Well-known Galax artist Lona Mae Cox has captured the spirit of the community by combining Galax leaves with a fiddle, which symbolizes the contribution Galax has made to the heritage of old-time mountain music. (Lona Mae Cox Collection.)

On the Cover: This undated photograph shows members of the Galax Fire Department in front of the Bluemont Hotel on North Main Street. Pictured from left to right are (first row) Walt Anderson, Ralph Todd, Walter Matthews, and Clarence Todd; (second row) Tom Trimble, unidentified, Bill Boaz, Garland Anderson, Emmon Todd, Dan Anderson, Badger Witherow, Gabe Lundy, Walter Elliott, Herman Webb, Jim Anderson, Sid Dotson, and George Callaway; (third row) Paul Phipps, Lance Todd, Fernoy Worrell, Roy Manning, and Lester Diamond. (Matthews Museum.)

IMAGES
of America

GALAX

John Nunn and Judith Nunn Alley

ARCADIA
PUBLISHING

ISBN 978-0-7385-8582-6

Published by Arcadia Publishing
Charleston, South Carolina

Printed in the United States of America

Library of Congress Control Number: 2009940725

For all general information contact Arcadia Publishing at:
Telephone 843-853-2070
Fax 843-853-0044
E-mail sales@arcadiapublishing.com
For customer service and orders:
Toll-Free 1-888-313-2665

Visit us on the Internet at www.arcadiapublishing.com

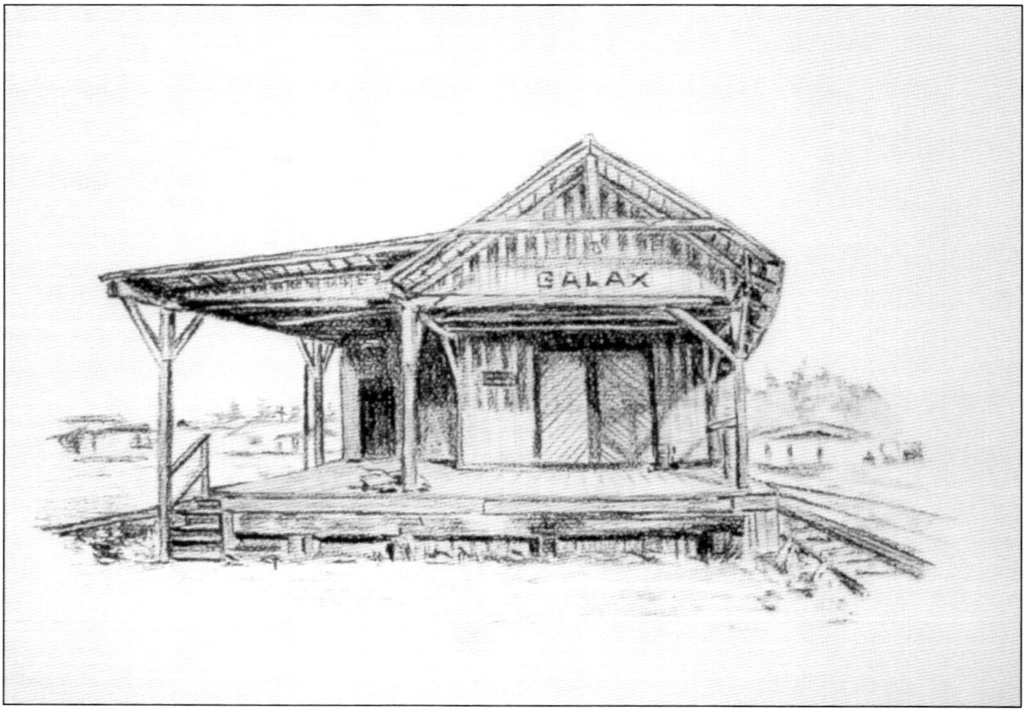

Well-known local artist Willard Gayheart has provided an excellent pencil drawing of the old Galax Norfolk and Western train depot. It is very appropriate that this has been included, because the railroad provided Galax with the necessary link to the outside world. (Willard Gayheart.)

Contents

ACKNOWLEDGMENTS

The journey for this book began many years ago when we both realized we loved history and old photographs. We have combined our mutual desire to preserve and document a photographic history of the early years of Galax for future generations. It became very apparent that time was critical, because the old photographs were rapidly disappearing through neglect, loss, or damage.

While our maternal family did not arrive in town until December 1927, we had the great fortune of being born in Galax and growing up during the best part of the 20th century. We lived on East Center Street in the former home of Lelia Burt Nuckolls Waugh, the original owner of the old Waugh Hotel on the corner of Main and Center Streets. Maybe that is when the history bug bit us.

As we sorted through the photographs to use for the book we not only realized we were missing records of some important events, but that we were not going to be able to use every single photograph that was so graciously loaned to us. We will be eternally grateful to each and every one of you who loaned photographs, old newspapers, booklets, and documents to us. A special thank-you goes to Odell Hampton, Mary Guynn, Skip Henderson, Penny Kyle, Harvey Neff, Louise Pollard, Jewel Melton, Etoile Morton, Elwood Newman (EN), Moe Weaver, Irene Alderman, and Ruby Lindamood (RL), who shared their memories with us. Our deep appreciation to the major contributors of photographs: *Galax Gazette* (GG); Laura Bryant at the Galax Library (GPL), who loaned us the centennial collection of photographs; Jerry Wolford (JW); Nicky Felts (NF); and Pat Bolt (PHB). To Tony Burcham and Joyce Sawyers at the Matthews Museum (MM), who dismantled their photo boards more than once; Dennis Morgan at M. C. Imaging, who provided us with his expertise; and Bob Welsh of Welsh Computers, for keeping our equipment running. C. L. Martin's history of Galax was a great source of information.

Our mother, Beatrice Messer Nunn, passed along her love of books, history, and photography to us, and our grandfather John Messer Sr. shared his belief that one should give back to their community. So this photograph history of early Galax is our special gift to the town we love. A Web site, www.galaxscrapbook.com, has also been created to share other written information about the history of Galax.

—John J. Nunn and Judith Nunn Alley

INTRODUCTION

They were all shapes and sizes and came from all walks of life . . . they were bankers, farmers, Civil War veterans, merchants, doctors, teachers, ministers, lawyers, builders, and everyday country folks. They were friends and neighbors from the surrounding counties in Virginia and North Carolina. Most importantly, they each possessed imagination, hopes, and dreams for a prosperous, productive, and secure life for themselves, their children, and the children that would come after them. Who were these men? They were the men of vision who banded together to create a new town in the mountains of southwest Virginia now known as Galax.

These founding fathers selected a wide expanse of meadowland, with Chestnut Creek running through the middle. The county line of Grayson and Carroll runs through the chosen site from the southeast to the northwest. It is surrounded by rolling hills, an ample supply of timber, and sits at an altitude of 2,500 feet on a valley-like plateau, which runs south all the way from the Potomac River deep into North Carolina. The Appalachian Trail runs down Main Street. The Thomas Roberts family once owned the land that became Galax. It was part of a grant of 800 acres given to James Buchanan in 1756 by England's King George.

The men who laid the cornerstone of the town's strong foundation included J. P. Carico, J. B. Waugh, B. F. Calaway, T. L. Felts, R. E. Jones, A. C. Painter, R. L. Dickerson, J. K. Caldwell, W. K. Early, the Ward brothers—Marvin, Monroe, and Frazier, J. W. Bolen, M. L. Bishop, M. T. Blessing, J. K. Kapp, W. F. Murphy, G. F. Carr, and numerous members of the Anderson, Nuckolls, Witherow, Matthews, Roberts, and Vass families. They set the examples, constructed the buildings, paved the streets, and led the way for those who followed.

The second wave of town fathers included B. D. Beamer, Floyd Landreth, John Messer Sr., T. G. Vaughan, Nathan Potolsky, Glenn Pless, B. C. Vaughan, Warren Giersch, Earl Nuckolls, Joe Parsons, R. V. Morris, Virgil Cox, Hubert White Sr., Gordon Felts, Cliff Kyle, Robert Waddell, Jack Matthews, J. T. Pollard, and W. M. Jones Sr.

None of these men were out for glory or to make a name for themselves. You will rarely find schools, streets, or buildings named in their honor. In fact, you would have to read the old, dusty minutes of church, civic, school, and business meetings to find their names. All these men had one common goal. They wanted to create a prosperous town that would be the best place to raise their children. Were they successful? Just ask any descendent of these men who had the great fortune to grow up in Galax, if their father, grandfather, or great grandfather made the right decisions, set the right examples, or provided the right guidance, and one will find an answer.

These men built a firm foundation for Galax based on the love of God, country, and their fellow man. By their examples, they showed the next generations the importance of close-knit families, hard work, honesty, integrity, and patriotism.

In 1956, local historian Ed Cox wrote that J. P. Carico, a native of Stevens Creek, was perhaps the most successful promoter of enterprises this section has produced. Carico not only helped to establish industry in the town of Fries, but he set his eyes on something even grander . . . to create an entirely new community. He convinced the railroad to extend tracks from the main line in Pulaski to the site on Chestnut Creek that would become Galax.

The first building in town was the small structure for the Grayson Real Estate Company, located on the west side of North Main Street. J. H. Kapp built the first family residence, and Lelia Nuckolls Waugh owned the first hotel, located on Main and Center Streets. B. F. Calaway became the first mayor when the town was incorporated in 1906. The first town council consisted of Elbert F. Wright, Dr. J. K. Caldwell, E. C. Williams, M. L. Bishop, J. H. Kapp, and Dr. J. W. Bolen. The first school was conducted on the second floor of R. E. Jones and Son. Jones was also the first undertaker, as well as the first postmaster. G. F. Carr was the first principal of Galax High School. The Presbyterians built the first church, located on the corner of Center and Jefferson Streets. The Ward brothers built the first movie theater in town in 1906. It was located on the second floor of their business on the east side of North Main Street and had only been opened for a few months when the building burned to the ground. Galax was home to 600 residents when the first Galax Agricultural Fair was held in September 1908.

After the town suffered several devastating fires that destroyed major portions of Main Street businesses, the mayor, town council, and citizens of Galax called a meeting. They all agreed that there was a need for a fire department and a town water system. Residents had fought the fires using the bucket-brigade system. The water resources at that time were hand-pump wells located at the Central Hotel on South Main Street and the Waugh Hotel on North Main Street. Citizens who built their own homes in residential areas owned their own hand-pump wells. The first Galax Volunteer Fire Department was organized in 1912. Through the efforts of the citizens, a reservoir was constructed, water lines were laid along the streets to supply water to homes, and fire hydrants were in place by 1914.

The 1920 federal census indicated that the population of Galax had increased to 1,700 residents. In 1922, Galax's charter was amended and adopted to have a town manager form of government approved by the Commonwealth of Virginia. I. G. Vass was appointed as the first town manager. Under his directions, major improvements were made. In 1923, the town began grading streets; laying storm drains, water, and sewer lines; and contracting sidewalks. The first street to be paved was Main Street, from East Stuart Drive to the entrance to the fairgrounds. Another project was the installation of a modern water filtration system. The new waterworks plant began operation in late 1924.

From the laying of the first railroad tracks, auctioning lots, and realizing the importance of a steady payroll, these men set about building factories, churches, schools, and businesses that would allow this small community to grow into the business center for the twin counties. By the 1950s, Galax was home to six furniture factories, a mirror plant, Carnation Milk, Coca-Cola Bottling Company, Clover Creamery, a major lumber company, at least four textile companies, and two large department stores. The success of these companies was largely due to the fact that most of them were locally owned. The owners, managers, and employees attended the same churches, shopped at the same stores, banked at the same banks, and possessed a healthy respect for each other.

Only a personal visit to Galax can convey the full strength of the quality of life, the wealth of possibility in its environment, the beauty of its surroundings, and the high quality of its residents.

One

Scenes

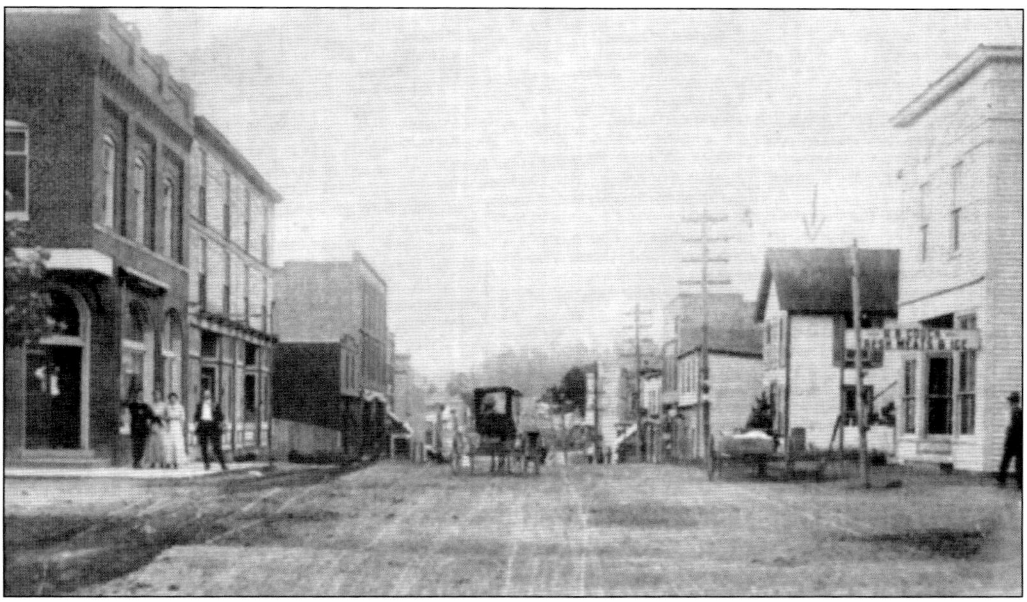

This is an early photograph of Main Street looking south. On the left is the First National Bank, which later became city hall when the bank moved to the corner of Main and Grayson Streets. On the right is a building erected by Dr. J. K. Caldwell and his associates. The storefront was home to several businesses over the years. The rest of the building was used as medical offices. (JJN.)

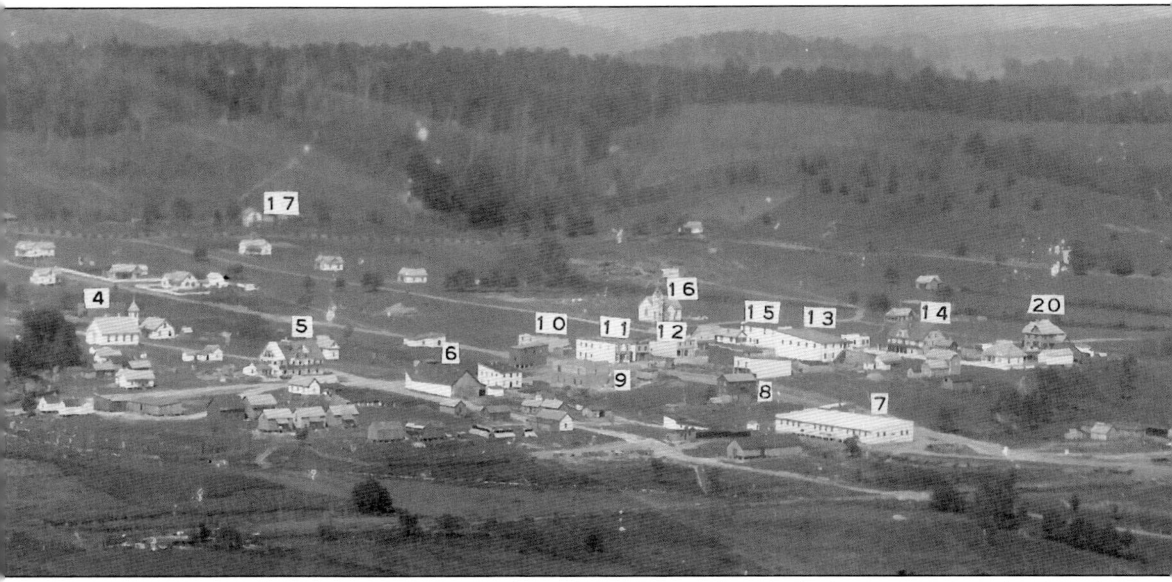

This is an early panoramic view of Galax. The numbers identify the locations. Note that Mt. Airy Street on the plat map on the following page was changed to Main Street, and Main Street was changed to Center Street. Identified are 4. Missionary Baptist Church: Lot 1 and 2, Block 17; 5. Hotel Central: Lot 1, Block 16; 6. Bishop Livery Stable: Lot 4, Block 4; 7. Blair Grocery: on Depot and East Grayson Streets; 8. Blair Bank: Lot 8 or 9, Block 1; 9. J. B. Waugh and Son: Lot 1, Block 1; 10. Galax Drug Company: Lot 9, Block 14; 11. R. E. Jones and Son: Lot 10, Block 14; 12. Galax Hardware: Lot 7, Block 14; 13. First National Bank: Lot 1, Block 5; 14. Waugh Hotel: Lot 1, Block 6; 15. Crystal Drugstore: Lot 1, Block 14; 16. Presbyterian church: Lot 1 and 2, Block 20; 17. Home of Thomas Roberts: Northeast of Blocks 21 and 22; 19. N&W railroad depot: East end of Grayson Street; and 20. Home of W. K. Early: Lot 10, Block 6. (RL.)

The Grayson Real Estate Company was formed in 1903 and purchased 375 acres from T. F. Roberts. They hired C. L. Demott of Lynchburg to draft a plat map indicating lot and block numbers and streets. After advertising the sale, the auction was held on December 17, 1903. The most frequent comment heard that day was, "Why all these wide streets and sidewalks? The town will never grow to where the street cars will be needed; it's just a waste of good land." (GGA.)

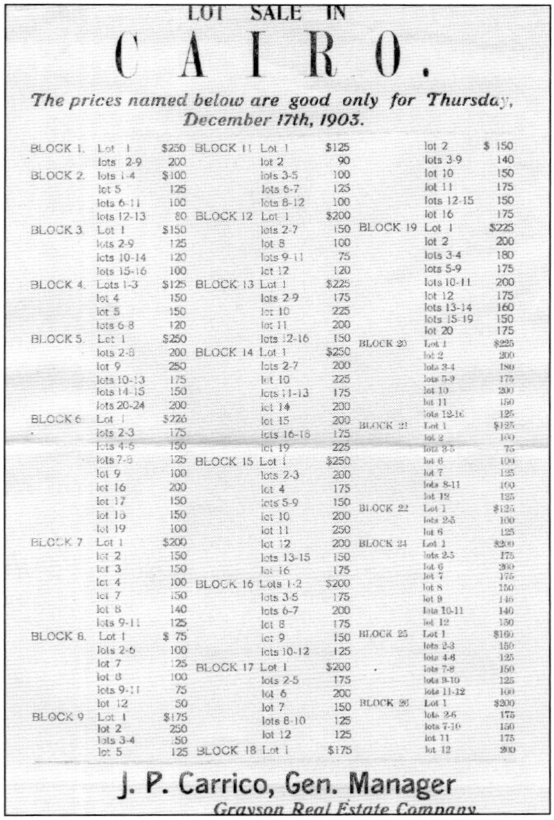

LOT SALE IN

CAIRO.

The prices named below are good only for Thursday, December 17th, 1903.

BLOCK 1.	Lot 1	$250
	lots 2-9	200
BLOCK 2.	lots 1-4	$100
	lot 5	125
	lots 6-11	100
	lots 12-13	80
BLOCK 3.	Lot 1	$150
	lots 2-9	125
	lots 10-14	120
	lots 15-16	100
BLOCK 4.	Lots 1-3	$125
	lot 4	150
	lot 5	150
	lots 6-8	120
BLOCK 5.	Lot 1	$250
	lots 2-8	200
	lot 9	250
	lots 10-13	175
	lots 14-15	150
	lots 20-24	200
BLOCK 6.	Lot 1	$226
	lots 2-3	175
	lots 4-6	150
	lots 7-8	125
	lot 9	100
	lot 16	200
	lot 17	150
	lot 18	150
	lot 19	100
BLOCK 7.	Lot 1	$200
	lot 2	150
	lot 3	150
	lot 4	100
	lot 7	150
	lot 8	140
	lots 9-11	125
BLOCK 8.	Lot 1	$ 75
	lots 2-6	100
	lot 7	125
	lot 8	100
	lots 9-11	75
	lot 12	50
BLOCK 9.	Lot 1	$175
	lot 2	250
	lots 3-4	150
	lot 5	125
BLOCK 11	Lot 1	$125
	lot 2	90
	lots 3-5	100
	lots 6-7	125
	lots 8-12	100
BLOCK 12	Lot 1	$200
	lots 2-7	150
	lot 8	100
	lots 9-11	75
	lot 12	120
BLOCK 13	Lot 1	$225
	lots 2-9	175
	lot 10	225
	lot 11	200
	lots 12-16	150
BLOCK 14	Lot 1	$250
	lots 2-7	200
	lot 10	225
	lots 11-13	175
	lot 14	200
	lot 15	200
	lots 16-18	175
	lot 19	225
BLOCK 15	Lot 1	$250
	lots 2-3	200
	lot 4	175
	lots 5-9	150
	lot 10	200
	lot 11	250
	lot 12	200
	lots 13-15	150
	lot 16	175
BLOCK 16	Lots 1-2	$200
	lots 3-5	175
	lots 6-7	200
	lot 8	175
	lot 9	150
	lots 10-12	125
BLOCK 17	Lot 1	$200
	lots 2-5	175
	lot 6	200
	lot 7	150
	lots 8-10	125
	lot 12	125
BLOCK 18	Lot 1	$175
	lot 2	$ 150
	lots 3-9	140
	lot 10	150
	lot 11	175
	lots 12-15	150
	lot 16	175
BLOCK 19	Lot 1	$225
	lot 2	200
	lots 3-4	180
	lots 5-9	175
	lots 10-11	200
	lot 12	175
	lots 13-14	160
	lots 15-19	150
	lot 20	175
BLOCK 20	Lot 1	$225
	lot 2	200
	lots 3-4	180
	lots 5-9	175
	lot 10	200
	lot 11	150
	lots 12-16	125
BLOCK 21	Lot 1	$125
	lot 2	100
	lots 3-5	75
	lot 6	100
	lot 7	125
	lots 8-11	100
	lot 12	125
BLOCK 22	Lot 1	$125
	lots 2-5	100
	lot 6	125
BLOCK 24	Lot 1	$200
	lots 2-5	175
	lot 6	200
	lot 7	175
	lot 8	150
	lot 9	145
	lots 10-11	140
	lot 12	150
BLOCK 25	Lot 1	$160
	lots 2-3	150
	lots 4-6	125
	lots 7-8	150
	lots 9-10	125
	lots 11-12	100
BLOCK 26	Lot 1	$200
	lots 2-6	175
	lots 7-10	150
	lot 11	175
	lot 12	200

J. P. Carrico, Gen. Manager

Grayson Real Estate Company.

This is the first plat map for Galax, dated December 1903. The Grayson Real Estate Company continued to develop and sell additional lots and blocks not shown on this original plat map. Ten years later, the town was described as a beautiful little city 2,500 feet up in the matchless blue skies of the Blue Ridge Mountains. (GGA.)

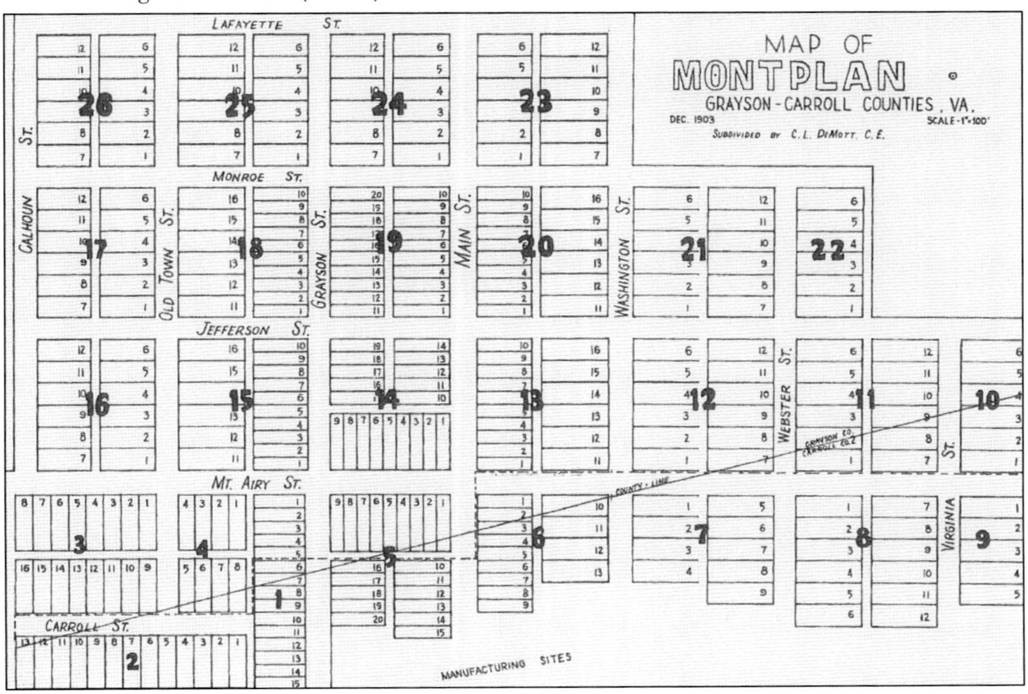

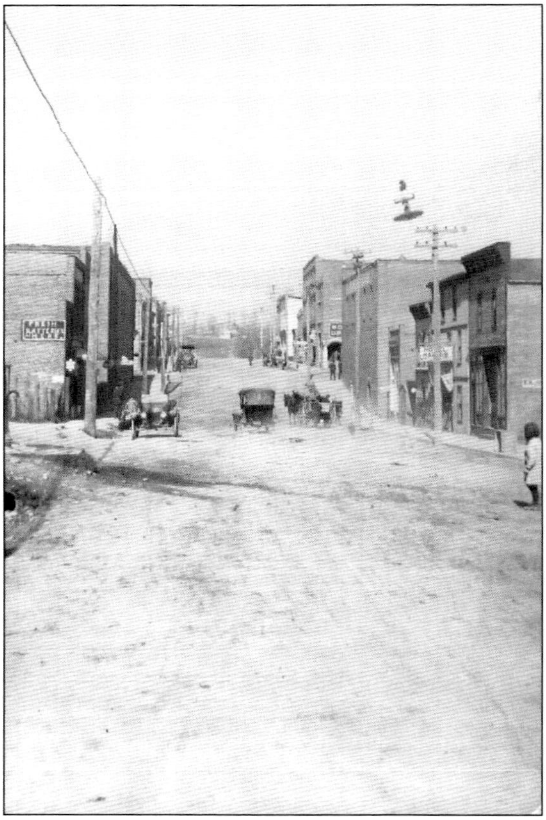

This is an early scene of Main Street looking north. It was taken before the town began grading and paving the streets in 1923. On the left is a hand-pump well near the Central Hotel and a sign for fresh batteries. At the far right, partially hidden behind a pole, is the sign for the Harris Hotel, which burned in 1911. The partial sign for Bolen Drugstore can also be seen farther up the street on the right. (James Ballard.)

Below is an undated photograph looking north on Main Street. The sidewalks are in place, and the street has been paved. At right, it shows that Globman's Department Store has not moved into its new location on the corner of Main and Oldtown Streets. (MM.)

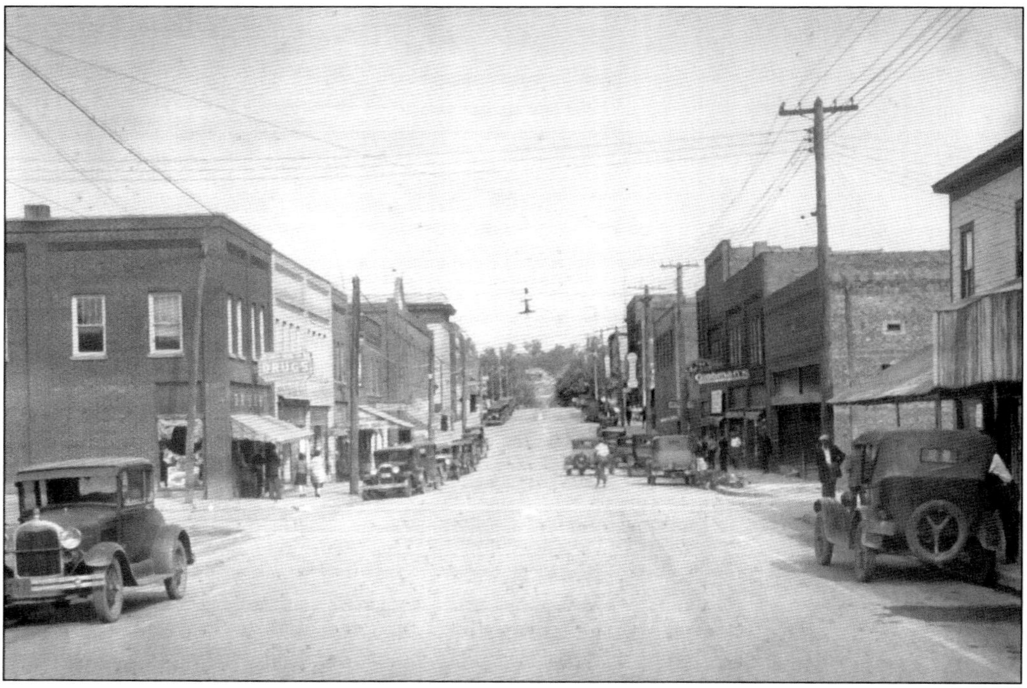

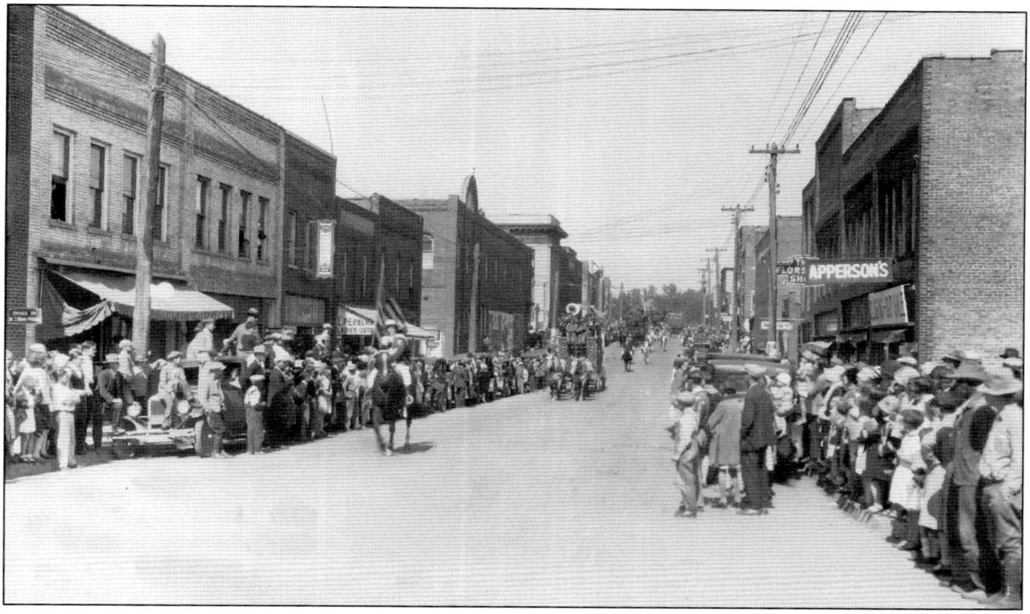

In the mid-1930s, the photographer was standing on South Main Street looking north when this photograph was taken of a parade. If one looks close, they will see a brass band sitting on top of the large wagon being pulled by a team of horses. Has the circus come to town? On the right are Apperson's and the Florsheim Shoe Shop. At left is a soda shop and Perelman's Ladies Shop. (GG.)

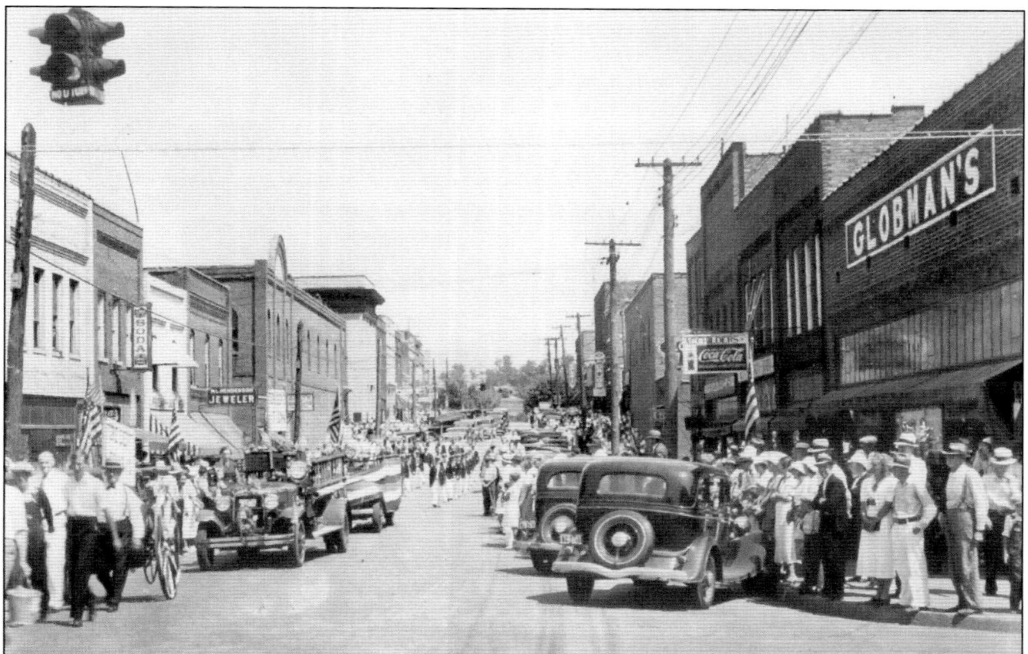

Everyone loves a parade, especially in Galax! The event would not be complete without one of its fine fire trucks participating. Note that Globman's Department Store has moved from its original location into its new building on the corner of Main and Oldtown Streets. (GG.)

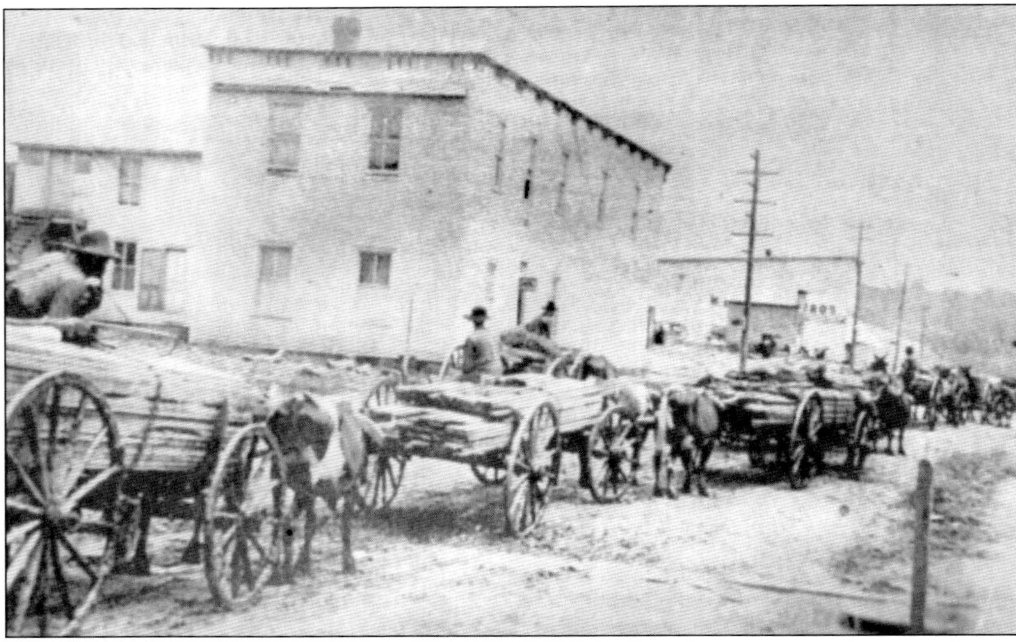

This 1905 photograph shows ox-drawn wagons going east on Grayson Street, bringing lumber into town. The large building on the left was Witherow's Drugstore. The First National Bank would later be built on this corner. The drugstore obtained ice from the frozen New River and stored it in the basement to use through the year at the soda fountain. (MM.)

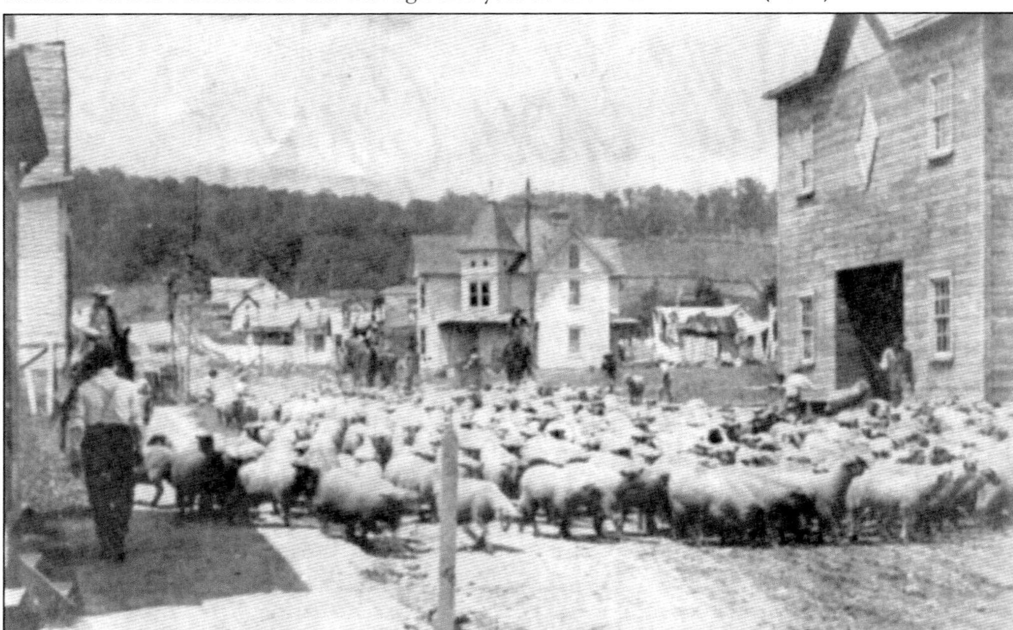

The streets of Galax were muddy and unpaved during the early years. While unsuitable for an afternoon stroll by ladies in long dresses, the sheep, horses, and other farm animals did not seem to mind the mud at all. Imagine the Whitley family sitting on their front porch and watching a large herd of sheep running past their home on the way to the market. (MM.)

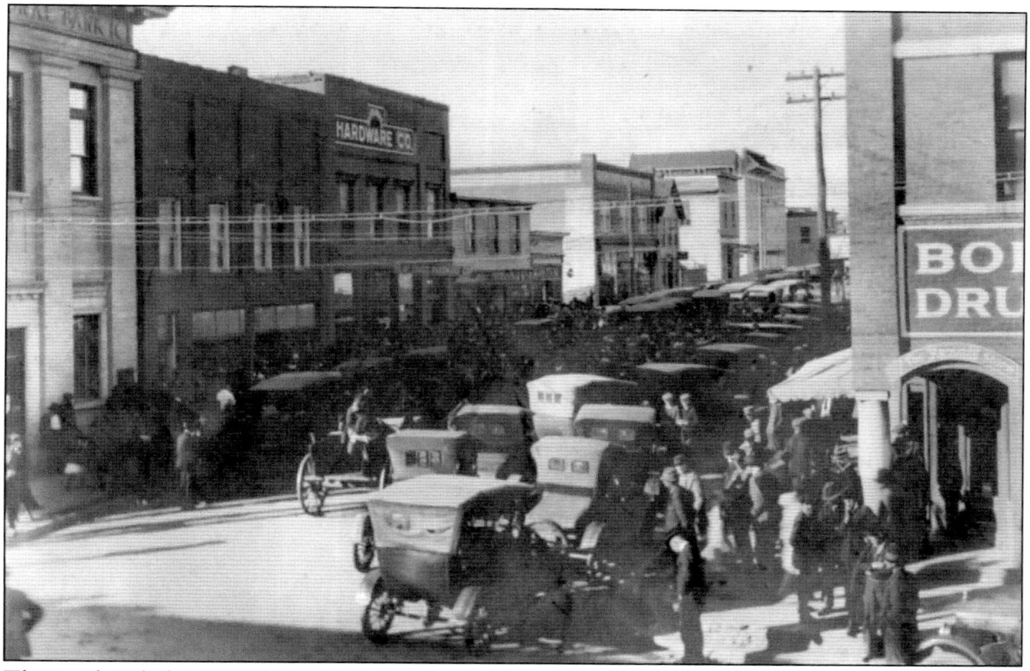

This undated photograph was taken at the intersection of Main and Grayson Streets. It appears that even though the town's population was still small, there seems to be an abundance of black cars on the street. (Susan Fackrell.)

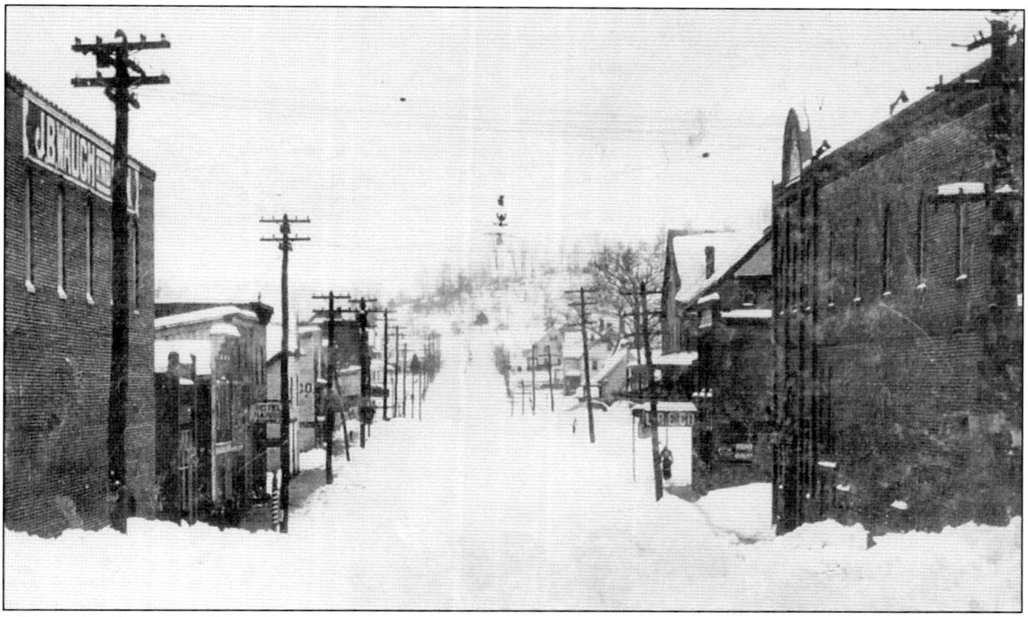

This is looking south at the intersection of Main and Grayson Streets. At left is the Harris Hotel, and at right is the new Matthew Hardware building. Records indicate that the Harris Hotel was one of the buildings that burned in 1911. Residents united to organize the Galax Volunteer Fire Department in 1912. Under all that snow is frozen mud because it would be another 11 years before the streets were paved. (Jewel Melton.)

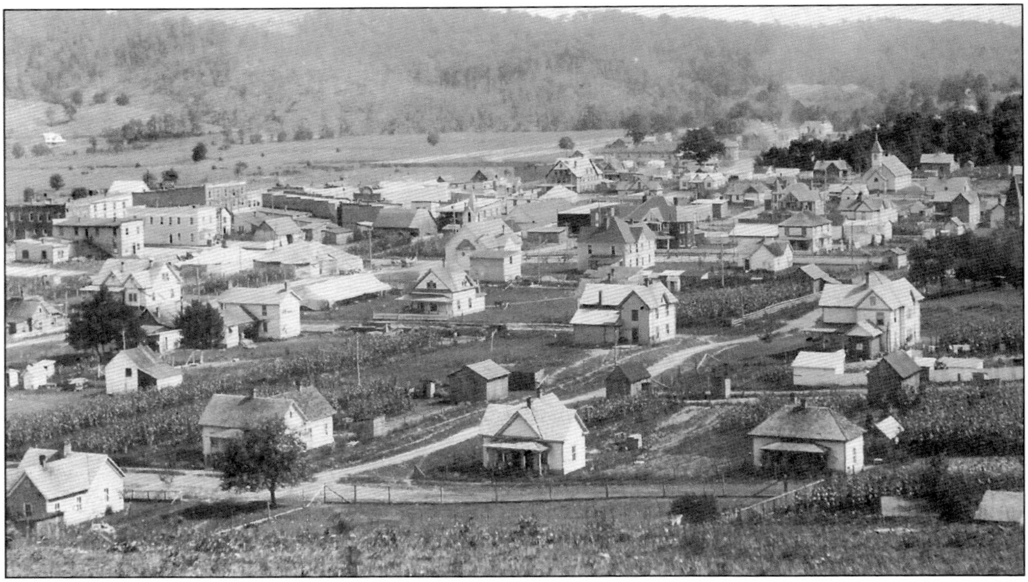

This is an excellent view of early Galax looking south from Fries Hill. The Central Hotel is visible at top center, directly left of the Missionary Baptist Church on the corner of Oldtown and Jefferson Streets. Monroe Street runs from north to south, with the large Vass-Robinson house at center right. At center left are Dr. J. K. Caldwell's building and the Ward brothers' brick building. The First Presbyterian Church of Galax is in the center. (Jewel Melton.)

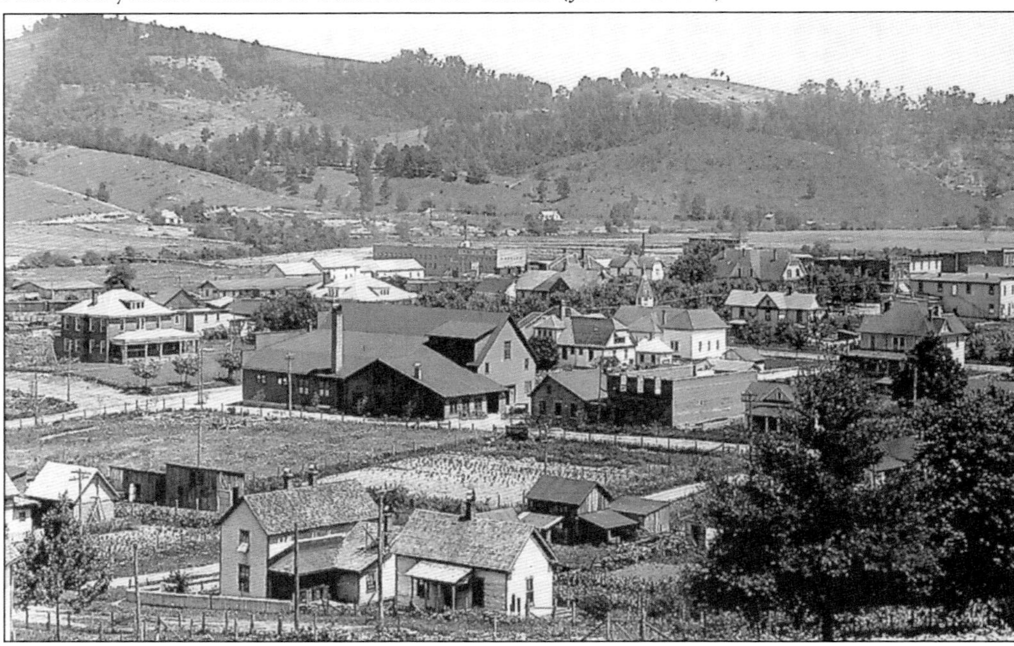

This is another north-to-south view of Galax. At center is the Twin County Livery Stable, next door to the new addition (with tall smokestack) that will become the Twin County Motor Company. The roofless building directly to the right is the company's garage under construction. South of the livery stable is the Bowie home, which was later moved to North Main Street to become the chamber of commerce office. (MM.)

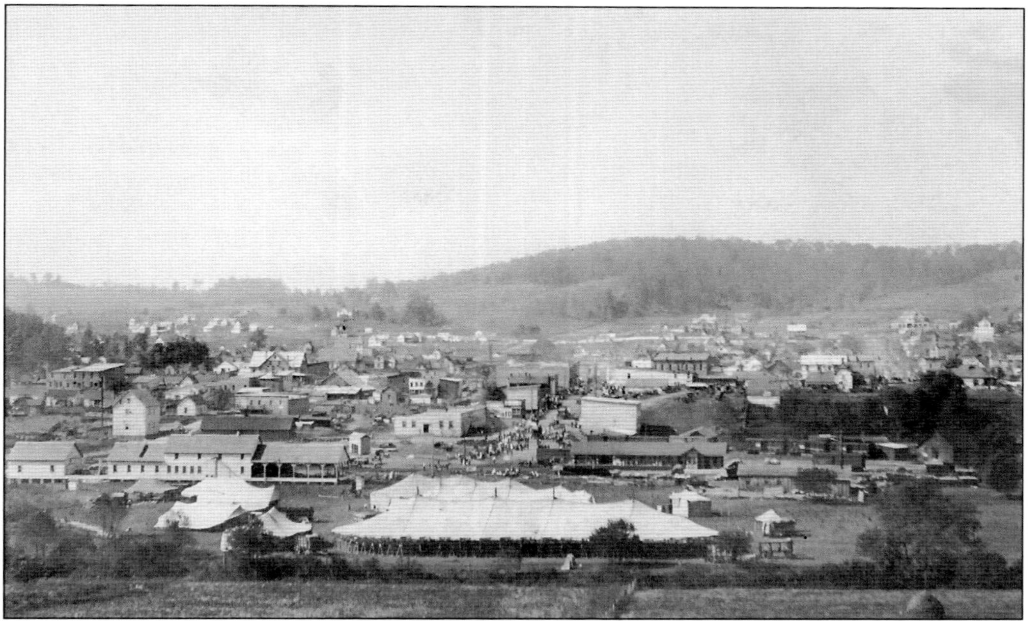

This is an undated photograph looking at Galax from the east toward the west. The purpose for the large tent at the bottom of the picture is unknown. It appears that a large group of people is making their way toward the tent. (Jewel Melton.)

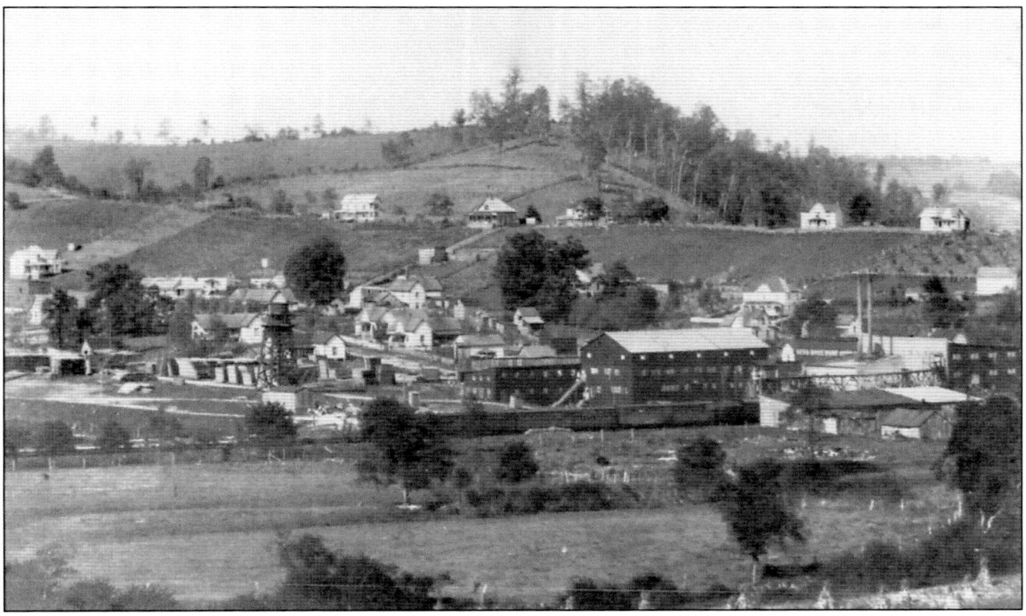

This is an excellent photograph of the first furniture factory built in town. The Galax Furniture and Lumber Company began business in 1906. However, it burned to the ground in 1907. It was rebuilt at the same location in 1908 but burned to the ground again in 1917. (James Ballard.)

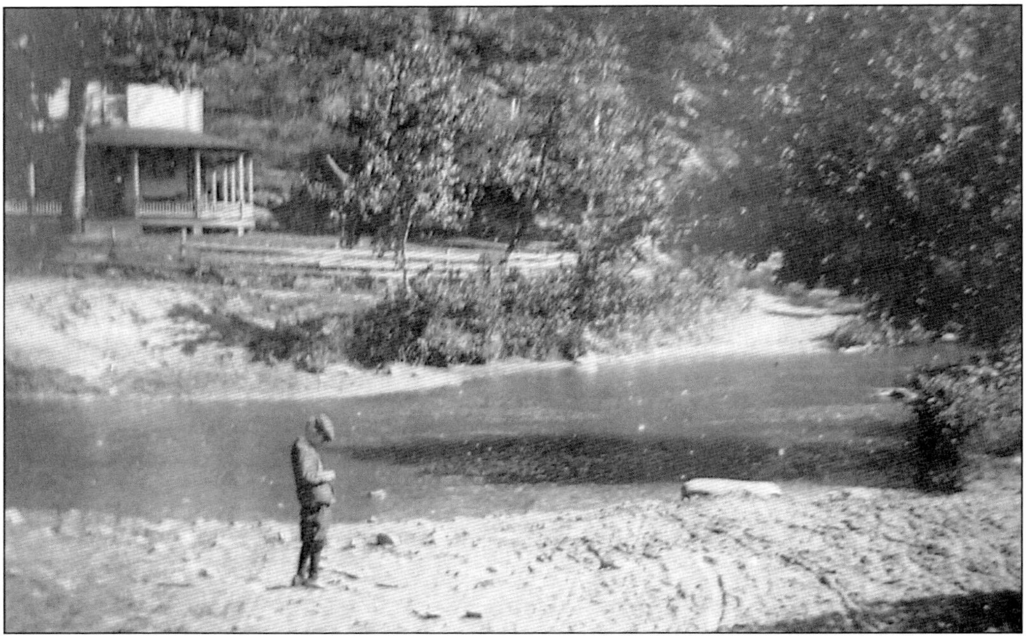

This undated photograph was taken near Robert Caldwell's home on the east side of Chestnut Creek. During the early days, the creek was shallow at that location. Tire tracks can be seen, indicating that people could drive their cars or wagons across the creek before the bridge was installed. (MM.)

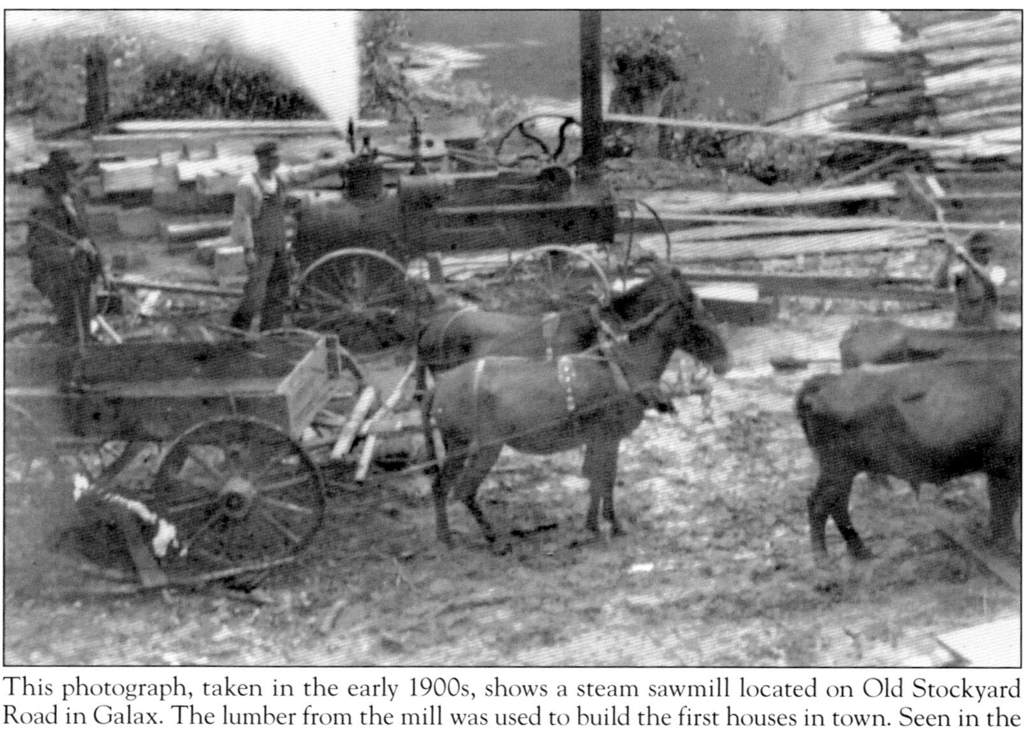

This photograph, taken in the early 1900s, shows a steam sawmill located on Old Stockyard Road in Galax. The lumber from the mill was used to build the first houses in town. Seen in the photograph, from left to right, are Floyd Leonard, Weart Leonard, and Walter Leonard. (MM.)

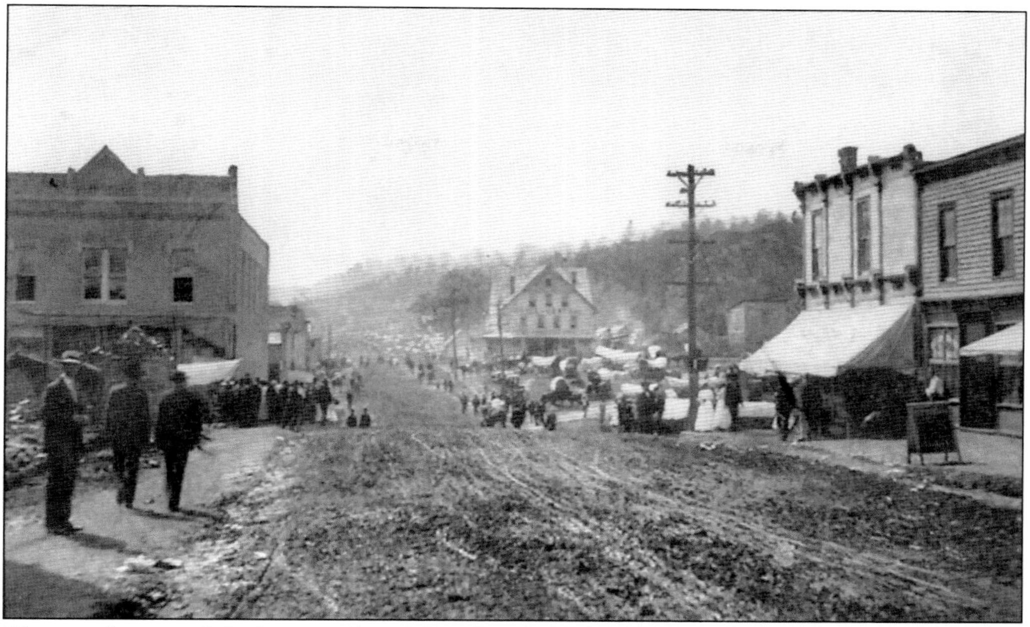

This is a photograph looking south on Main Street. Witherow's Drugstore and the R. E. Jones and Son building are at right. J. B. Waugh's store is at left. The Central Hotel in the background is at center. Notice the muddy street and the cluster of covered wagons in front of the hotel. (MM.)

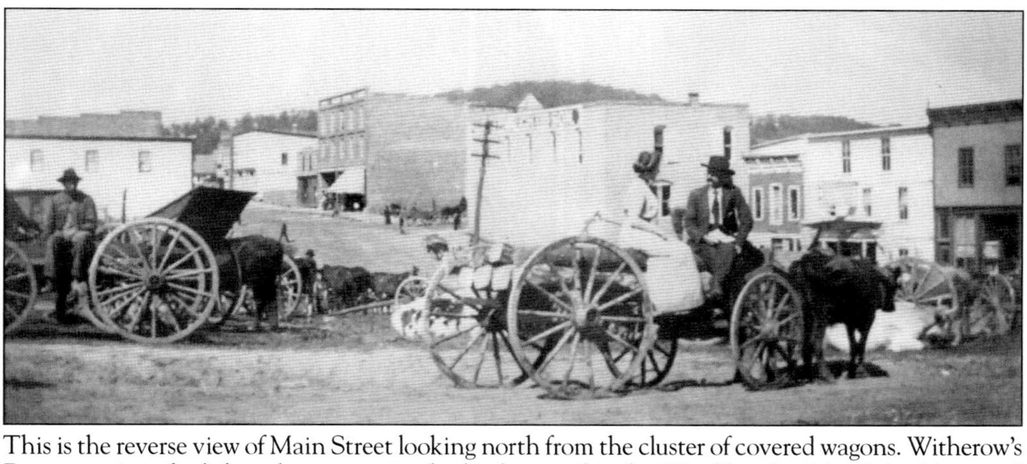

This is the reverse view of Main Street looking north from the cluster of covered wagons. Witherow's Drugstore is at far left and at center in the background is the Ward brother's brick building and J. B. Waugh's building. (GPL.)

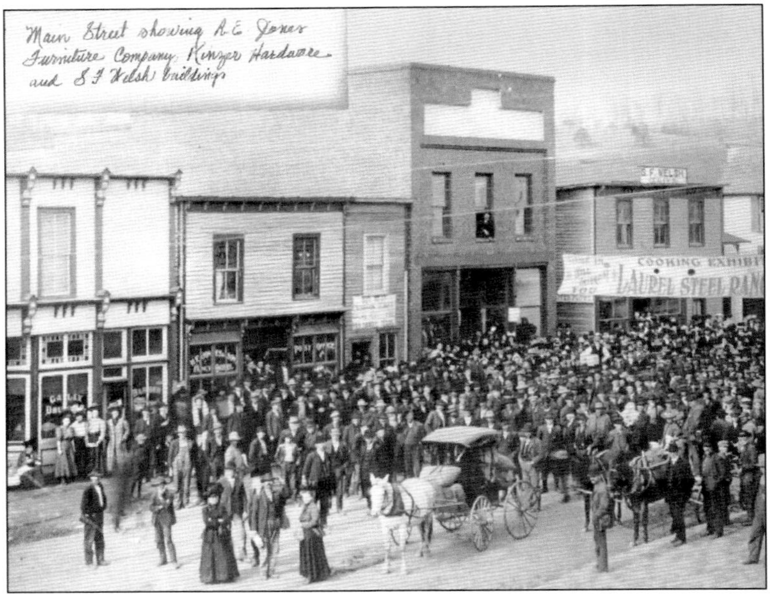

A cooking exhibition was held on Main Street in 1906. The first building at left is the Galax Drugstore, owned by the Witherow brothers. The next building is R. E. Jones and Son, which housed a post office, a school room, an undertaker business, and a fancy dry-goods store. Next to the Jones building is Kinzer Hardware (Galax Hardware) and the S. F. Welsh building. (MM.)

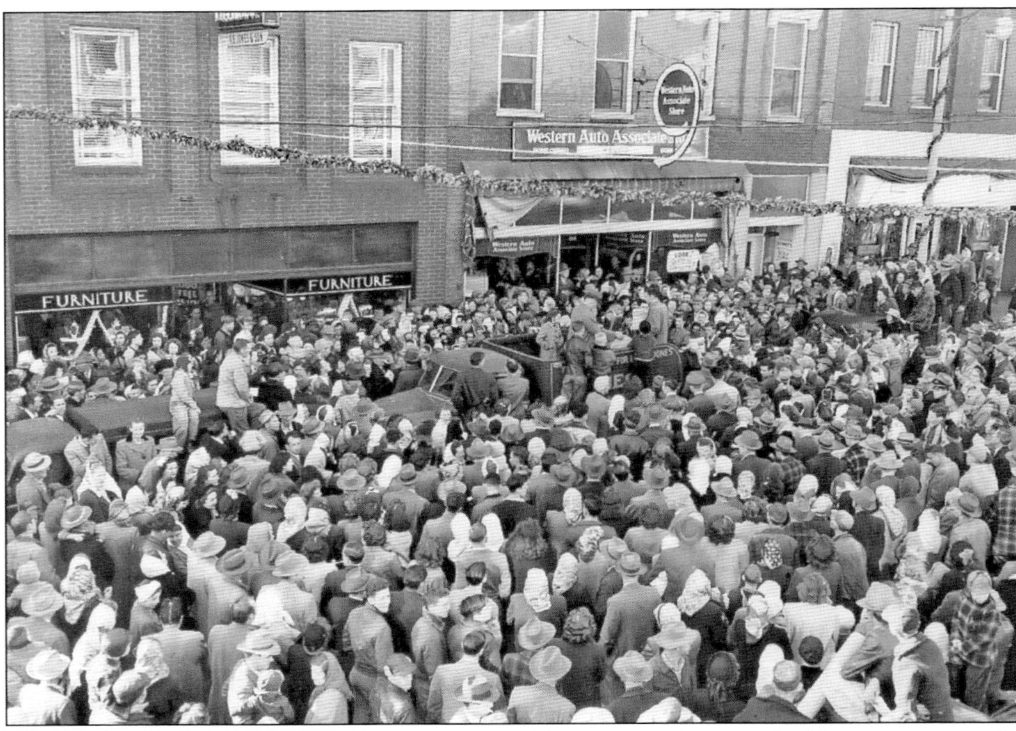

This photograph was taken on Main Street and focused on the same buildings shown in the cooking exhibition picture. This 1940s picture shows a large crowd gathered for a drawing conducted by R. E. Jones and Son. This building, as well as the rest of the buildings on the block, are now brick structures. (MM.)

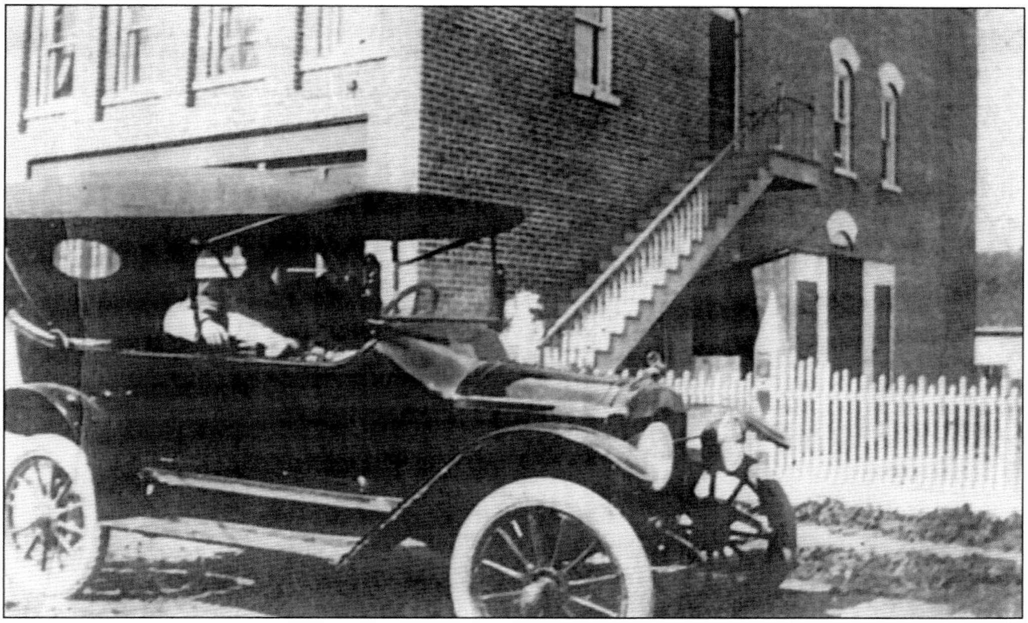

The location of this photograph is not known, and the people in the car are unidentified. The photograph was taken before 1923, because the street has not been paved. (MM.)

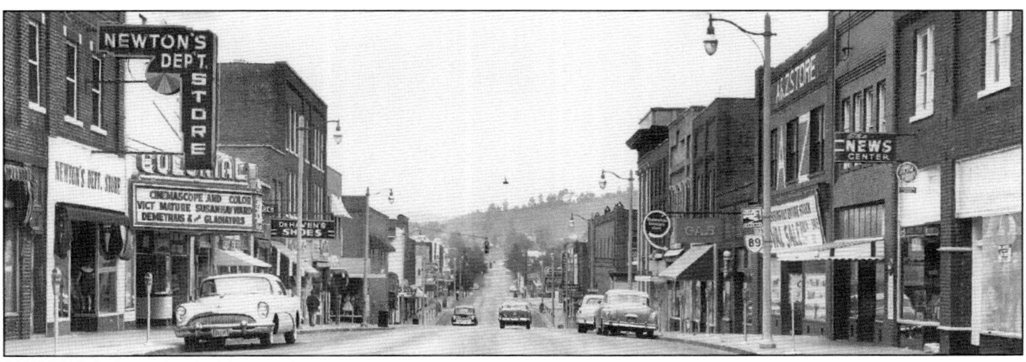

This photograph of Main Street looking south during the 1950s must have been taken early on a Sunday morning, the only time when the stores would be closed and the shoppers were still in bed or at church. (MM.)

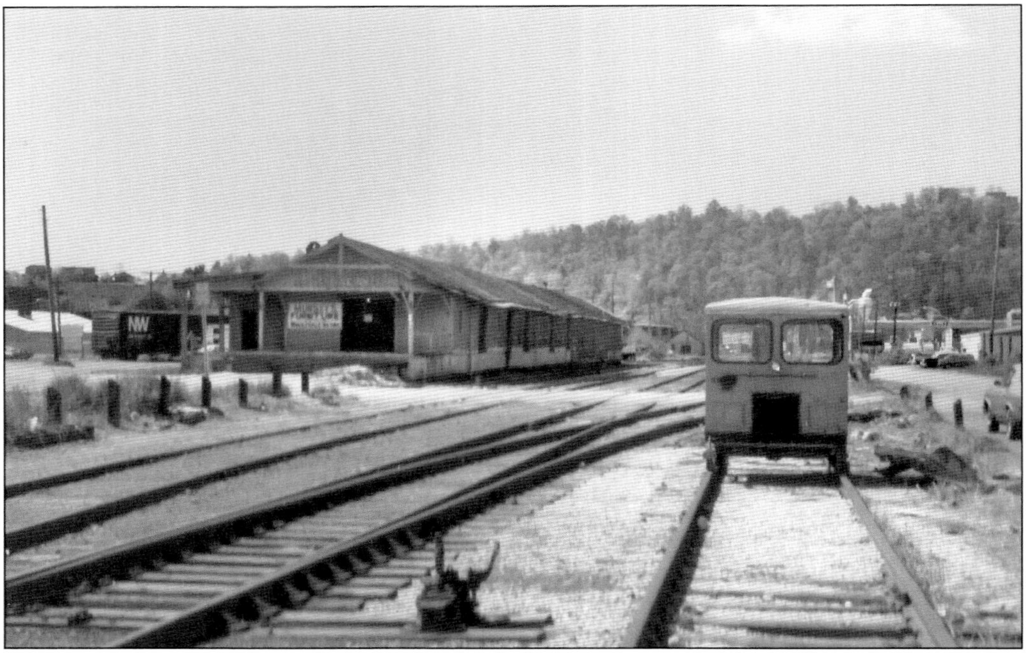

This is a rare photograph of the train depot on the east side of Galax. The depot and tracks disappeared in later years, and only the older generations have memories of the trains passing though town. (MM.)

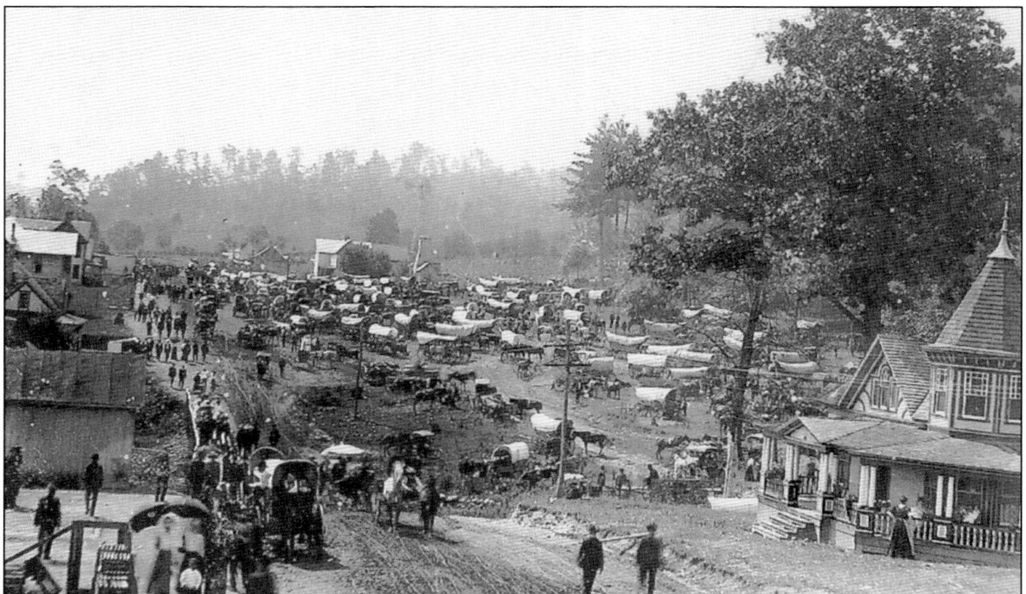

This is an excellent early photograph of South Main Street. The Collier home is on the right. All of the covered wagons may indicate that the owners are attending the Greater Galax Fair. Note how low the street becomes just past the house. A small creek was in this area and would later be placed underground when a large culvert system was installed before the street was paved. (MM.)

Two

PEOPLE

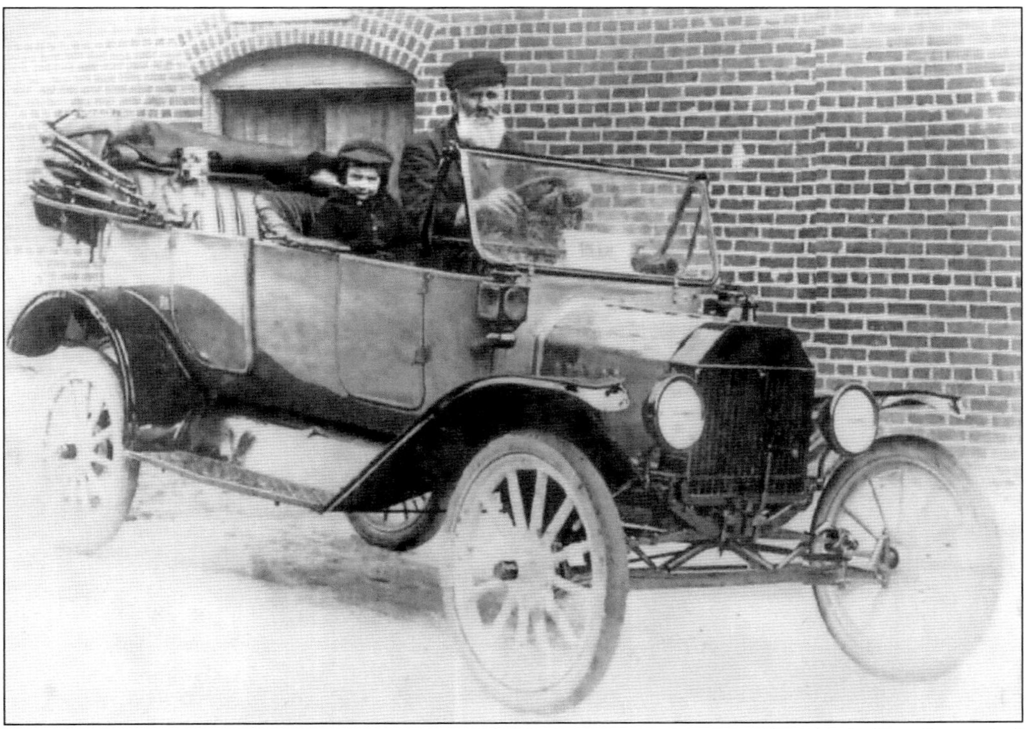

Dr. J. K. Caldwell and M. T. Blessing owned the first two cars in Galax. E. S. Lundy traded with Blessing for one of the Ford Model Ts and established the first taxi service in town. The car had a brass radiator, yellow wheels, black fenders, and a royal blue body. The year was 1918, the streets were unpaved, and the shiny yellow wheels became caked with mud during rainy weather. In this photograph, Lundy is giving his six-year-old grandson, Edward Lundy, a ride around town. (MM.)

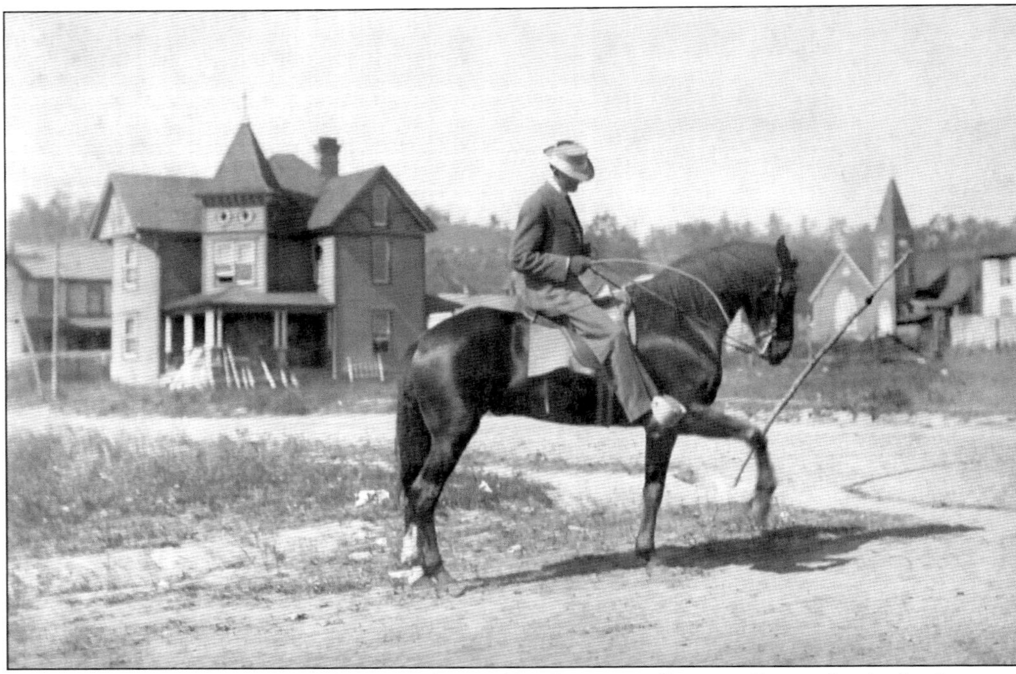

E. L. Whitley is exercising his horse in front of his home on Grayson Street. In the background on the right is the First Presbyterian Church of Galax on West Center Street. This was a dry, sunny day because the streets in Galax were known to be quite muddy at times. (MM.)

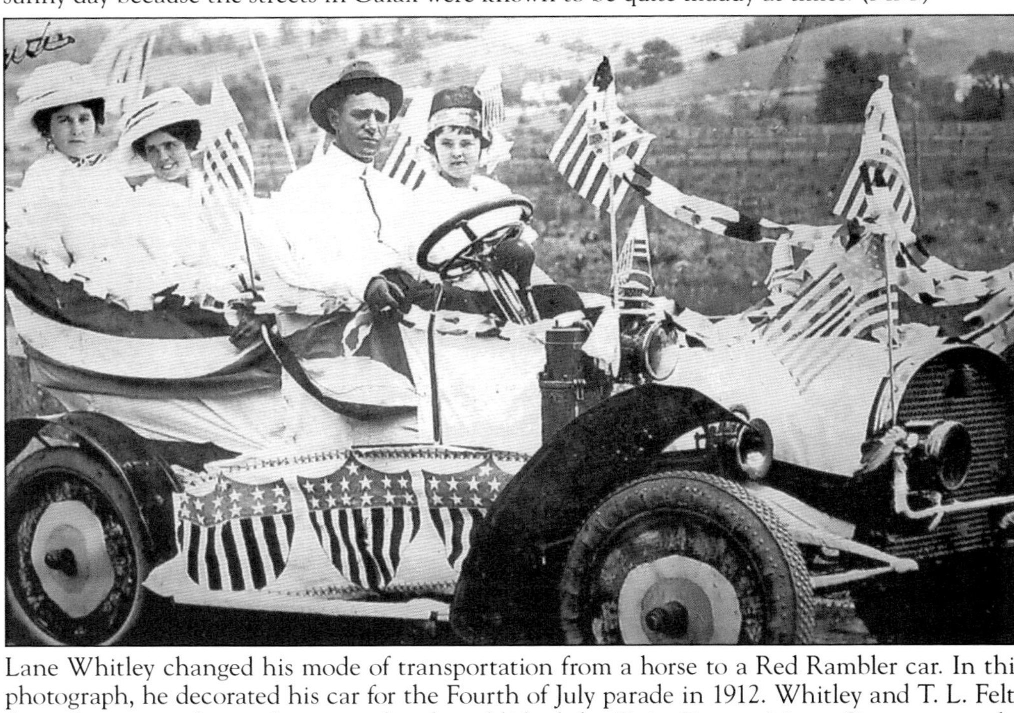

Lane Whitley changed his mode of transportation from a horse to a Red Rambler car. In this photograph, he decorated his car for the Fourth of July parade in 1912. Whitley and T. L. Felts formed a partnership and organized and established the Twin County Motor Company on the corner of North Main and West Webster Streets in 1915. (GG.)

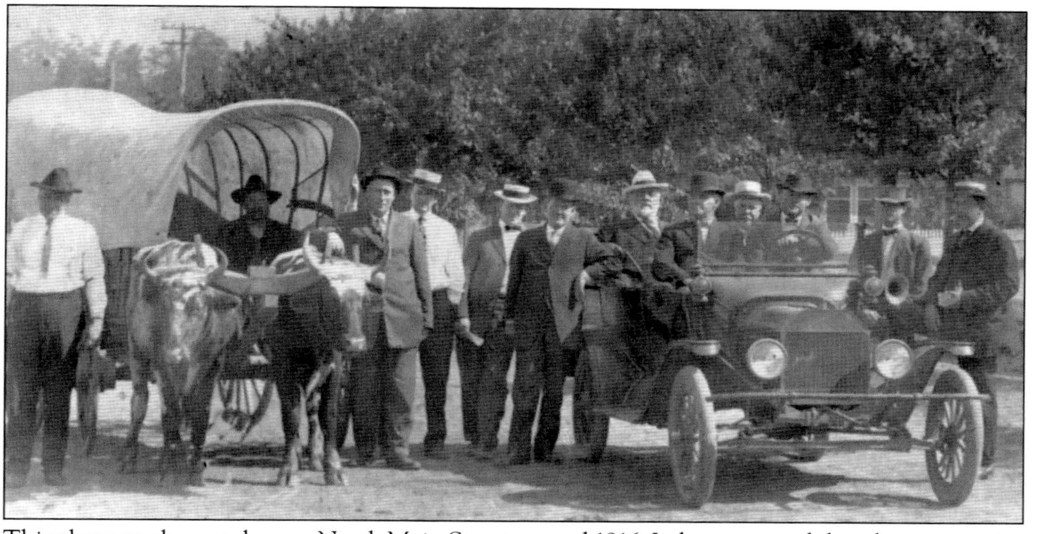

This photograph was taken on North Main Street around 1916. It demonstrated that the community was making the transition from oxen to cars. Shown in the photograph are, from left to right, Mark Jennings, unidentified man in the wagon, J. M. Cheek, Charlie Waugh, Floyd Landreth, Monroe Ward, D. W. Bolen (with whiskers), R. E. Jones (derby hat), Capt. J. B. Waugh (straw hat), Bob Caldwell (driver), Bert Williams, and Dr. J. K. Caldwell. (MM.)

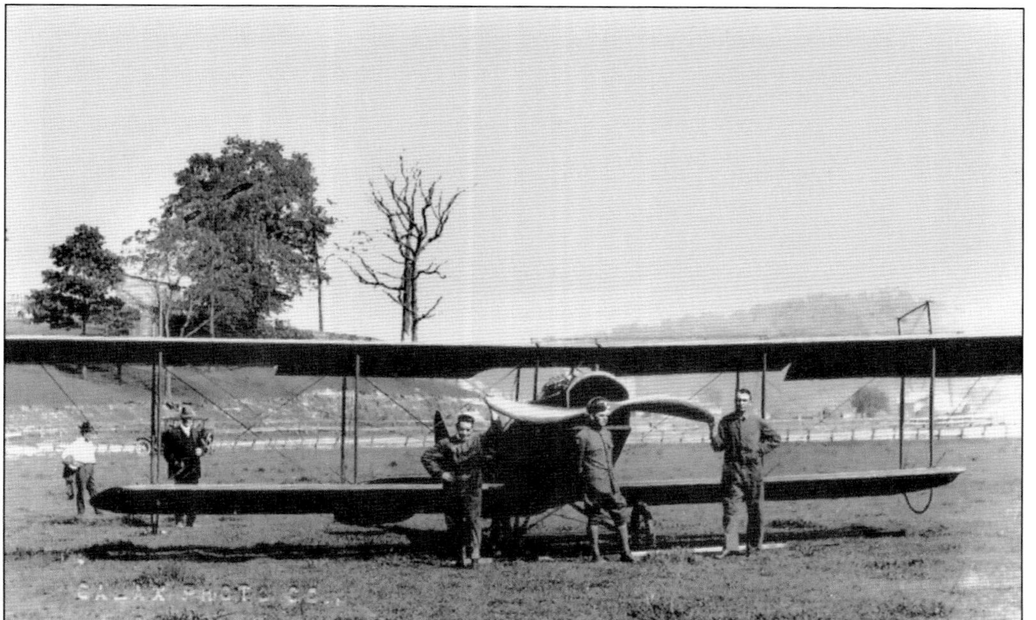

An airplane sits at the Galax Fair Grounds (now Felts Park) in this 1914 photograph. In the city's early days, airplanes would land and take off from the fair grounds, offering people free rides. The men are unidentified. (GG.)

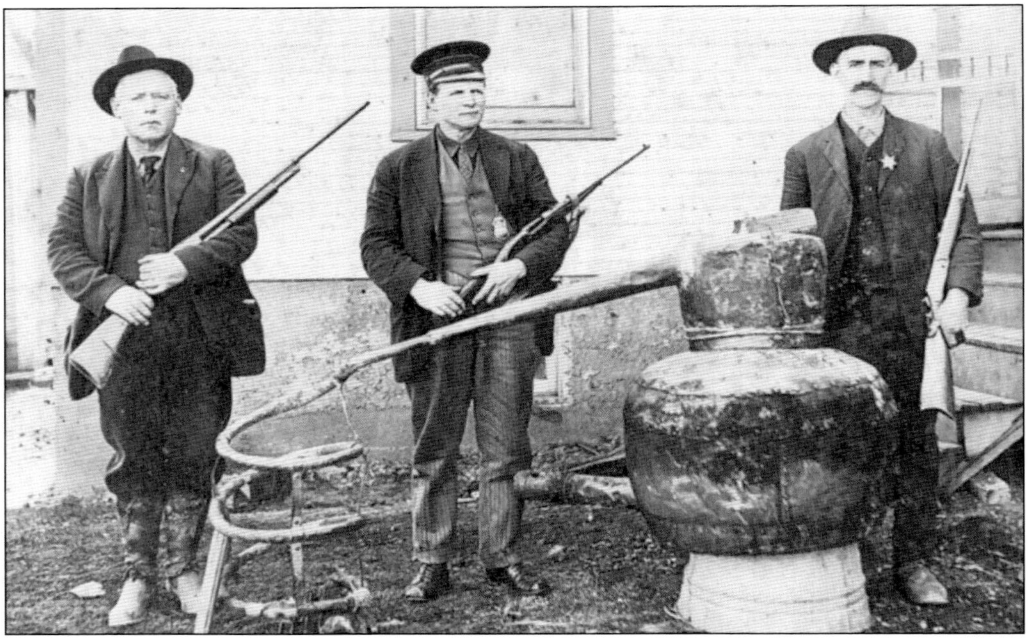

Bootleg whiskey was often made in the mountains of southwest Virginia to supplement one's income, as well as for personal use. Periodically a photograph would appear on the front page of the *Galax Gazette* showing the latest still that had been found. From left to right, Martin Moore, Troy Higgins, and Frank Dotson considered it a successful hunt when they found this still. Dotson was known as the town cop of Galax. (GG.)

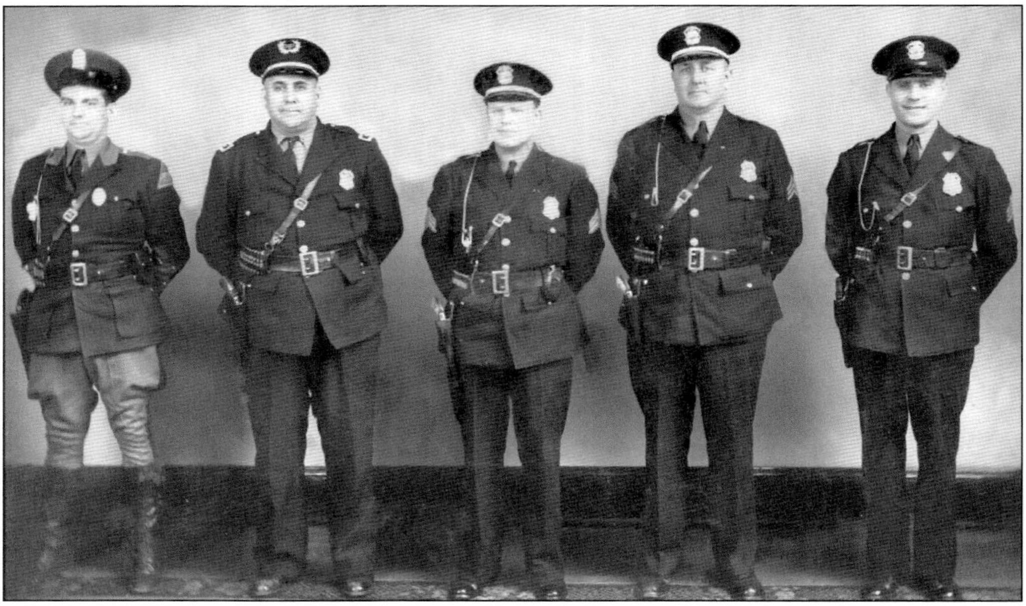

Citizens of Galax slept well and pursued their daily activities with the knowledge that they were under the watchful protection of the town's police force. This photograph was taken between 1930 and 1940. From left to right are Trooper Gibbs, chief of police Jack Higgins, Frank Vaughan, Hugh Turner, and Harold Williams. (GG.)

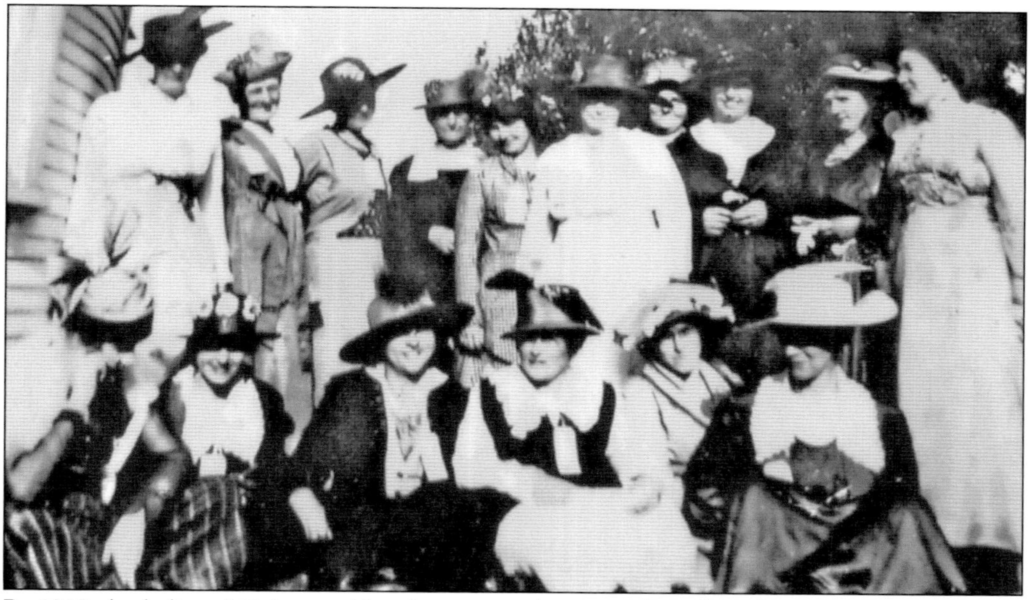

By 1919, the ladies of Galax could gather on neatly trimmed yards and not expect to see sheep trotting on residential streets as they made their way to market. Numerous social clubs were formed, including the Women's Book Club. A group photograph was taken when Hattie Whitley served as hostess at her home on Grayson Street. From left to right are (first row) Katherine Reavis, Mattie Hortenstine, Mamie Poole, a Mrs. Simmeron (Hillsville), Jennie Roberson, and Viola Dodd; (second row) Nettie Bolen, a Mrs. Tipton (Hillsville), Janie Waugh, Sarah Early, Blanche Early, a Mrs. Nuckolls (Hillsville), Josephine Witherow, Lola Landreth, Mae Kapp, and Hattie Whitley. (MM.)

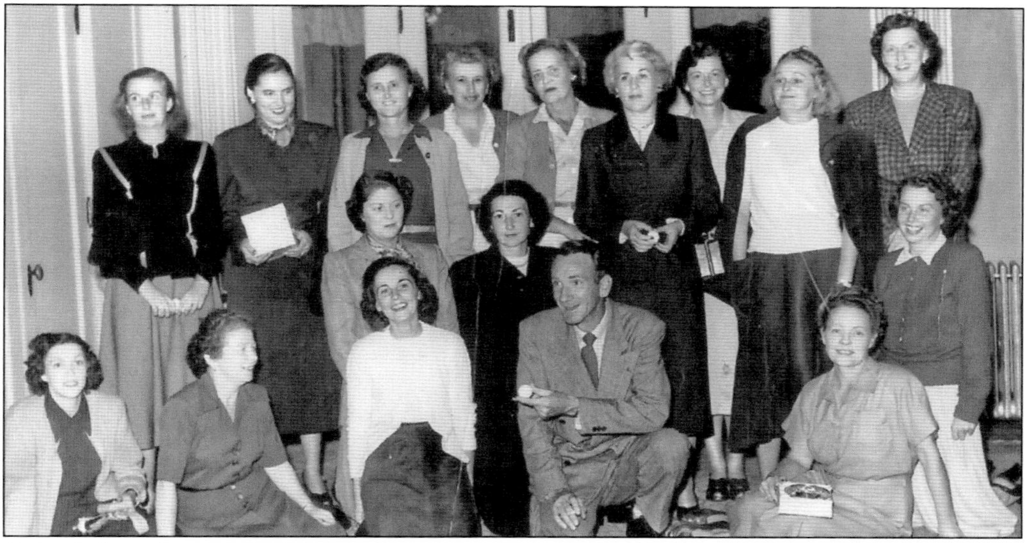

Galax ladies who attended the final 1949 Southwestern Golf Association Tournament are, from left to right, (first row) Reba Messer, Rose Potolsky, Winnie Messer, Galax professional Dorsey Meade, and Hazel Waugh; (second row) Elizabeth Chatham, Etoille Berry, and Margaret Higgins; (third row) Frances Exum, Ruth Felts, Nell Harris, Ida Coates, Alice Felts, Gladys Cox, Kenetta Pless, Juanita Phipps, and Virginia Nuckolls. (Celia Matthiesen.)

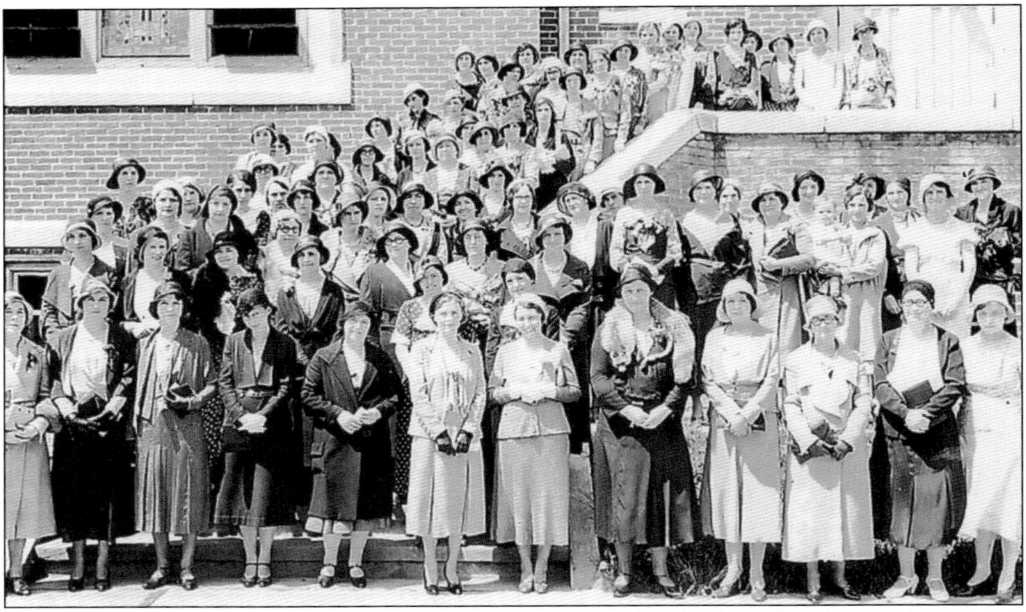

Ladies of the Woman's Friendship Bible class of the First Methodist Church pose for a group photograph on the east side of the church on Mother's Day in 1932. Tessie Williams began teaching the class in 1930 and held this position for more than 22 years. Members of the class included many of the wives of local Galax community leaders. (GG.)

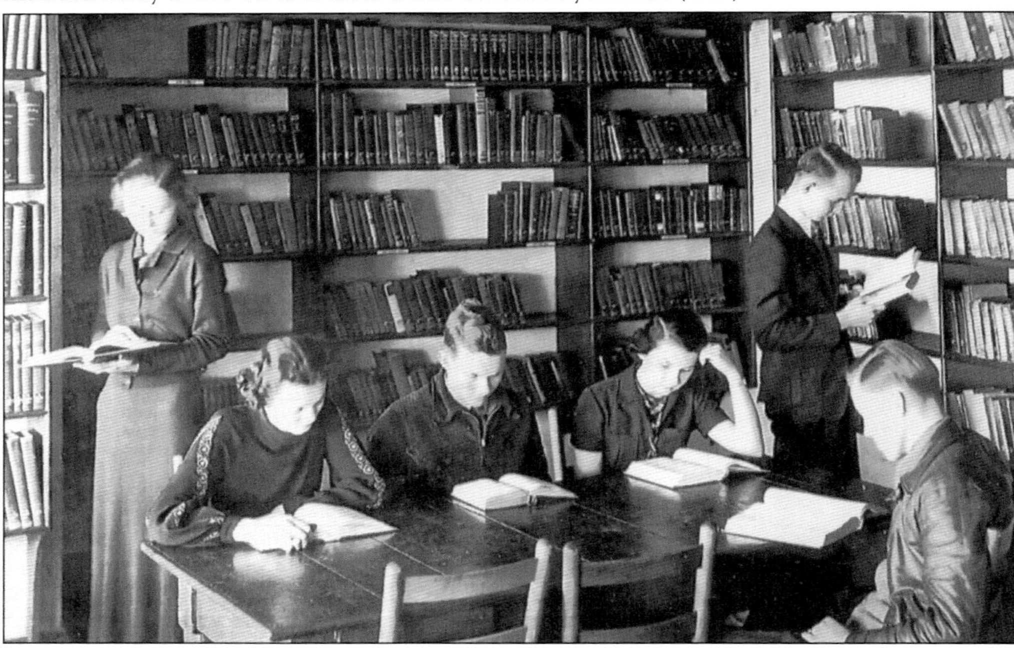

The auditorium was the center of the Galax High School building, with classrooms and the principal's office located around the perimeter. This photograph was taken in 1936 in the school's library. The floors were old and creaky, so it was difficult to maintain the required library silence. Students are, from left to right, Evelyn Troy (standing), Kathleen Wampler Rollins, unidentified boy, Ruth Warner, Tim Pollard (standing), and Curtis Delp. (GG.)

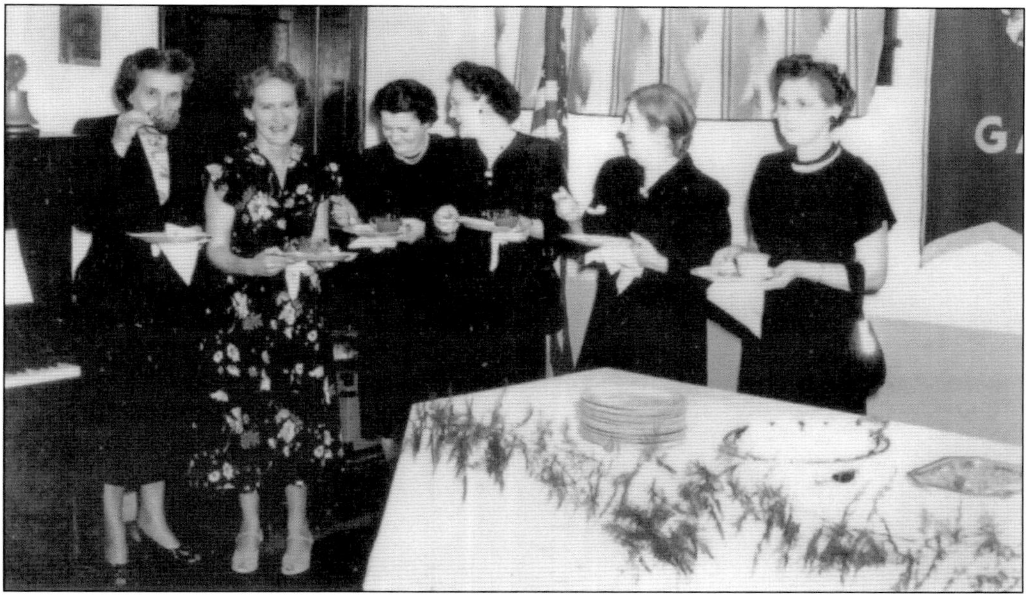

The patriotic ladies of Galax responded immediately following the attack on Pearl Harbor. The membership of the local Red Cross swelled to include almost every available woman in town. A surgical room was secured, and the women prepared bandages and surgical dressings by the thousands, which were shipped from Galax to all four corners of the world. Ladies attending a Red Cross tea are, from left to right, Plina Cox Roberts, Hattie Weatherman, Pauline Gentry, Mary Alice Henderson, Grace Bishop, and Grace Jones. (EN.)

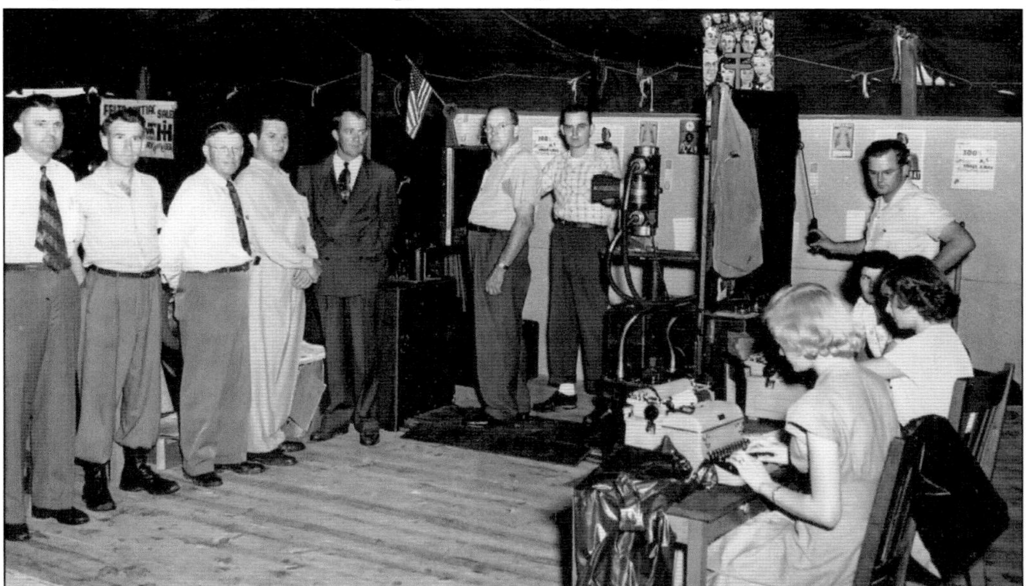

Members of the Galax City Council were among the first residents to have chest x-rays taken. Doctors used this machine to diagnose tuberculosis. The sign for Christmas seals can be seen on the wall behind the x-ray machine. From left to right, C. E. Hackworth, Clarence Alderman, Walter Andrews, Johnny Messer, and Milo Cockerham wait their turn while Victor Wilson stands in front of the machine. Bill McCarter is assisting the technician. (GG.)

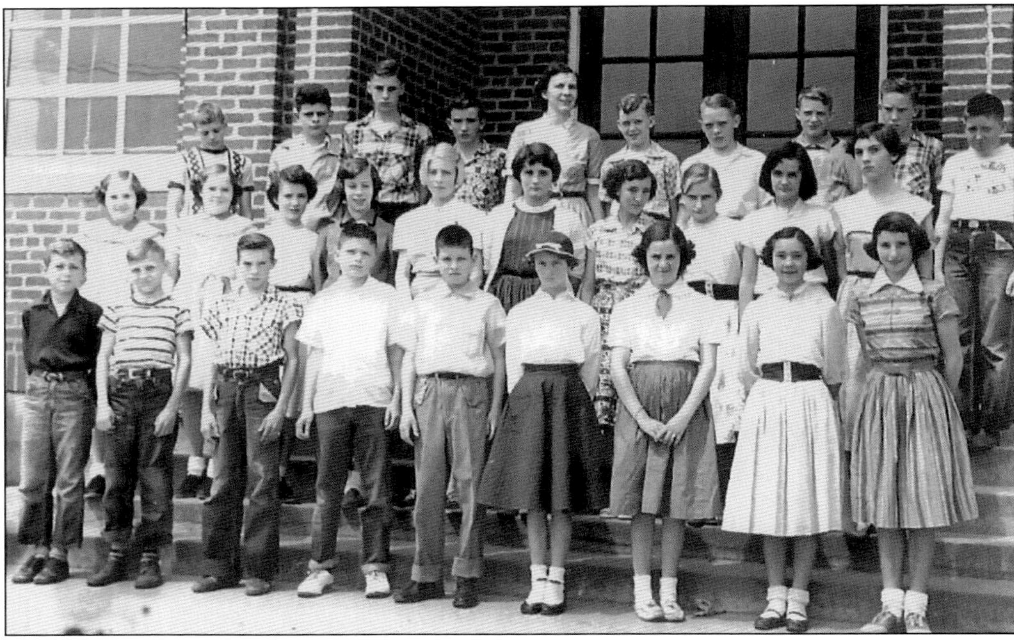

Sixth grade students in 1953 included, from left to right, (first row) Johnny Funk, Billy Horton, Bobby Worrell, Conley Harris, Harvey Hennis, Patsy Carr, Norma Evans, Shirley Brown, and Lucy Evans; (second row) Sarah Price, Charlotte Price, Mary Ann Spinks Dotson, Pat Exum, Bund Gallop, Augusta Messer, Marie Simpson, Lettie Mae Ayers, Ammy Carico, and Sue Morris; (third row) Mike Cook, J. M. Hall, Jeff Morris, Kerman Cummins, Lacona Diamond (teacher), Freddie Crouse, Jei Kimby, unidentified, Willard Miles, and "Topper" Franke.

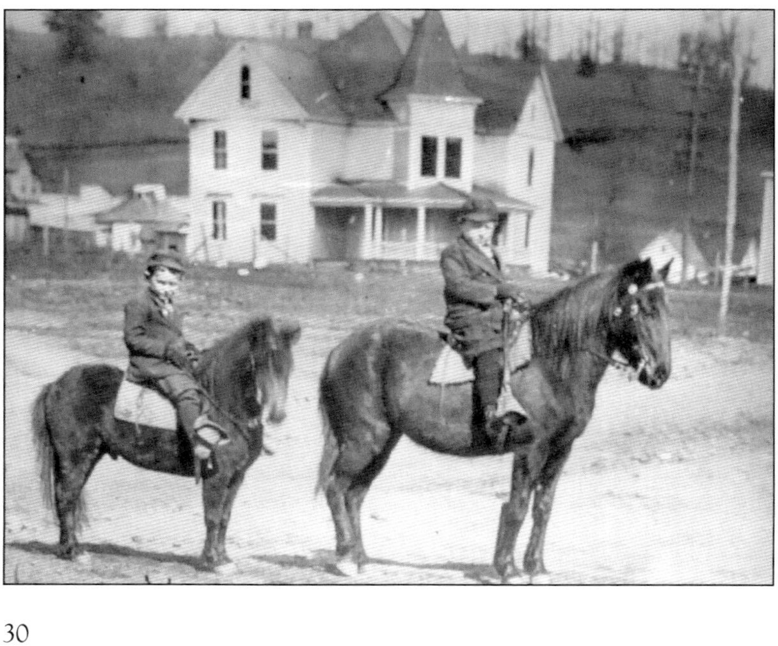

David Bolen (left) and Paul Kapp ride their horses around town together. Not only are they neighbors on North Main Street, they later became dentists and shared a practice together. Their offices were located above Bolen's Drugstore on Main Street. The E. L. Whitley home is in the background. (MM.)

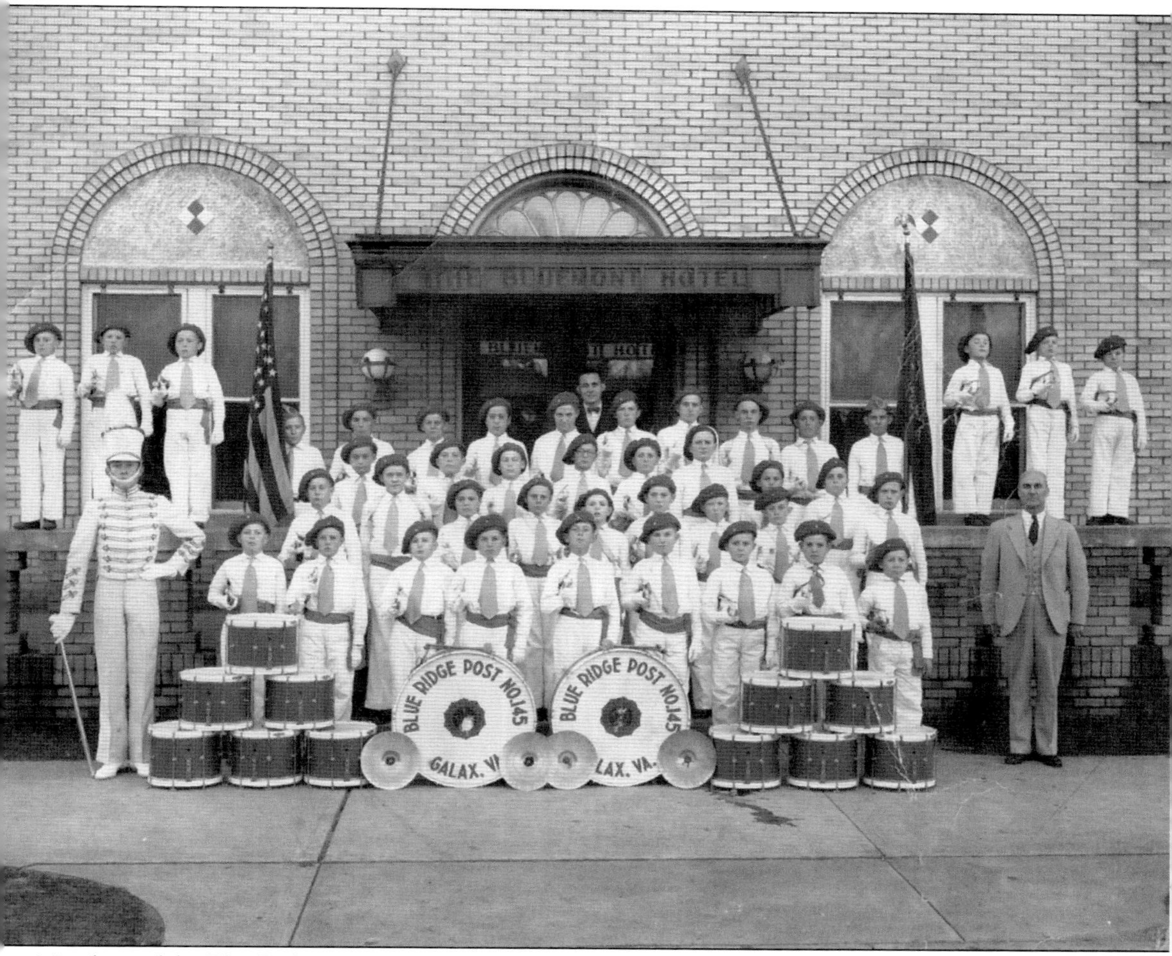

Members of the Blue Ridge Post No. 145 band stand on the steps of the Bluemont Hotel. Pictured from left to right are (first row) Jack Williams, Edward Weaver, James Carico, James Welsh, Elwood Wilson, Dale Parsons, J. B. Jones, Bill Owens, Johnny Lemons, Joe Lundy, and a Mr. Thompson; (second row) James Bartlett, James Cox, Charles Burroughs, Jimmy Henderson, Garland Higgins, Marvell Owens, Junior Andrews, George Vaughan, and Creed Harmon; (third row) Paul Shores Jr., Joe Williams, Scott Nicholls, Joe Chappell, Virgil Catron, Babe Harris, Bobby Nelson, and Bob Jones; (fourth row) Edward Newman, Bill Matthews, Hollis Burroughs, George Day, Harry Chipman, Bill Nelson, Billy Hanks, Gene Jones, Dan Vass, Joe Crockett, Tim Pollard, Cob Adams, Billy Thompson, Buddy Fisher, Frank R. Vass, and Tommy Matthews; (fifth row) Floyd Williams. (EN.)

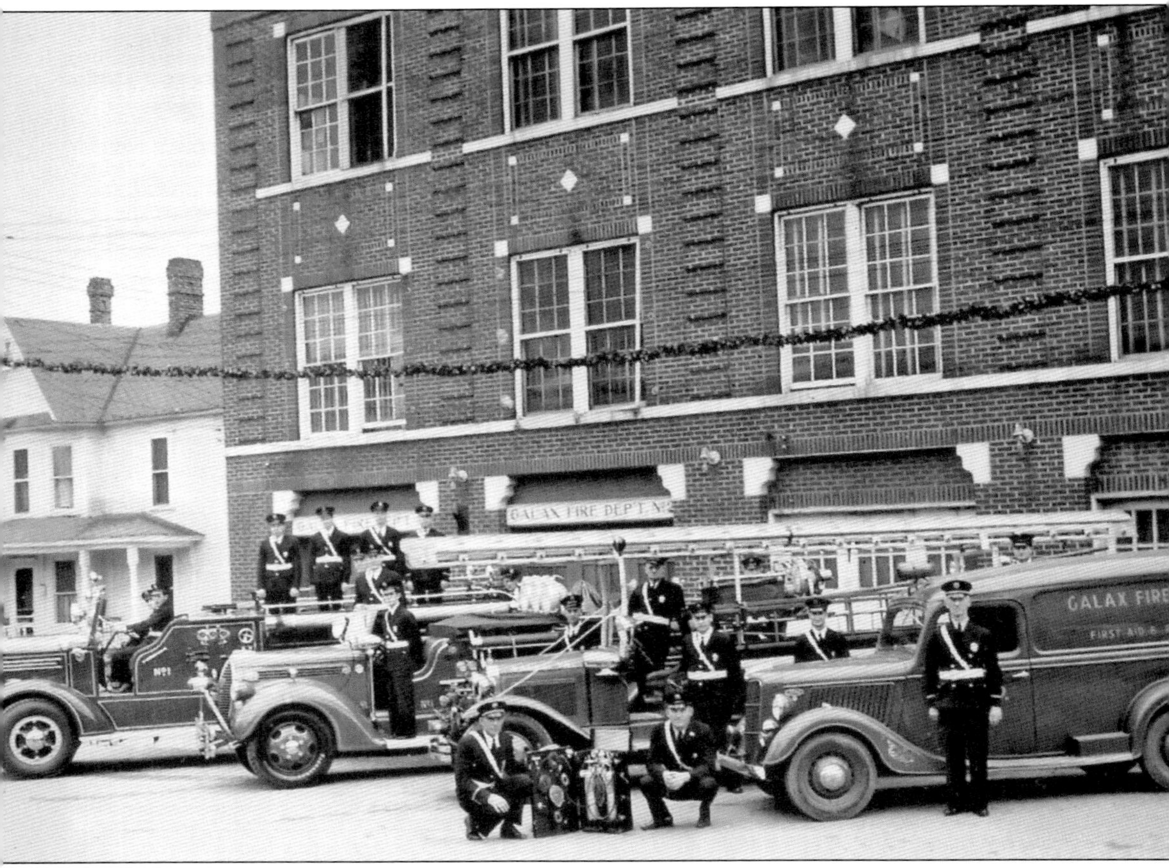

Many of the earliest buildings in Galax were made of wood. The town suffered devastating fires that destroyed the Central Hotel, the Galax Furniture and Lumber Company, the Ward brothers' first building, the Red Star Hotel, Dr. D. W. Bolen's boardinghouse, Netti Bolen's millinery shop, M.L. Bishop's livery stables, the Harris Hotel, F. S. Dobyn's livery stables, the Galax Produce Market, J. W. Poole's general store, Hightower's Studio, Novelty 5 and 10 Store, and A. E. Disher's grocery store. There were two public water hand pumps in Galax during the early days. One was located on the corner by the Waugh Hotel on North Main Street, and the other was near the Central Hotel on South Main Street. The first firefighting in town was done by the people's bucket brigade when the church bells sounded the fire alarm. Finally, the town council, mayor, and citizens held a meeting to discuss and organize a town water system and a volunteer fire department. The Galax Volunteer Fire Department was organized in 1912 with Edd D. Perkins serving as fire chief. (Jack Pless.)

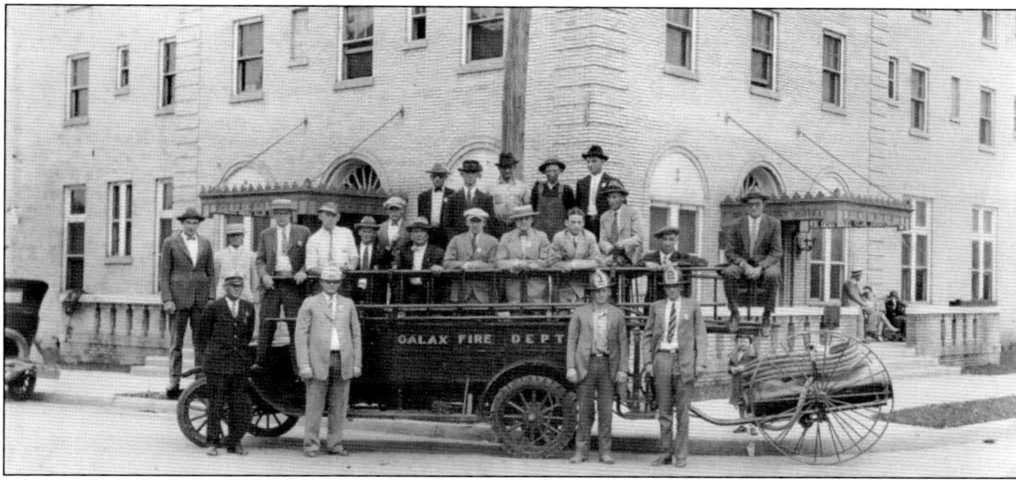

This undated photograph shows members of the Galax Fire Department in front of the Bluemont Hotel on North Main Street. Pictured from left to right are (first row) Walt Anderson, Ralph Todd, Walter Matthews, and Clarence Todd; (second row) Tom Trimble, unidentified, Bill Boaz, Garland Anderson, Emmon Todd, Dan Anderson, Badger Witherow, Gabe Lundy, Walter Elliott, Herman Webb, Jim Anderson, Sid Dotson, and George Callaway; (third row) Paul Phipps, Lance Todd, Fernoy Worrell, Roy Manning, and Lester Diamond. (MM.)

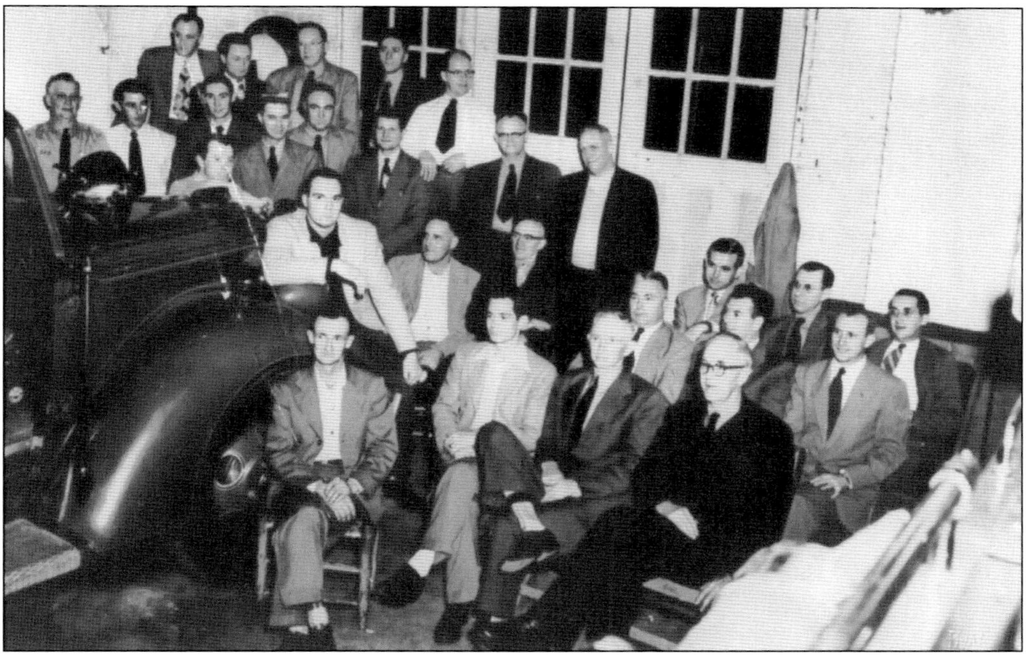

Galax Fire Department volunteers in 1953 included, from left to right, (first row) G. W. Todd, Clifton Manning, Roy Manning, and Clifton Sutherland; (second row) Winfred Boaz, Orba Whitt, Lance Todd, Harmon Dickerson, Elmer Sells, and Elwood Newman; (third row) Marvin Honeycutt, Lawrence Dalton, Duard Burnette, Ray Fortner, Raymond Burnette, Bays Roberts, Cicero Lineberry, R. V. Morris, Joe Crockett, Guy Leftwich, and Edwin Sutphin; (fourth row) Roy Hale, John Reavis, Victor Wilson, John Bryant, and Gabe Lundy. Elmer Carpenter is learning on the truck. (GG.)

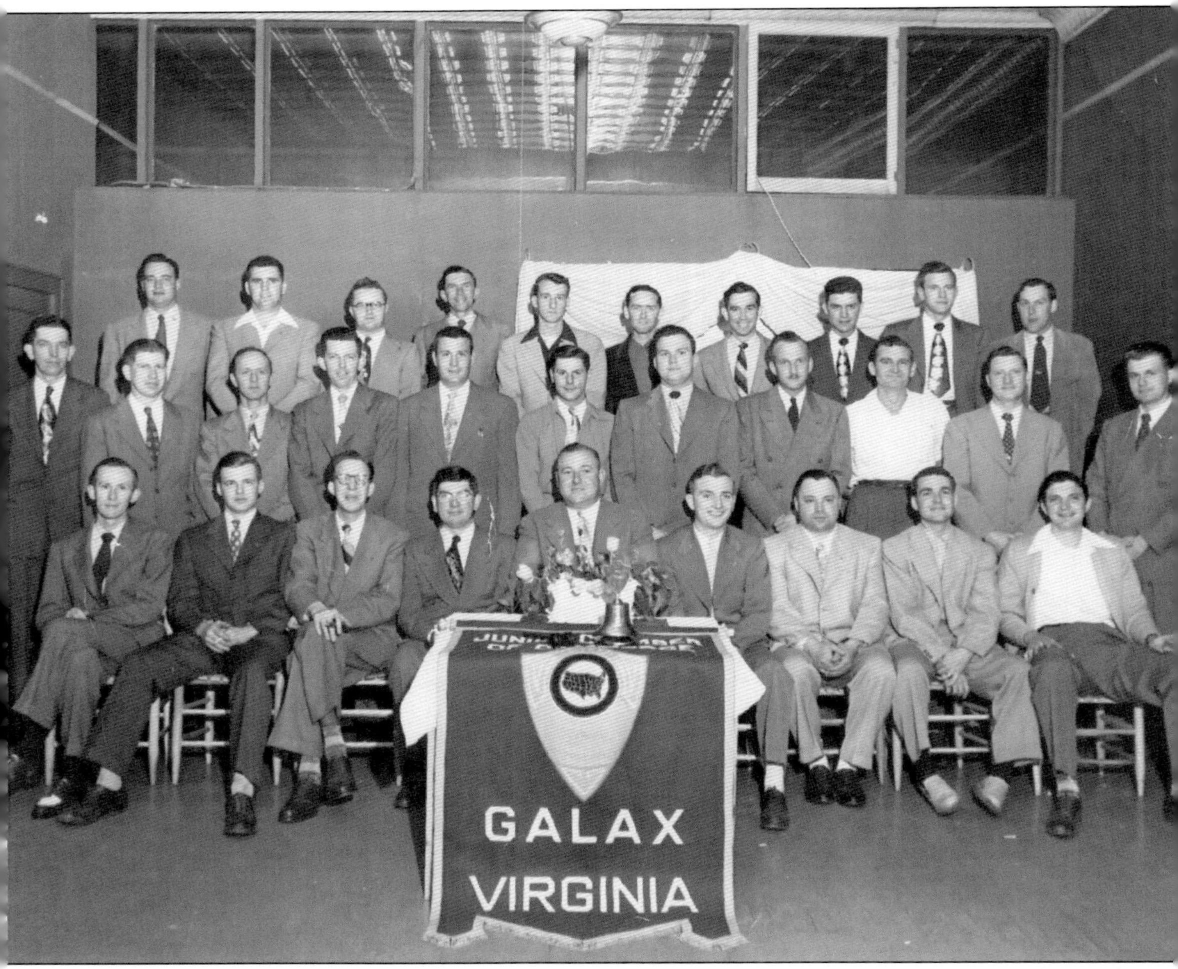

The Galax Junior Chamber of Commerce was organized in 1947 and has continued to make major contributions to enhance the life of the city and its citizens. The organization consists of men, aged 21 to 45, who are hard working, intelligent, and have a keen sense of patriotic duty and commitment to their community. They decorate the streets for Christmas and participate in the Fourth of July parade. They started the Galax Christmas Party Fund for local needy families. They purchased and delivered food and toys to the children. Pictured from left to right are (first row) Sam Burnette, Dean Sutherland, Jim Jackson, Irving Key, Walter Jones Jr., Buford Lindamood, Charles Burroughs, Gene Nuckolls, and Dennis Vass Jr.; (second row) Gilmer Smythers, Chester Cochran, Bruce Galyen, Giles Cochran, Fred St. John, unidentified, Elbert Wampler, Frank Osborne, Walter Harris, Raymond Martin, and Bill McCarter; (third row) Jack Stanley Jr., Ellis Reeves, Van McCarter, Ralph Edwards, Richard Perry, Ralph Sexton, unidentified, Bob Williams, Carl Duckett, and Laurence Wensel. (RL.)

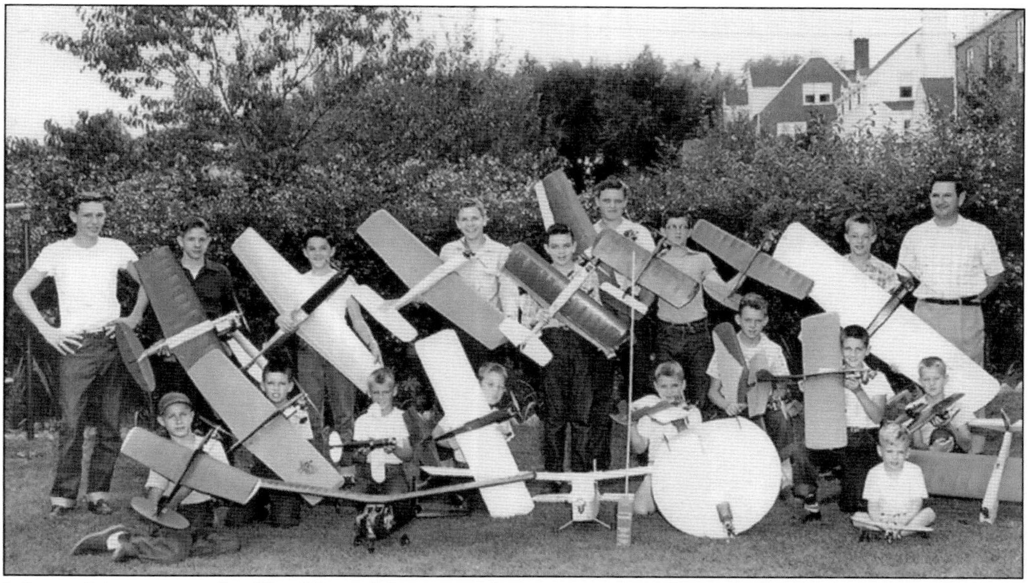

Johnny Messer was the "Pied Piper" for young boys in town in the early 1950s. During the winter months, the boys gathered in his basement on McArthur Street, where an elaborate system of model trains was set up. In the early spring, the boys began to work on their model airplanes, which they would fly during the summer. Pictured here are, from left to right, (first row) Jack Faddis, Harvey Hennis, Buster Combs, Tom Reason, Mike Combs, Freddy Crouse, Doug Messer, Alan Messer, and Jimmy Ward; (second row) Charles Frye, Roger Lineberry, Jack Messer, Warren Frye, Joe Stacy, Johnny Ashby, Johnny Eller, Jim Anderson, and Johnny Messer. (GPL.)

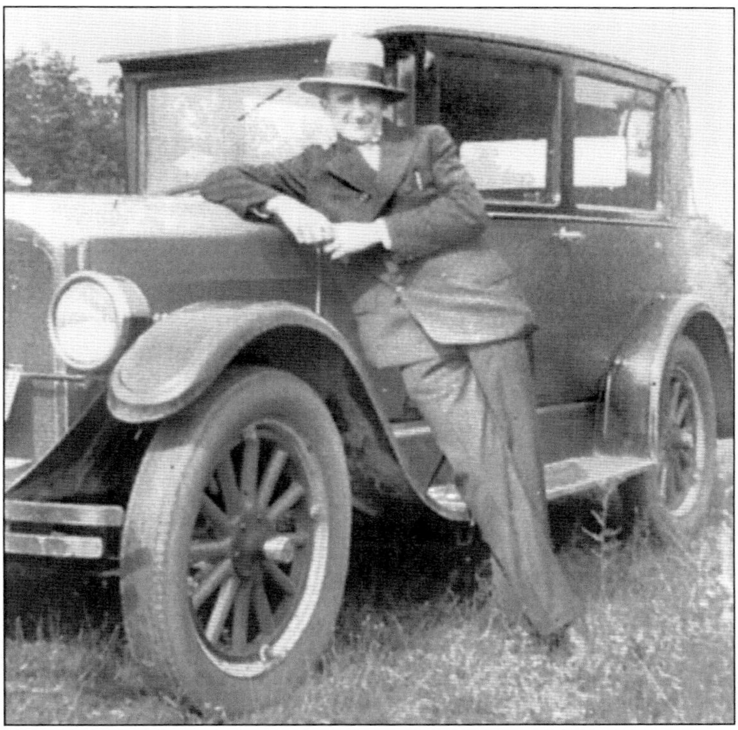

Everette V. Newman leans against a 1924 Star car. His father-in-law, Onnie B. Hackler, was the local dealer of Star and Durant touring cars in Galax. Newman owned and operated the City Barbershop on Main Street for more than 50 years. He then operated a barbershop next to N&H Grocery on West Stuart Drive until his death at age 85. (GG.)

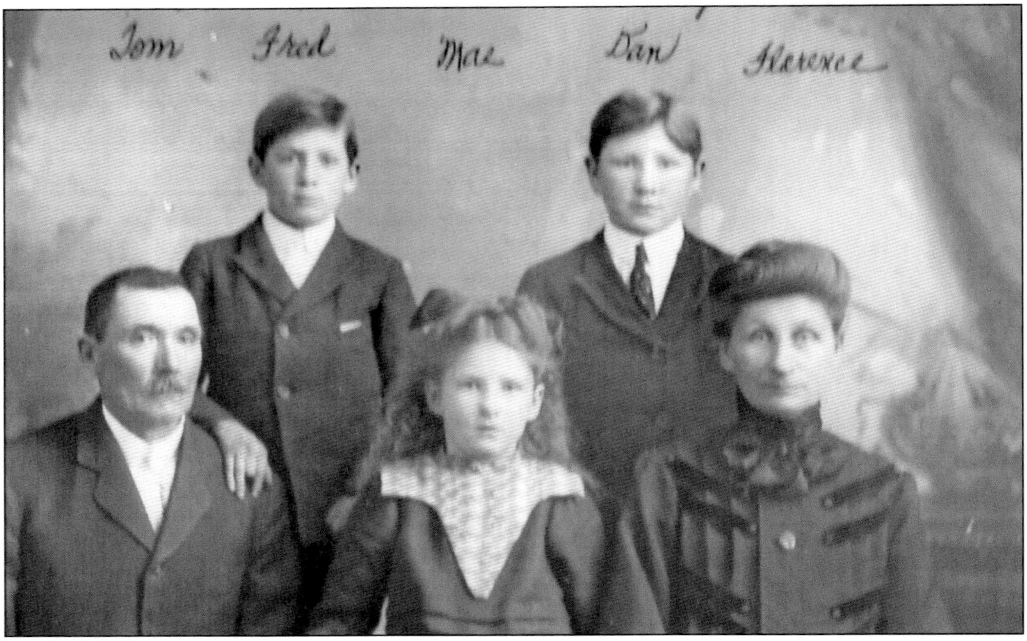

Thomas F. Roberts was a major landowner in the area known as Anderson's Bottom, the future site of Galax. His sons, Dan and Fred, attended the first school in Galax, located on the second floor of R. E. Jones and Son. Fred later married Grace Bishop, who was also in the class. Dan married Plina B. Cox, and Frances Maye married Newton Floyd Burge. Pictured from left to right are (seated) Tom Roberts, Mae Roberts, and Florence Roberts; (standing) Fred Roberts and Dan Roberts. (MM.)

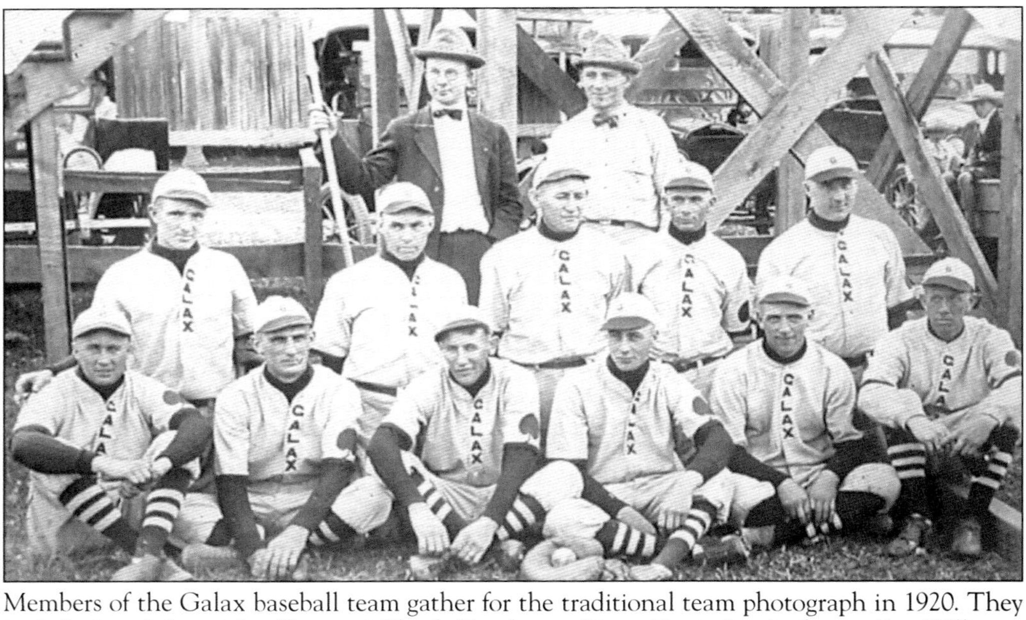

Members of the Galax baseball team gather for the traditional team photograph in 1920. They include, from left to right, (first row) Claude Henderson, Pierce Davis, Jim Anderson, Rex Williams, Baron Todd, and Bert Wright; (second row) Joe Todd, Carl Kirby, Walt Anderson, Fred Roberts, and Charlie Schrader; (third row) Dr. Heath A. Dalton and Breece Todd. (GG.)

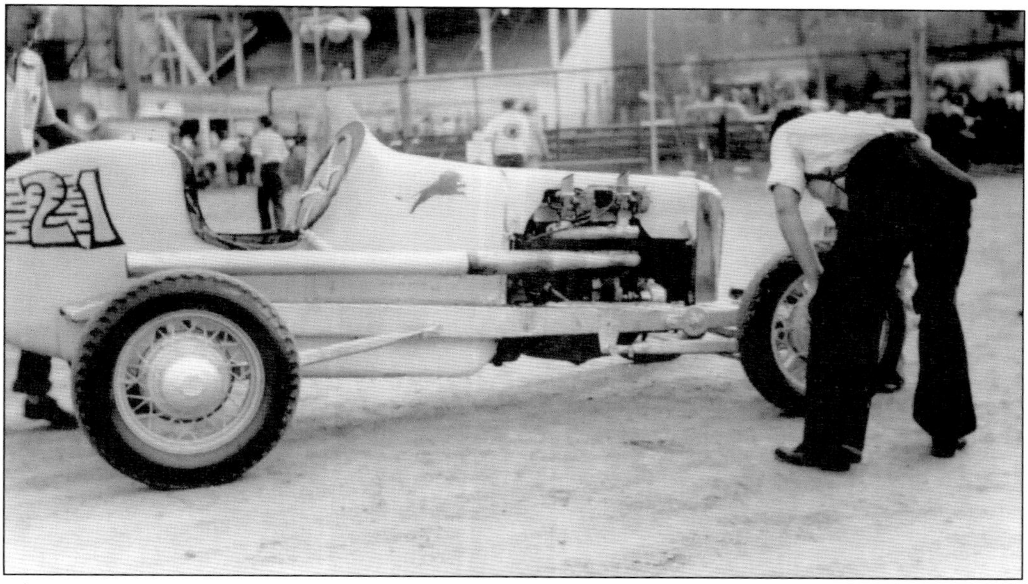

The Galax fairgrounds at Felts Park have always been a busy site. Activities have included high school football and baseball games, horse shows, the Fiddlers Convention, summer softball games, car races and demolition derbies, the circus, and the Galax Fair. This car is making a pit stop. (GPL.)

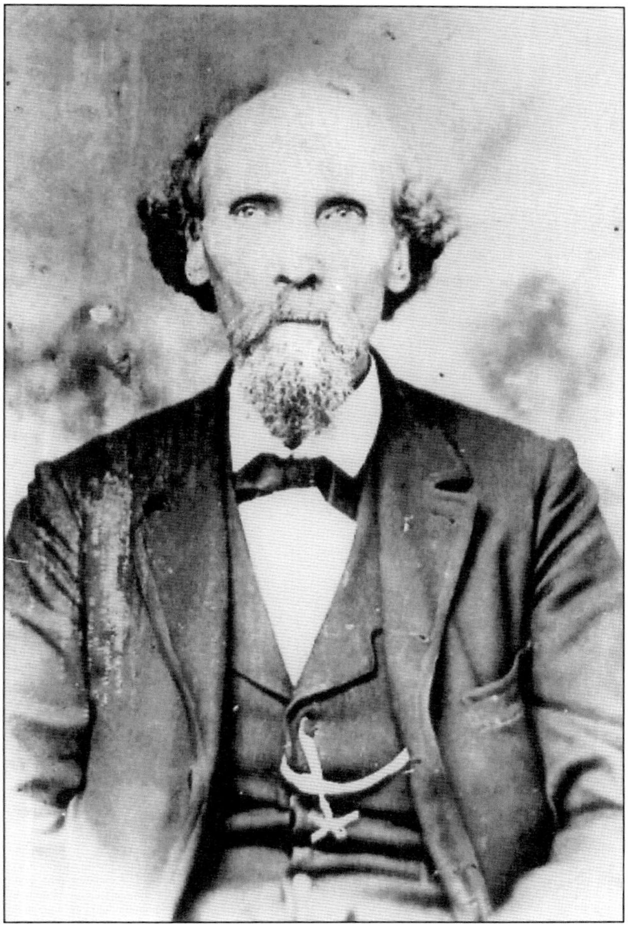

In 1904, C. H. South built the Central Hotel on the southwest corner of Main and Oldtown Streets. He served three meals a day and charged $1.50 per night for lodging. The hotel and the R. L. Rupe buildings were destroyed by fire in 1905. South had insured the hotel and its furnishings for $1,700. He rebuilt the hotel and ran it for several more years before leasing it to Oscar Higgins, who changed the name to the New Galax Inn. (MM.)

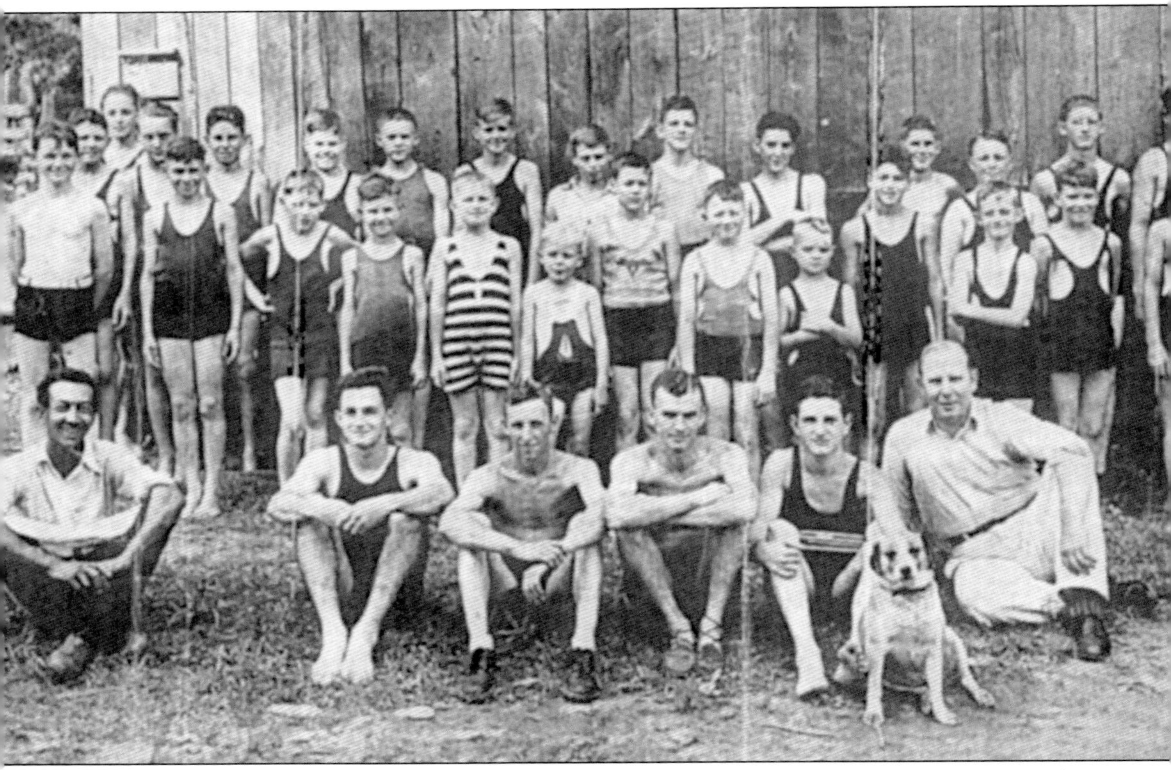

Rev. A. C. Meadows was the pastor of the Galax Christian Church, but to many young boys in town, he was known as "Scoutmaster." This photograph was taken of the Galax boys at Camp Pot Rock in Carroll County in 1931. Pictured from left to right are (first row) unidentified, Kenneth Messer, J. K. Davis, Ned Hawks, John Messer Jr., and Reverend Meadows; (second row) unidentified, Roy Manning, Rex Hampton, Roy Lee Spivey, Junior Nelson, J. B. Jones Jr., Alfred Meadows, Daniel Webb, Blair Waugh, unidentified, George Vaughan, Charles Redd, and Joe Chappell; (third row) three unidentified, Pete Atkinson, unidentified, Buford Crockett, Joe Crockett, Jody Harmon, unidentified, Linwood Blair, Rupert Hampton, Joe Kirby, John Davis, and James Lemons. (GPL.)

Each year, the local Loyal Order of Moose selected a man they considered to be the "Outstanding Citizen of the Year." The honoree was presented with a plaque in recognition of his many unselfish and dedicated contributions to the Galax community. In this photograph, John A. Messer Sr. (far left) is accepting his special award from Dale LaRue (far right). Also in the picture is Bob Hash (second from left). The other man is unidentified. (JJN.)

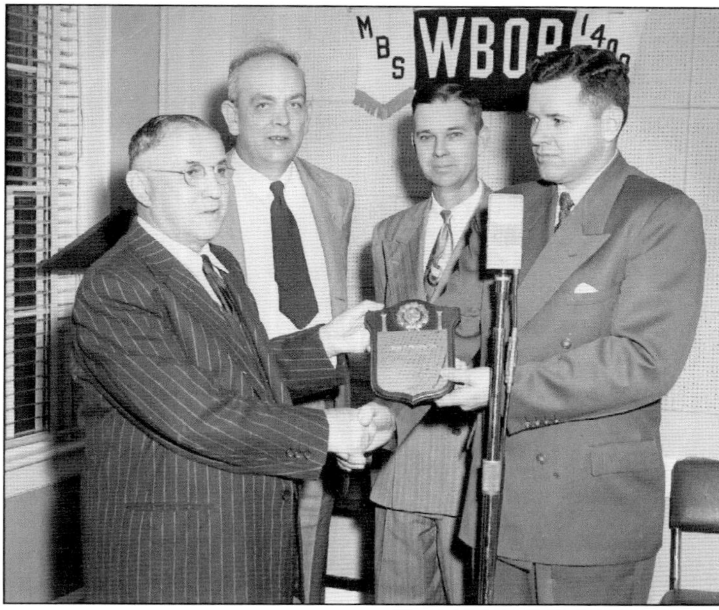

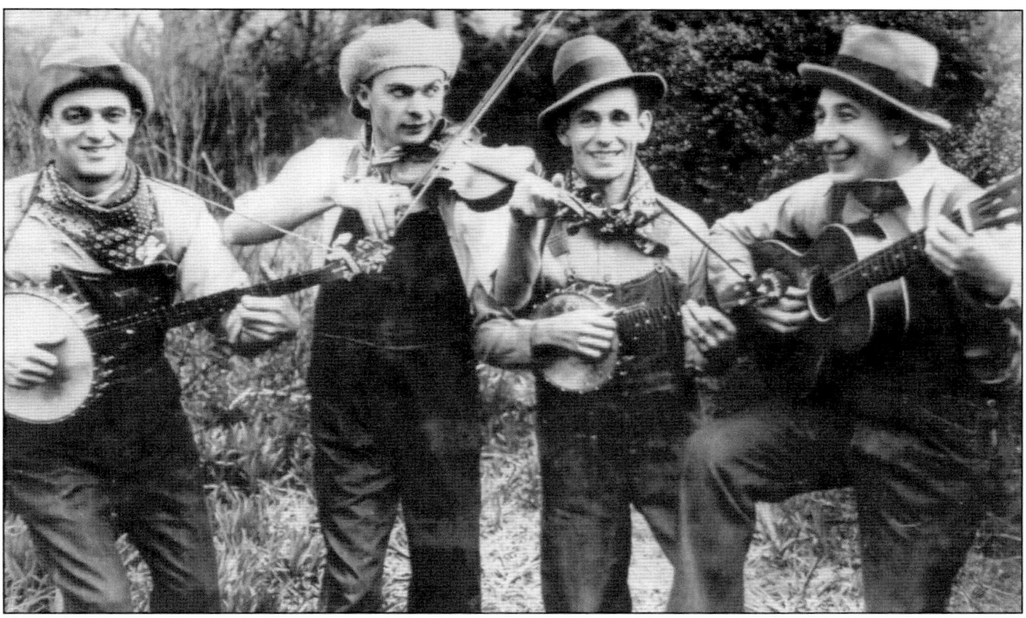

Members of the Hill Billies, a Galax band from the 1920s and 1930s, were credited with popularizing the term "hillbilly music" to describe rural music. The group relocated to Washington, D.C., to broadcast on the radio and tour the national vaudeville circuit. They were the first big country music group in show business. Hundreds of others made important records, but this band, originally from Galax, helped invent the business called country music. (Bob Patterson.)

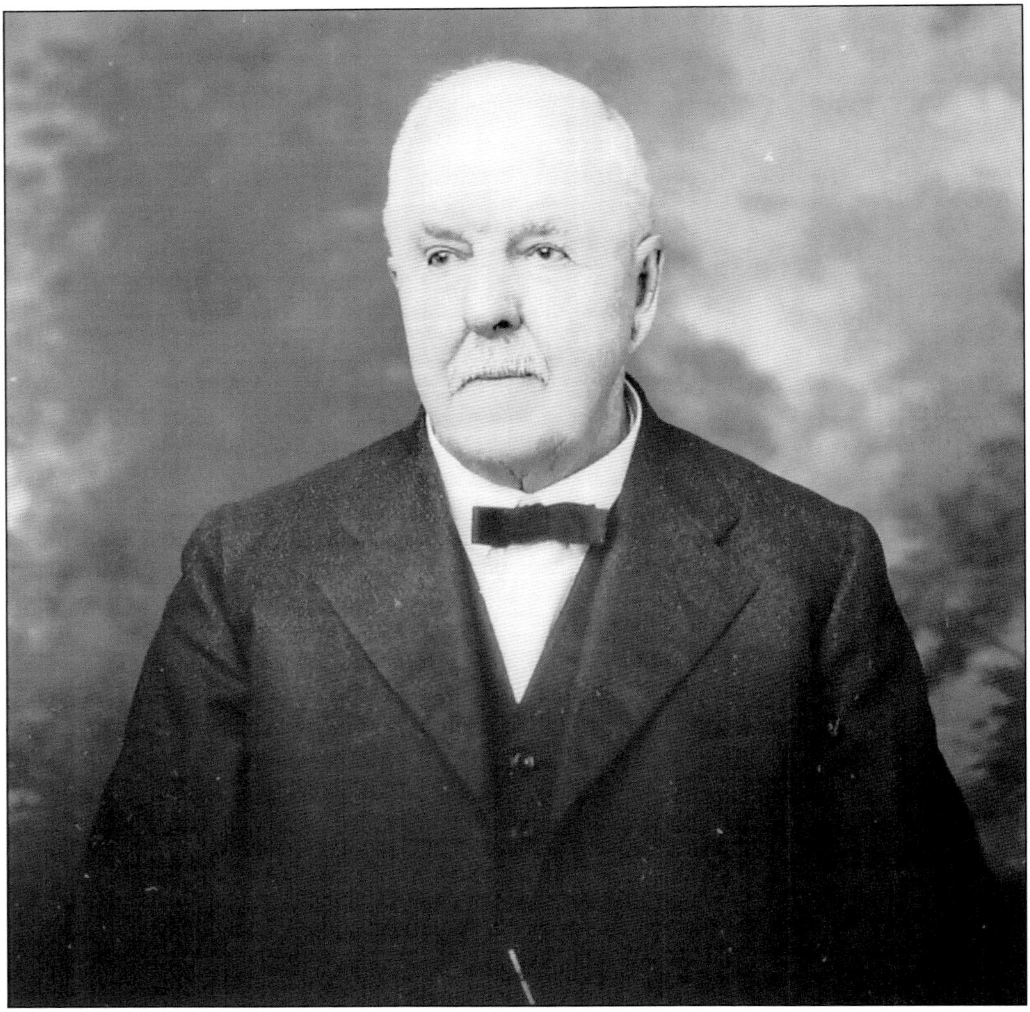

John Blair Waugh, son of James and Elizabeth Blair Waugh, served as a captain in the 61st Regiment during the Civil War. He returned home to take over his father's mercantile business in Blair. He was one of the founders of Galax and moved his business to Galax in 1904. His store was one of the first brick buildings to be constructed in the new town. Captain Waugh was a man of large means and varied business interests. He was a leading figure in the civic, commercial, and industrial life of southwestern Virginia. He was involved in farming, banking, real estate, mineral lands, furniture manufacturing, and many other enterprises. Captain Waugh was married to the former Jennie Perkins, and they were the parents of four children, Berta Carson Waugh, Charles Perkins Waugh, Dan Blair Waugh, and Richard Johnston Waugh. He built a stately home on Stuart Drive that provided a panoramic view of the town he loved so dearly. Waugh died in 1934 at age 92. His casket was covered with 7,000 Galax leaves. (MM.)

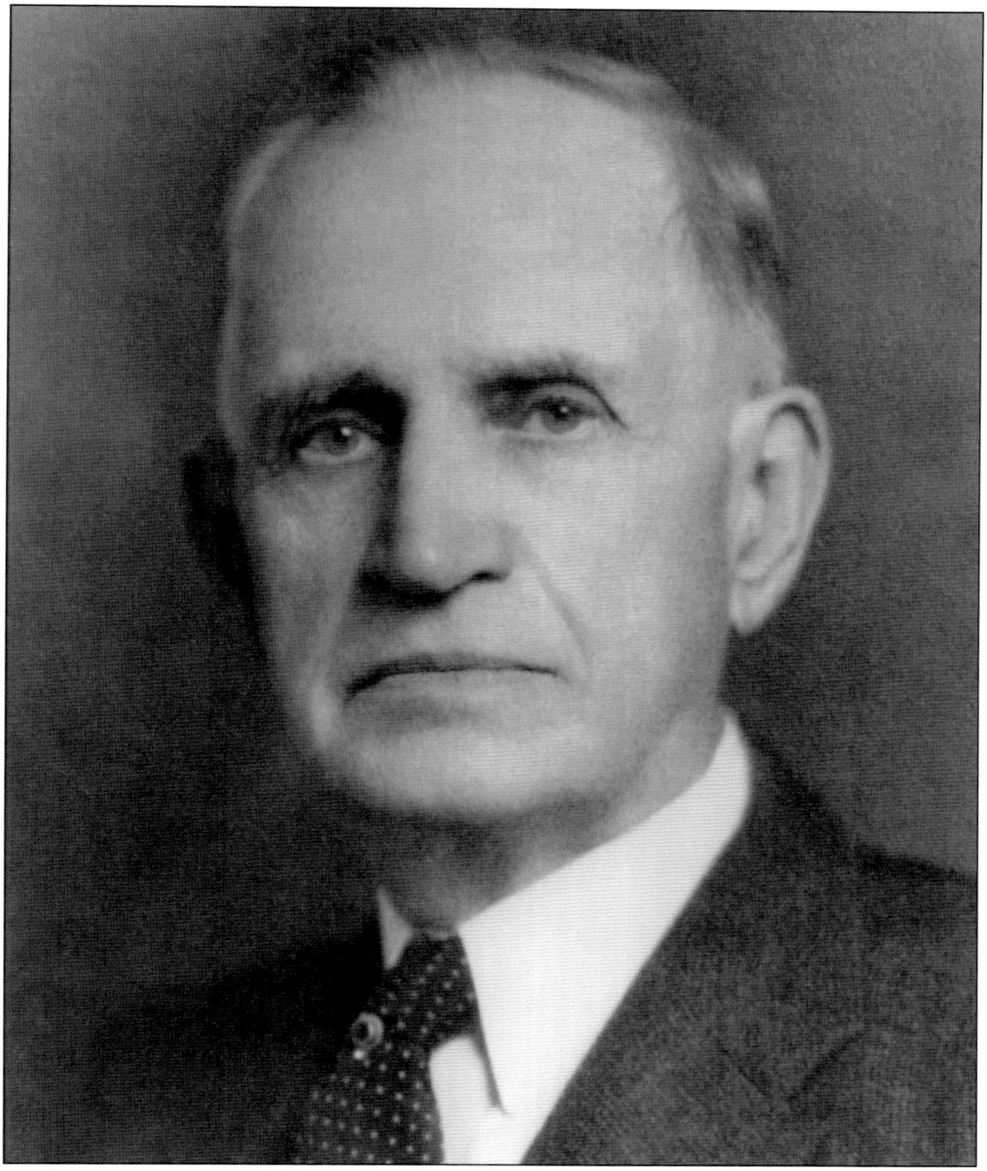

James Piper Carico was perhaps the most successful promoter of enterprises this section has ever produced. As manager of the Grayson Real Estate Company, it was his task to plan the layout of the town and to promote the sale of the lots. He remained as manager of the land company until it was dissolved. Carico was one of the town's most active and influential civic and church leaders. The name of James Piper Carico has been interwoven, directly or indirectly, with the establishment and development of practically every industry and outstanding enterprise that was carried on during the early years of the town. He was one of the organizers of the First National Bank, the Twin County Fair, and the first hospital in Galax. Carico was always active, connected, and deeply interested in any program that, in his judgment, would improve the city he loved so much. Carico was married to the former Elizabeth Bourne for more than 52 years. Six of their eight children are Lucy, Harry, Eugene, Nell, James, and Kate. James was the first child born in Galax. Carico died in 1936 and is buried in Felts Cemetery. (Jim Carico.)

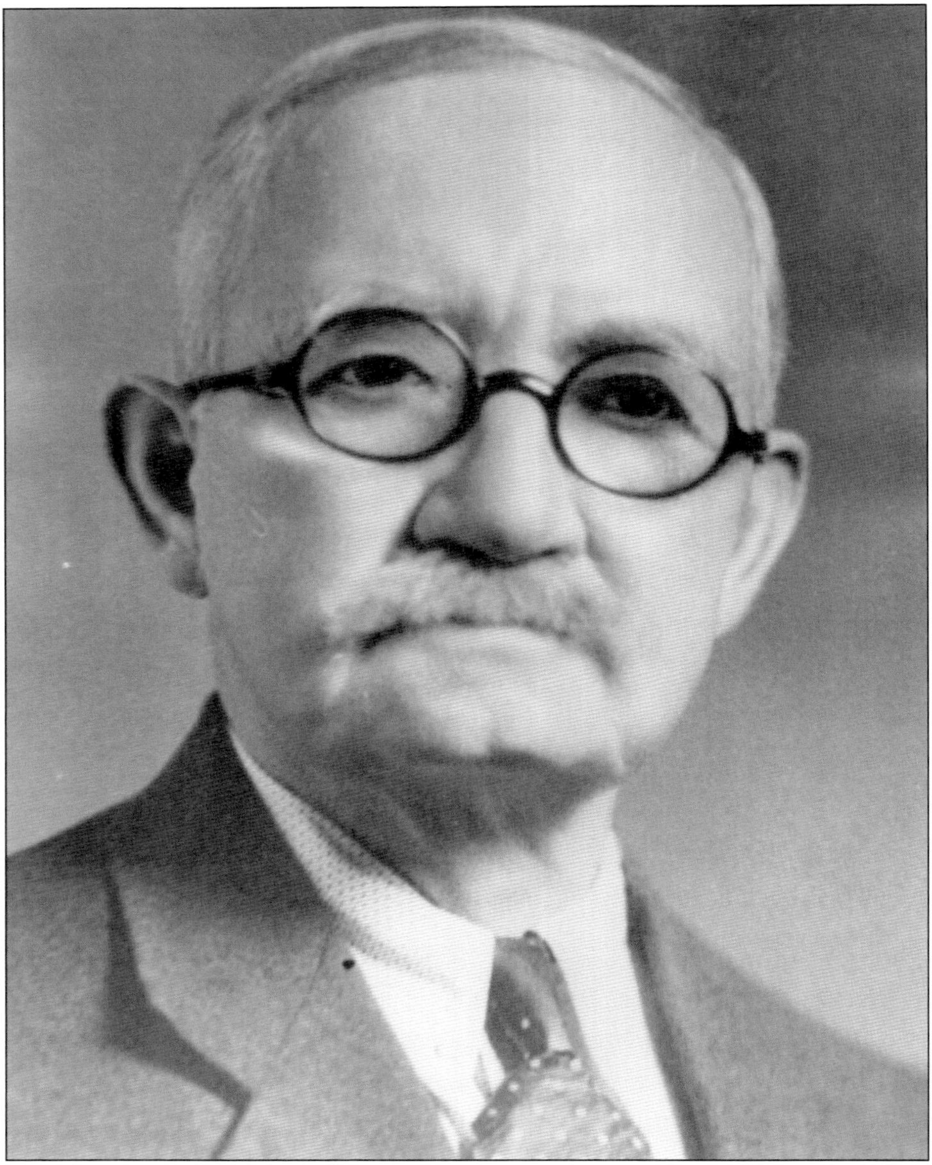

Robert E. Jones was a highly respected pioneer citizen who was affectingly known as "Daddy of Galax." He wore many hats in his illustrious career as a citizen and leader of the community. Jones built R. E. Jones and Son, one of the first stores in town. He was the first mayor, the first postmaster, and the first undertaker in Galax. He also established the first lumber company. He provided space for a school on the second floor of his store, where classes were held until the new school was completed. It has been said that if one was a customer at Jones's store in the early days of Galax, they could get everything they needed, from the cradle to the coffin. In 1912, Jones and his son, Walter, began construction on a modern brick building for their furniture store and funeral home; it was located on the west side of North Main Street. Jones was a leader in school affairs and in the political, social, and religious life of the community. He and his wife, the former Lithia Kirby, were the parents of Samuel E., Nelson Clyde, Ellie, Robert Luther, Stella B., Walter M., and Emmett. Jones died in 1937. (City of Galax.)

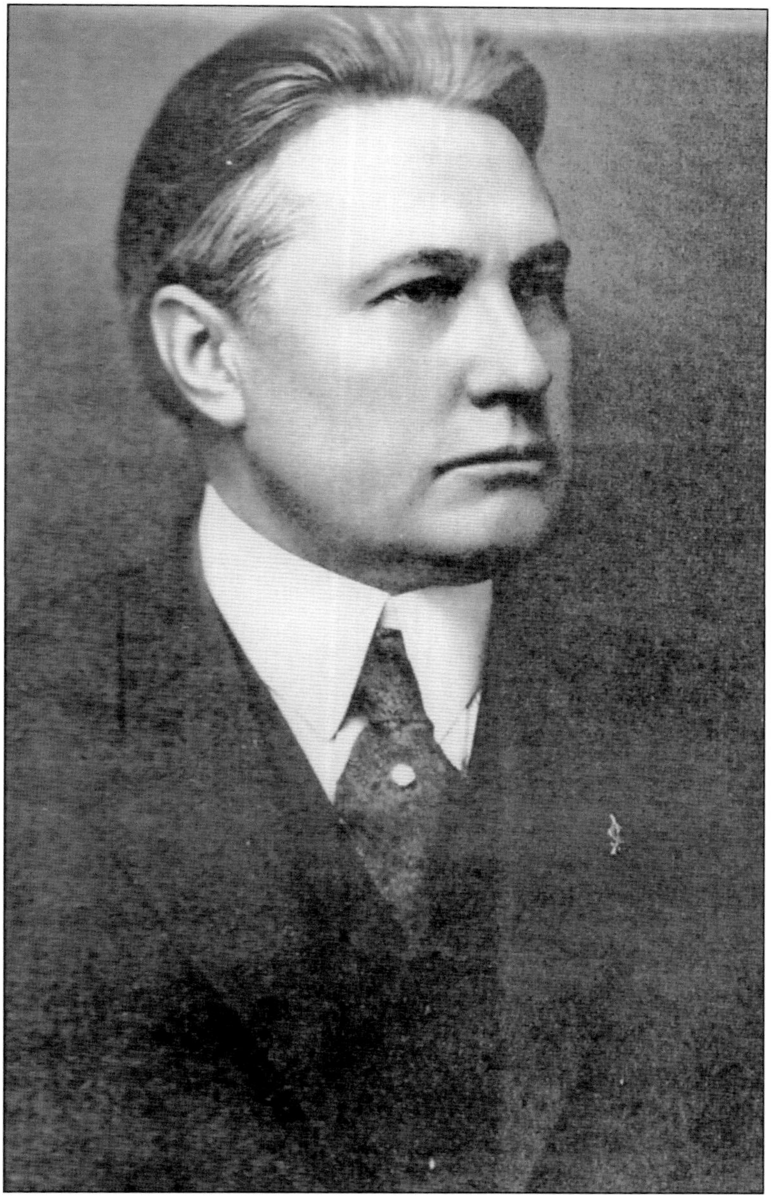

At age 21, Tom Felts entered into a partnership in the Baldwin-Felts Detective Agency and was prominent in political, farming, and banking circles. He was a member of the Masonic order, a Shriner, and a member of the Elks and Odd Fellows. Felts was the founder and president of the First National Bank and served on the board of directors of Mountain Trust in Roanoke. He served in the house of delegates and later as a state senator representing the counties of Grayson and Carroll. Felts, long identified with the development of this area, was a man of pronounced convictions. Felts married Elizabeth Houseman in 1891, and they were the parents of one son, Gordon. Following his death in 1937, a local resident remarked, "Mr. Felts was an influential business man and a leader in the progressive growth of Galax. He was a handsome man who drove the prettiest horse-and-buggies in town. Stories about his experiences as a brave detective excited us as youngsters. Mr. Felts was our hero, a sort of living Dick Tracy." (MM.)

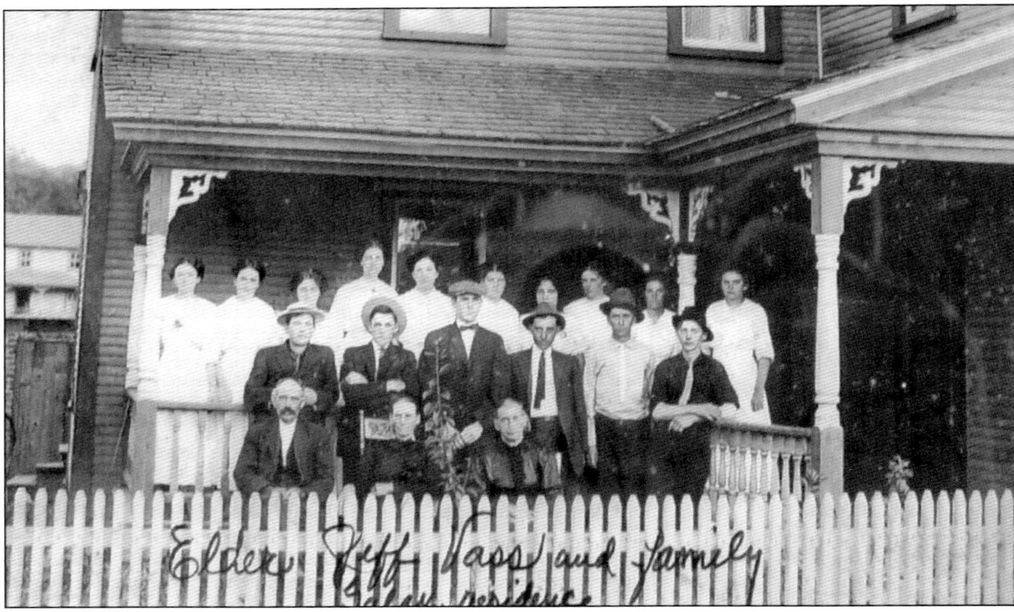

This is a photograph of the elder Jeff Vass family in front of their home in Galax. J. F. Vass and J. H. Vass were partners with J. C. Matthews, J. H. Kapp, L. J. Todd, John H. Faddis, Charlie Dobyns, and B. D. Beamer in the J. C. Matthews Hardware Company. In 1921, Matthews established his own hardware company, and J. H. Vass and J. P. Kapp established the Vass-Kapp Hardware on the corner of Main and West Grayson Streets. (MM.)

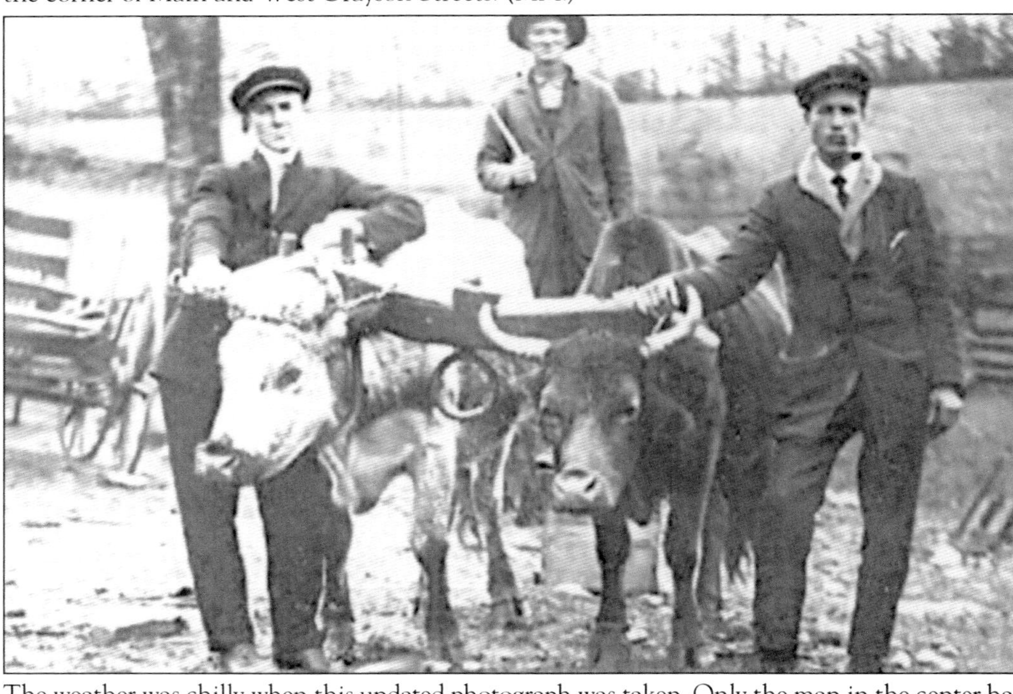

The weather was chilly when this undated photograph was taken. Only the man in the center has been identified, as Daniel Redd. The names of the other two men are unknown. A team of oxen was a valuable asset for farmers, not only for farm labor, but for transportation as well. (GPL.)

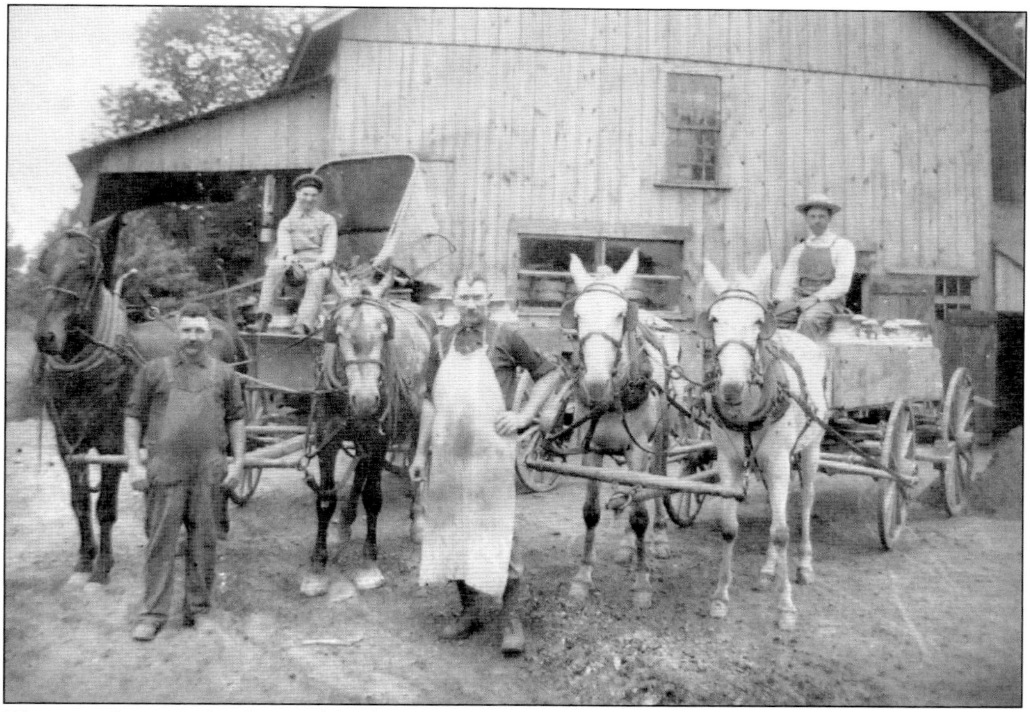

This is a photograph of one of the local dairies in the area during the early 1900s. Note the milk cans in the wagons. The men would go from house to house delivering milk. By the 1940s, local dairymen were involved with Carnation milk, which provided them with a dependable market for their fresh milk. (MM.)

Alexander Chapman and Ada May Cooper Anderson were both from old pioneer Grayson County families. They raised a large family of their own in a two-story white frame house in the southwest section of Galax. Their children included Lula Belle, Virginia, Pauline, Juanita, Alice, Helen, Ned, and Dan. (Barbara Eanes.)

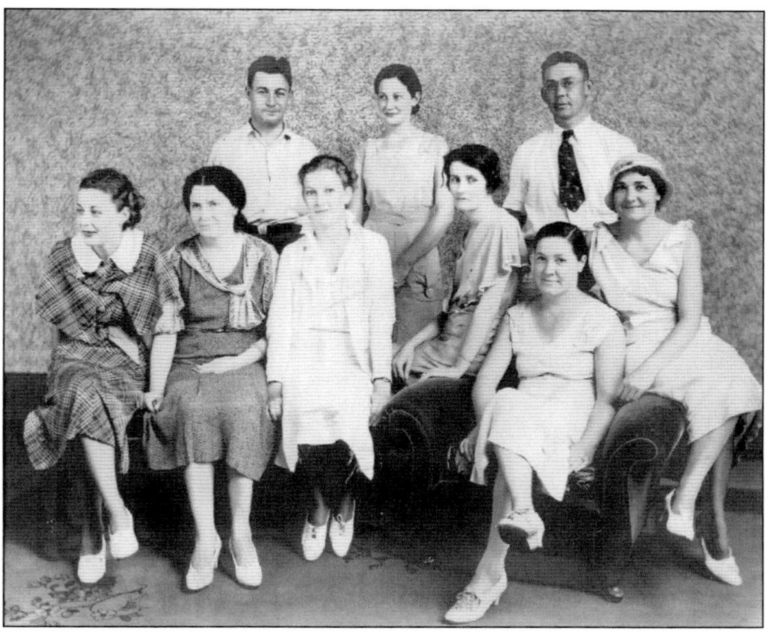

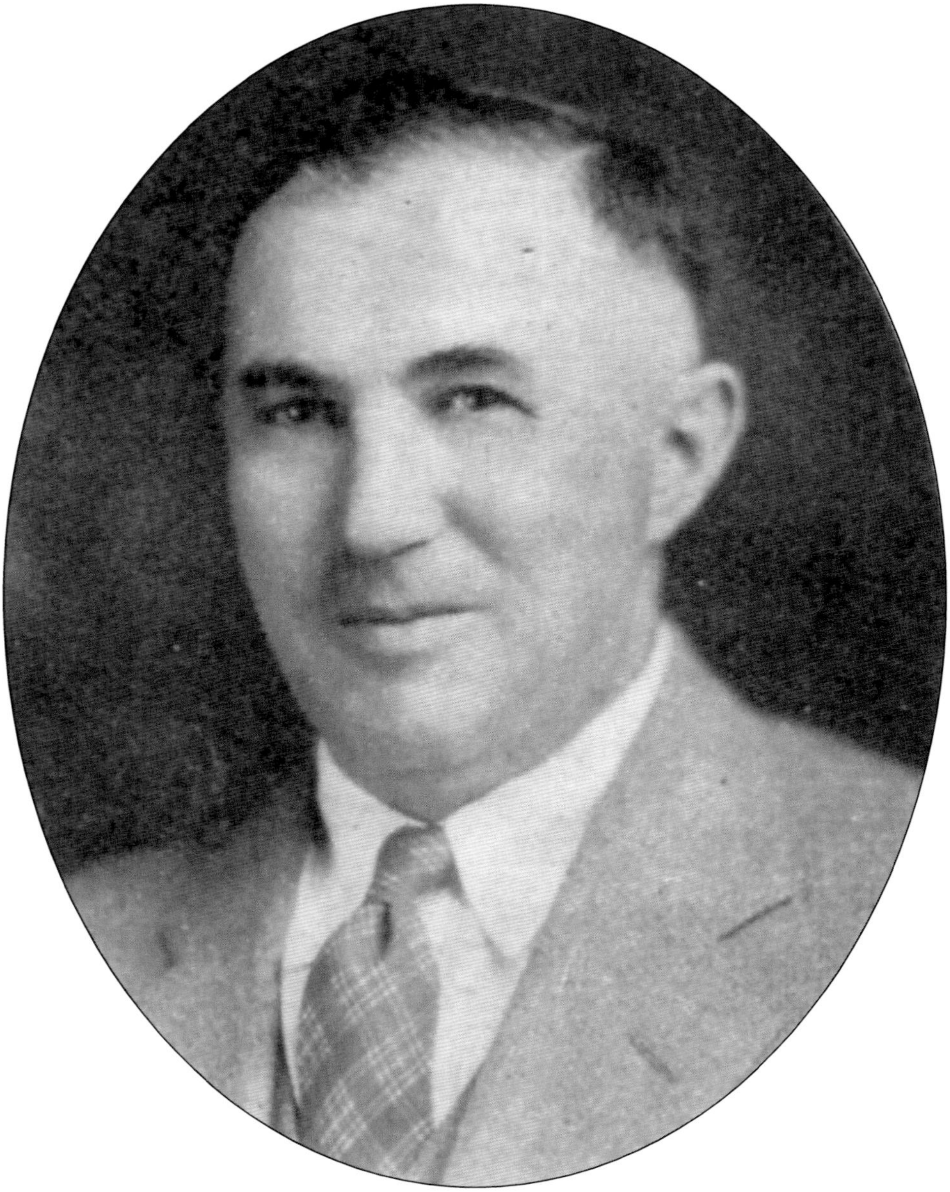

John A. Messer Sr. was a Russian immigrant who arrived in the United States in 1897. He moved to Galax in December 1927 with his wife, Augusta, and their four children. He arrived with $1,200 in his pocket and a strong faith in the future of Galax as an industrial center. He established the Galax Mirror Company, and during the next 15 years, he added Webb Furniture, Mr. Airy Mirror, Galax Furniture, and Carroll Furniture to Messer Industries. He was a member of the Methodist church, serving on the board of stewards and on the board of trustees. He was a member of the Loyal Order of Moose, the Masons, and the Kazim Temple in Roanoke. Not seeking recognition, he quietly went about giving a helping hand to his fellow men. He could always be depended upon to provide support when asked, because he believed that one should always give back to their community. He was a strong civic and business leader, and a staunch member of the Republican Party, attending the National Convention as an alternate delegate in 1956. (JJN.)

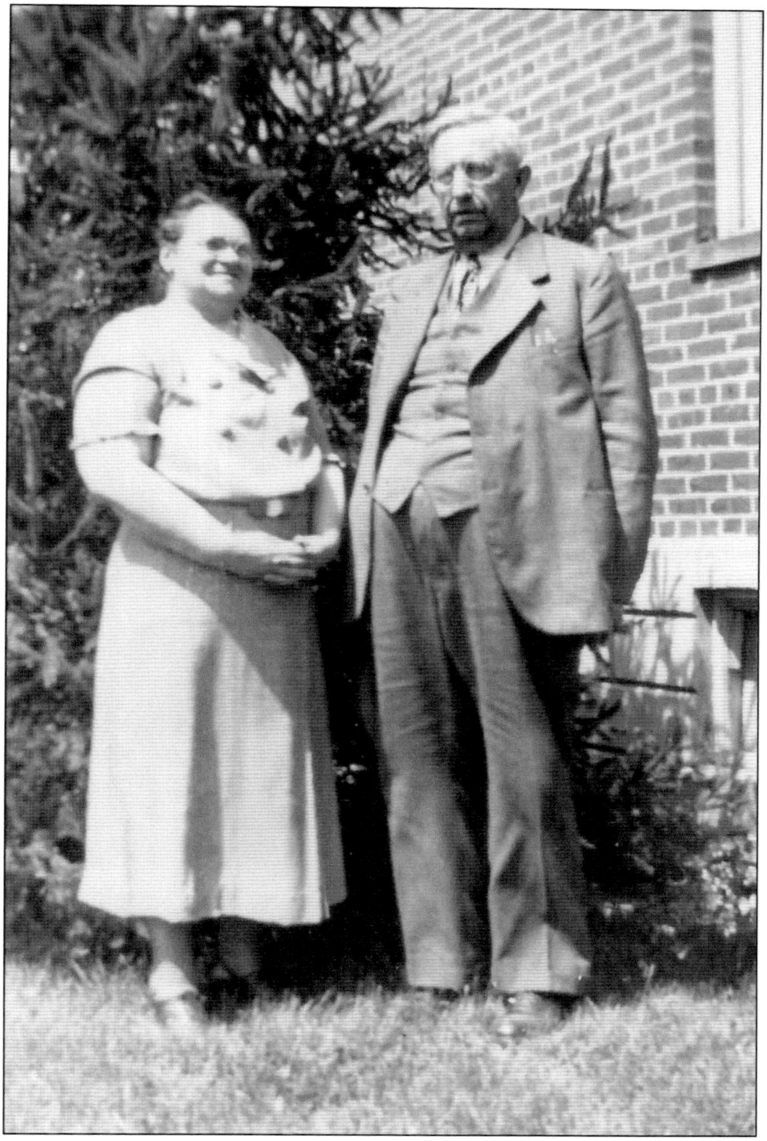

When interviewed in 1952, Dr. John Kingsbury Caldwell talked about his 53-year career of traveling the back roads of the county, delivering more than 5,000 babies. His mode of transportation included everything from walking and horseback, to buggies, cars, and even sleds pulled by steers. He was the perfect example of an old-time country family doctor. Dr. Caldwell helped organize the Grayson Real Estate Company and encouraged the Norfolk and Western Railway (N&W) to recognize the potential for growth in this area. When he moved to Galax in 1903 to set up his medical practice, he also treated the young town as if it was a patient as well. Dr. Caldwell nurtured the community by serving on the town council, taking on the task of improving sanitary conditions, working diligently to build a new school for the community, and organizing the Galax Hospital and clinic that opened on Center Street in 1925. It was Dr. Caldwell's dream to help Galax develop into an industrial manufacturing center. In his lifetime, he saw the town rise from its mud hole to become an amazingly neat and bustling trading center; his dream came true. Pictured with Dr. Caldwell is his wife, Hattie Roberta Caldwell. (NF.)

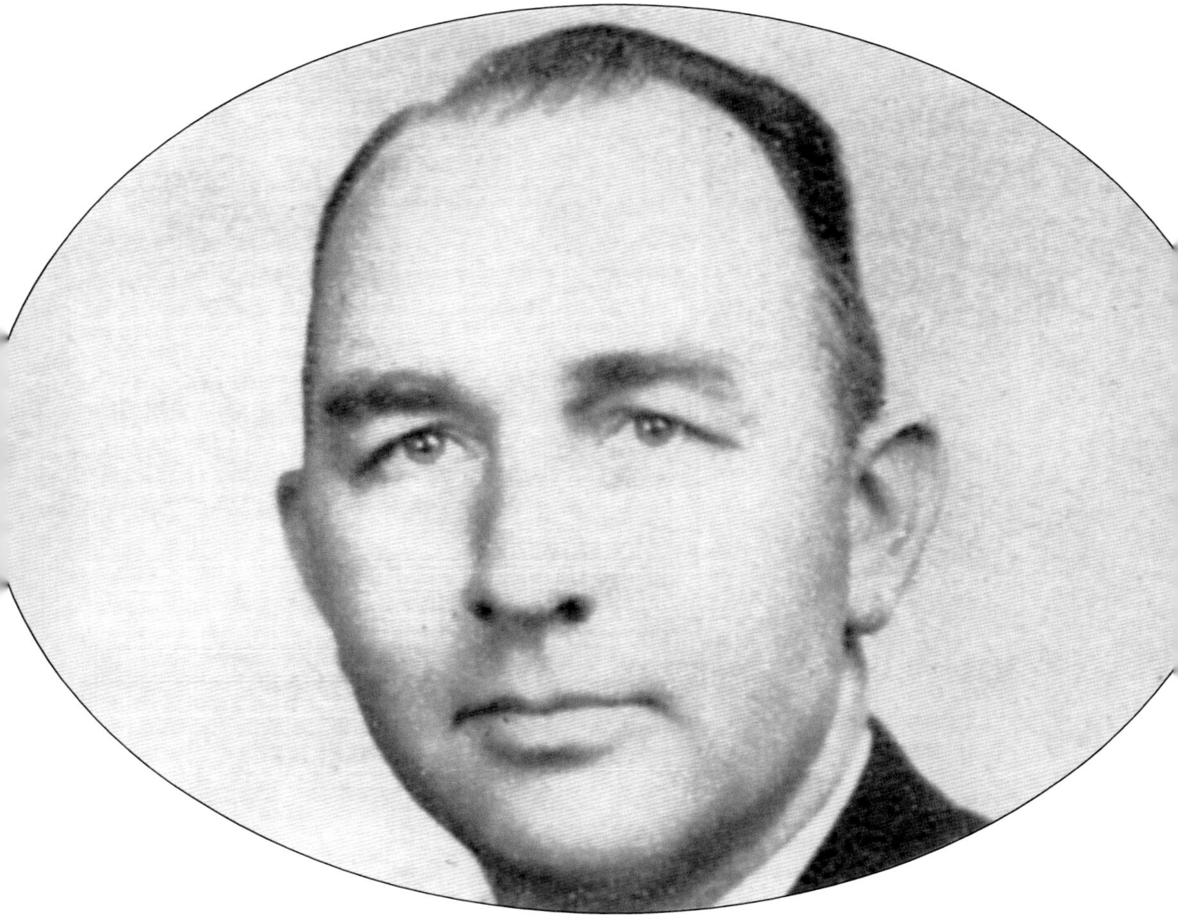

A. Glenn Pless Jr. spent his entire adult life serving the community he loved. In 1931, he took over the General Electric franchise in Galax and two years later added furniture. When financial times became hard for the local residents, Pless was one of the first who accepted purchases made on credit. When Galax flooded in 1940, he cancelled a majority of debts to his store. He was one of the men who helped secure federal funding to widen Chestnut Creek. Pless spent 40 years on the board of the Merchant and Farmers Bank. He was a member of the Galax Rotary Club, the First Methodist Church, the Galax YMCA, Galax-Carroll-Grayson Chamber of Commerce, and Galax Country Club, and a member of the Sons of the American Revolution. He also served on the board of the Vaughan Memorial Library and the Twin County Regional Hospital. Pless was not just a joiner; he was a worker who could always be depended upon to do more than his share. (JJN.)

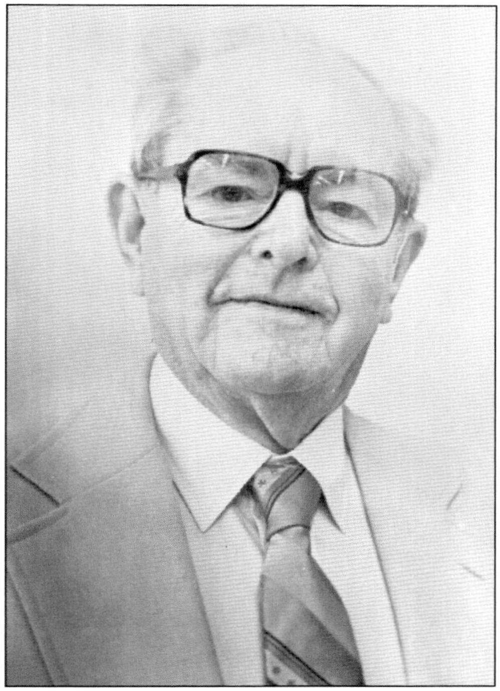

Dr. Virgil Cox set up his medical practice in 1936, and from the day of his arrival, the health and welfare of the residents of Galax was his No. 1 concern. He was an excellent example of the old-time country doctor who made house calls at any hour of the day or night. His office, located on Grayson Street, was expanded into a 44-bed hospital in 1952. (GG.)

Nathan Potolsky arrived in Galax in 1929 and immediately became a hardworking, dedicated citizen of the community. As manager of Globman's Department Store, he served as president of the Galax Merchants Association. His involvement with the Boy Scouts earned him the coveted Silver Beaver Award for noteworthy service to scouting. He served as Rotary Club president and was an active member of the Masons. (JJN.)

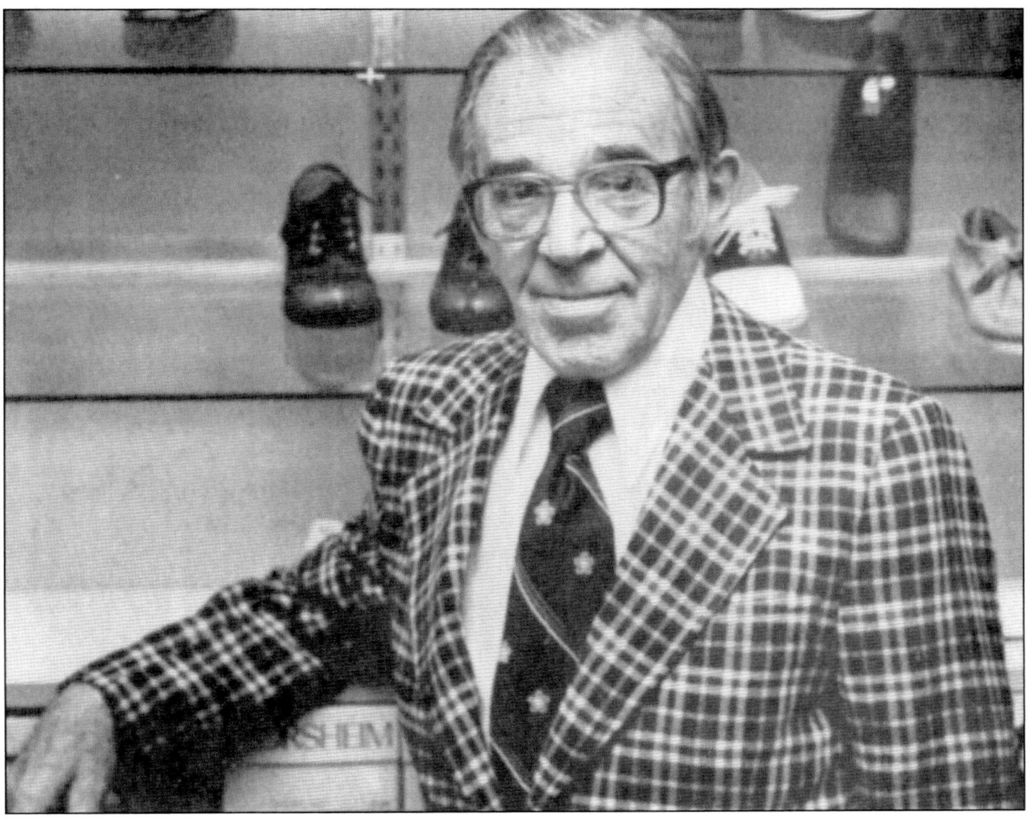

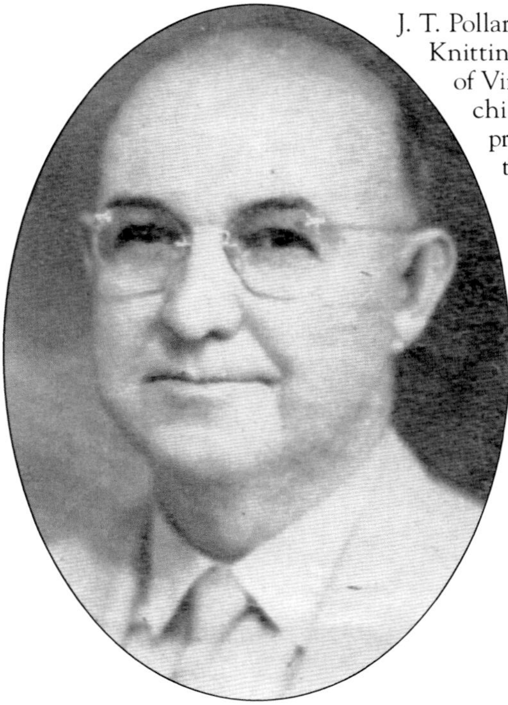

J. T. Pollard came to Galax in 1923 to organize the Galax Knitting Company. The business, located on the corner of Virginia and Madison Streets, produced men's and children's socks and ladies seamless hosiery. The products were sold to the jobbing trades throughout the United States. (JJN.)

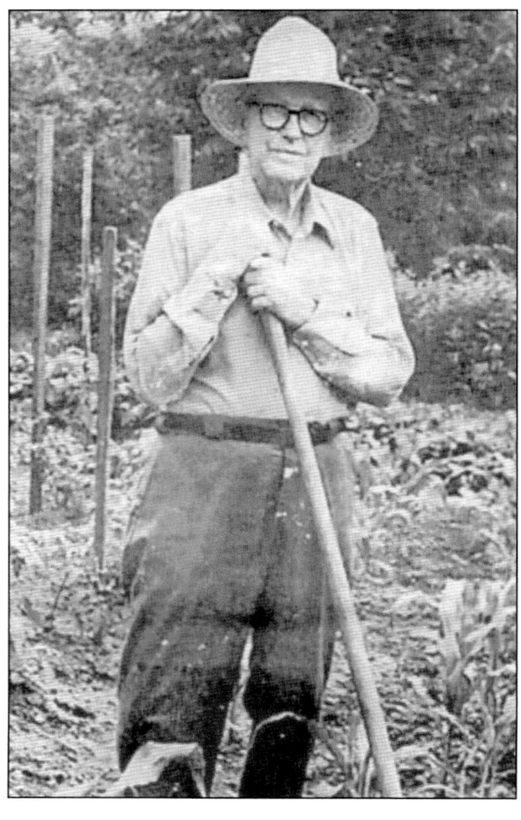

Walter G. Andrews became the Galax town manager in 1947, and under his guidance, several major improvements took place. Chestnut Creek was widened, the town became a second-class city, a new water and sewer plant was built, the new high school was completed, and the Galax Fire Department complex was erected. Because of Andrews's hard work and dedication to the city, the firemen named their new station the Walter G. Andrews Fire Station. (JJN.)

Taylor G. Vaughan was founder and president of Vaughan Furniture Company. Even with his commitment and attention to his factory, he still found time to devote to civic and community affairs. Vaughan also served as a state senator from the 14th Senatorial District, which is comprised of the counties of Grayson and Carroll. When T. G. Vaughan suddenly died at age 50, the furniture industry lost a man of vision. (JJN.)

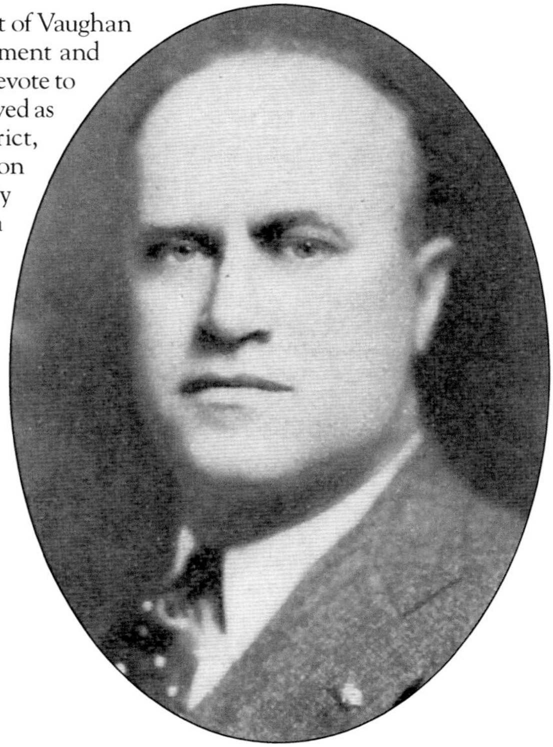

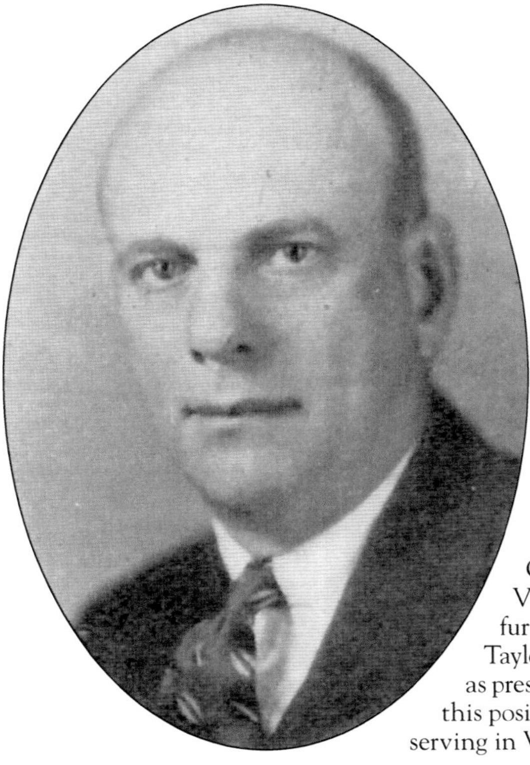

Bunyan Charles Vaughan was president and treasurer of the Vaughan Bassett Furniture Company, which was established in 1919. Vaughan has long been identified with the furniture industry in the South. When his brother Taylor died in 1940, B. C. Vaughan succeeded him as president of Vaughan Furniture Company. He held this position until Taylor G. Vaughan Jr. returned from serving in World War II. (JJN.)

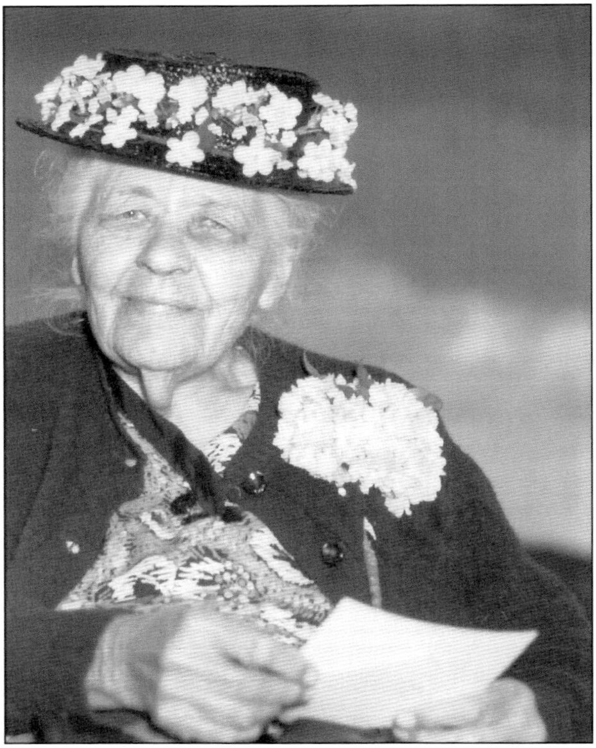

Nancy Melvina "Miss Vinnie" Caldwell was born in Carroll County in 1868 near what would eventually become Galax. She was the daughter of J. Barger and Fannie Givens Caldwell and the sister of Dr. J. K. Caldwell. She was one of the first four women to serve in the Virginia State Senate. She returned to Galax in 1912 when Galax was expanding its early growth. She became active in the advancement of the town and the surrounding counties. She served as a volunteer social worker for more than 20 years. (NF.)

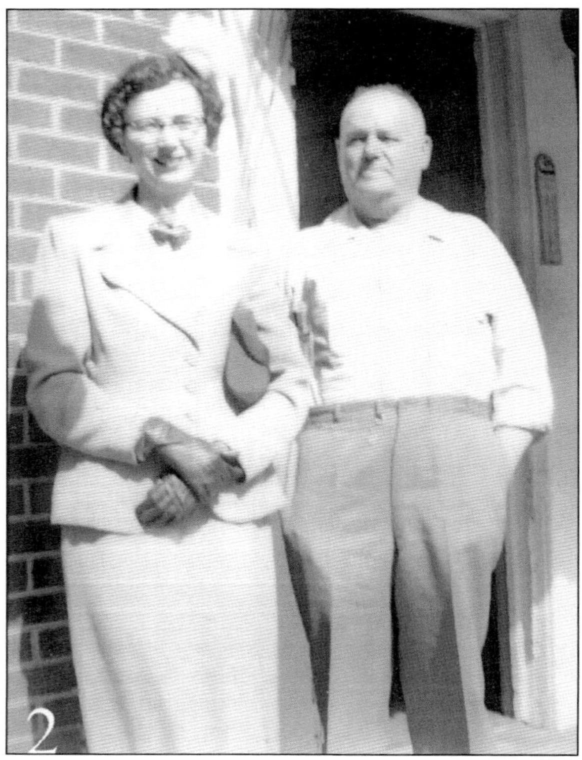

Troy Goodson was well known to thousands of people from this section of the state through the many years he spent as the owner and operator of Goodson's Café. He began his business on the east side of South Main Street next to Apperson's Store but later moved it to the north side of West Grayson Street. Goodson's Café served three hot meals daily; it was common knowledge that Goodson could never turn away a hungry individual. (GG.)

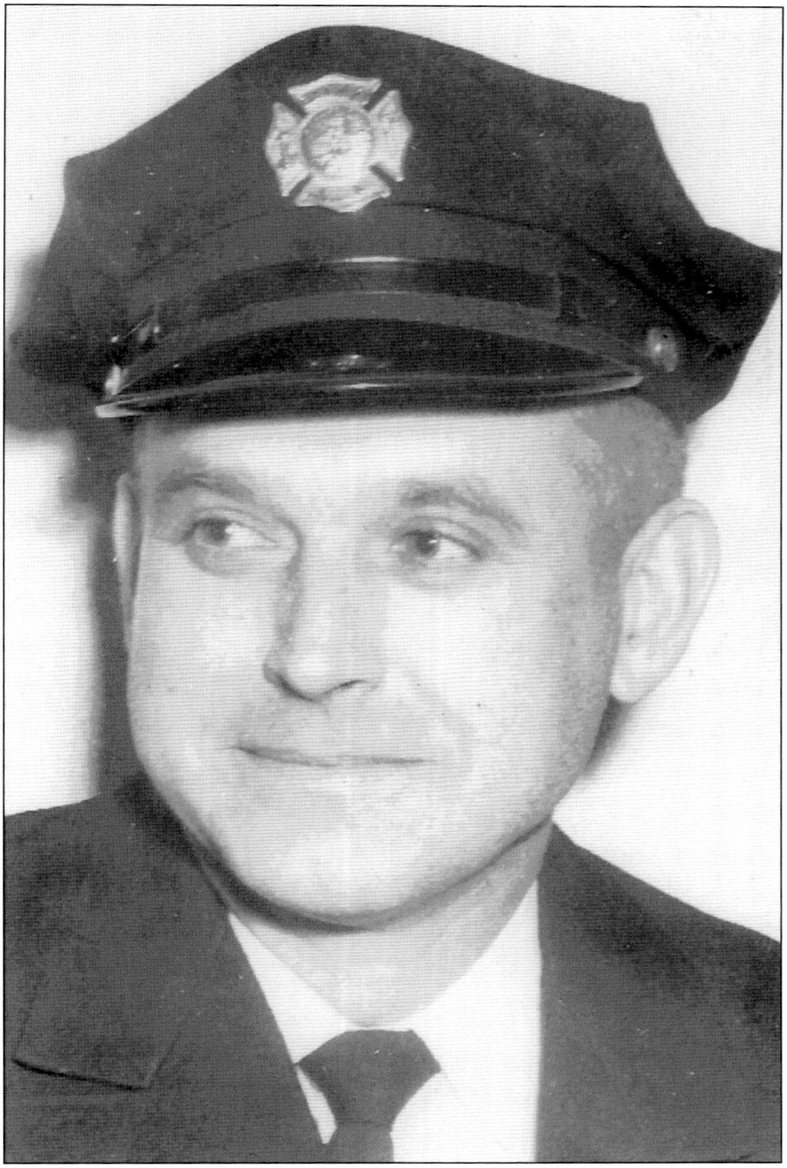

Joe Crockett was a patriotic member of America's "Greatest Generation" and will long be remembered as the driving force behind the Galax Volunteer Fire Department. When he died at age 88, he had dedicated more than 60 years to the organization, 32 years as chief. Crockett led by example in terms of his work ethic and dedication. He set an outstanding example for the men who spoke of him with such deep respect. Joe Crockett always made the welfare and safety of his men his No. 1 concern. A fellow fireman said that people respected Joe, because he was proud of the department and he believed in it. He was affectionately known as the "Great White Father" because of his wisdom and experience. Joe was also in the radio business for 38 years, during which he served as station manager for WBOB, now WWWJ-AM. He was a lifelong member of the Methodist church and the Lions Club, won the Citizen of the Year Moose and Boss of the Year awards, the last given by the Jaycees. Joseph Pierce Crockett was called a leader that saw beyond the present and planned for the future. (JW.)

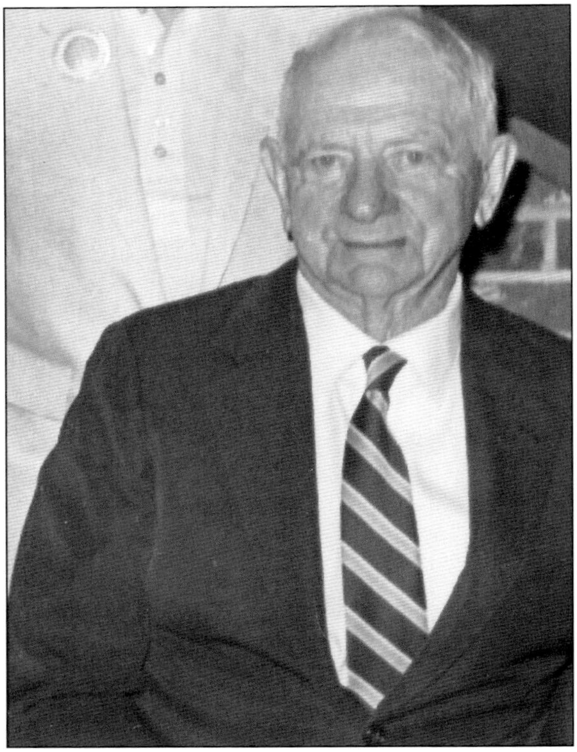

Judge Jack Matthews possessed a deep and abiding interest in the cultural heritage of this area. Through his efforts and generosity, the Matthews State Forest was established on 566 acres. The judge enjoyed all forms of outside activities, and it was his vision to provide for the scientific, educational, and research needs of those interested in protecting and improving water quality, wild habitat, and the native biological diversity. (Margaret Thomason.)

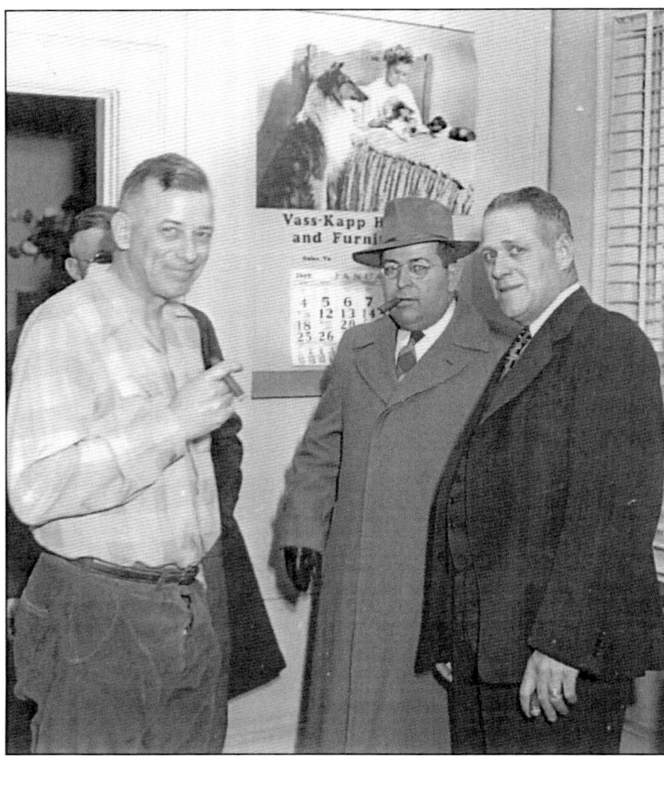

This is a photograph of three civic leaders—Mike Crabill (left), Ross Penry (center), and Bob Morris. Each man helped to improve the quality of life in Galax in a different way. Crabill was editor of the *Galax Post Herald*, with the motto "a local newspaper for local homes." Ross Penry was the general manager of the Old Dominion Knitting Company, which provided jobs for a large female workforce. Bob Morris was active in the Boy Scouts, owned the radio station WBOB, and was a member of the Galax Fire Department. He was also a wise investor in many local businesses. (JW.)

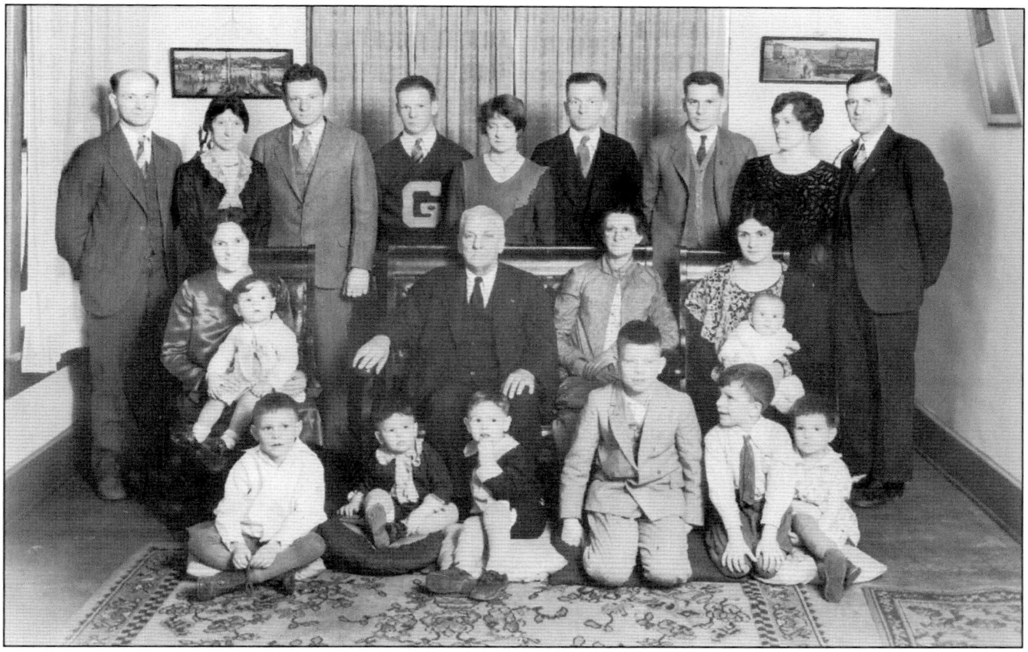

The family of John Creed and Cora Cox Matthews assemble for a family photograph. Pictured from left to right are (first row) Jim Vass Sr., Tommy Matthews, Billy Matthews, Eldon Vass, Gene Johnson, and Mildred Johnson; (second row) Zelle Thomas Matthews holding Bobby Matthews, John C. and Cora Matthews, and Blanche Alderman Matthews holding Frances Lee; (third row) Jeff Matthews, Mary Matthews Johnson, Jack Matthews, Claude Matthews, Blanche Matthews Clark, Edd Matthews, Walter Matthews, Alice Matthews Vass, and I. G. Vass. (Margaret Thomason.)

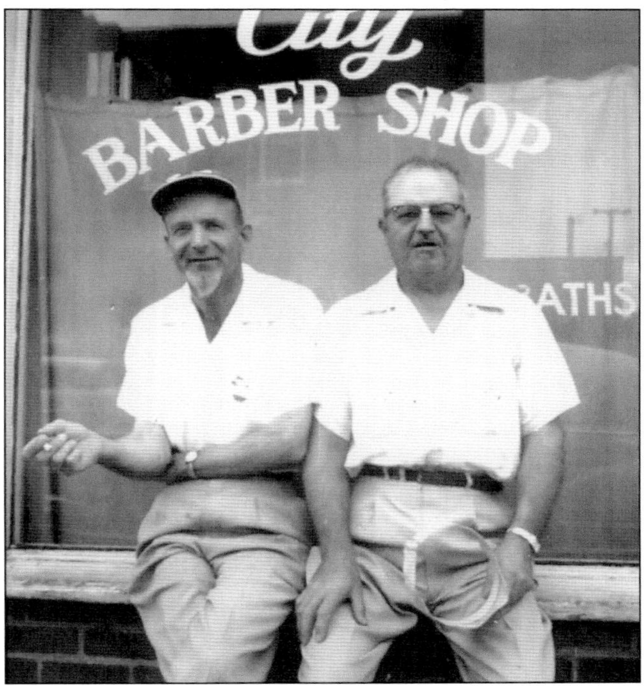

Charlie Newman (left) and Bob Murphy sit in front of their barbershop on South Main Street. It was located half way between Waugh's and Globmans on the north side of the alley. This has been the site of barbershops since the early days of Galax. The photograph was taken during the Golden Jubilee Celebration in the summer of 1956. (MM.)

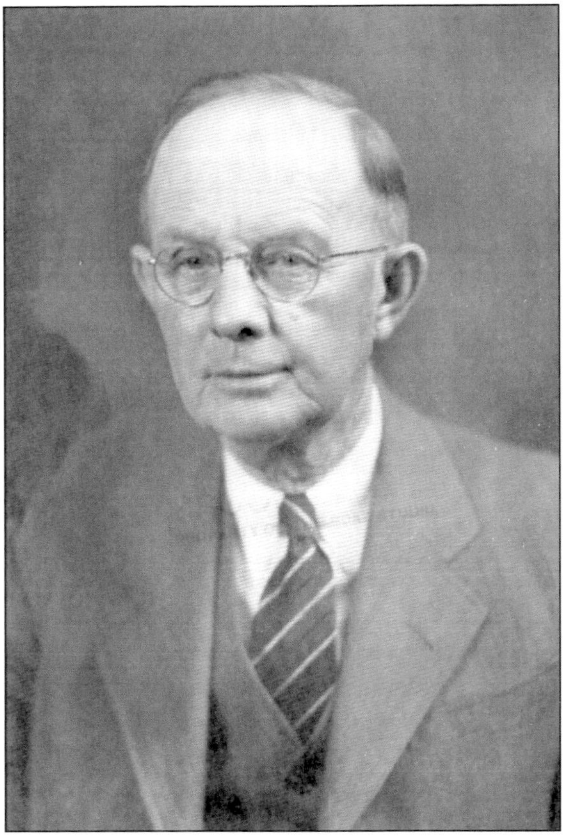

When William K. Early died in 1927, his son George took over as president of W. K. Early and Son. George Belo Early was a prominent businessman, a member of the original Galax Volunteer Fire Department, served on the town council, and was on the board of directors of the old Peoples State Bank. He was a Mason, a Shriner, and a member of the Rotary Club. (Louise Pollard.)

Lester Jennings was an employee of the Vaughan-Bassett Furniture Company. His job was operating the lathe turning machine to make bedposts. His son, Raymond Jennings, provided this photograph, taken around 1940. (MM.)

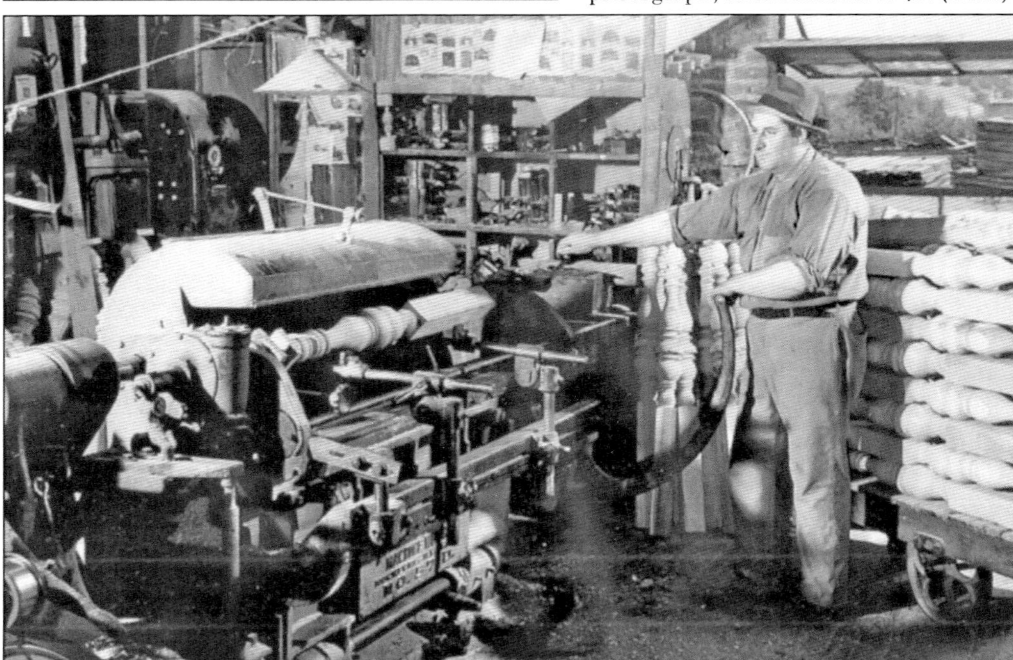

Three

Buildings and Businesses

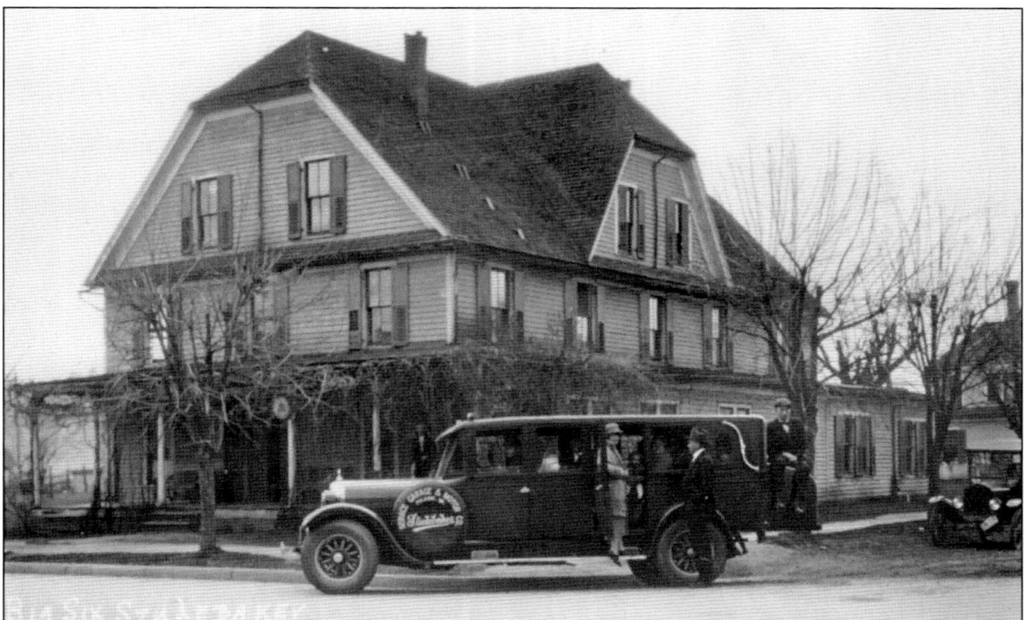

The Waugh Hotel was located on the corner of North Main and East Center Streets and was a popular gathering place for the local residents. "Service Garage and Motor Company, Pulaski, Virginia" was on the wheel cover of this Studebaker bus. It was part of the Blue Ridge Bus Line, servicing Galax, Hillsville, and Pulaski. The date of the photograph is unknown, and the people are unidentified. The house, partially visible on the right, is the home of Lelia B. Waugh, the first owner of the hotel. (GPL.)

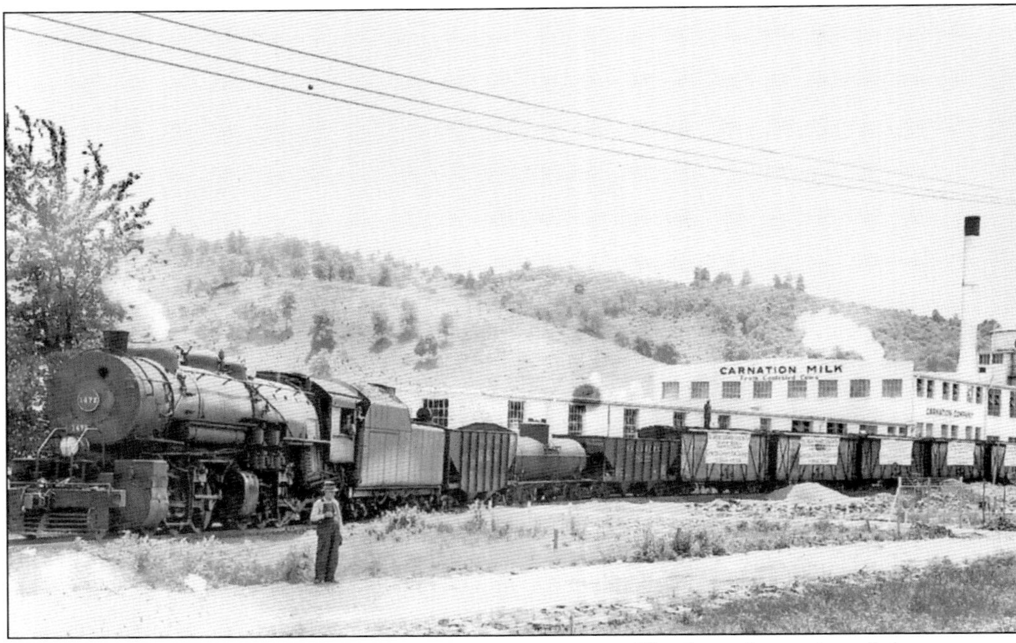

The formal opening of the Carnation company's new plant in Galax on July 23, 1937, was called Cow Day. Most of the business owners gave their employees a half holiday, so they could inspect the new plant, listen to Gov. George C. Peery speak, attend the picnic, and participate in all the games that had been planned by the organizational committee. (MM.)

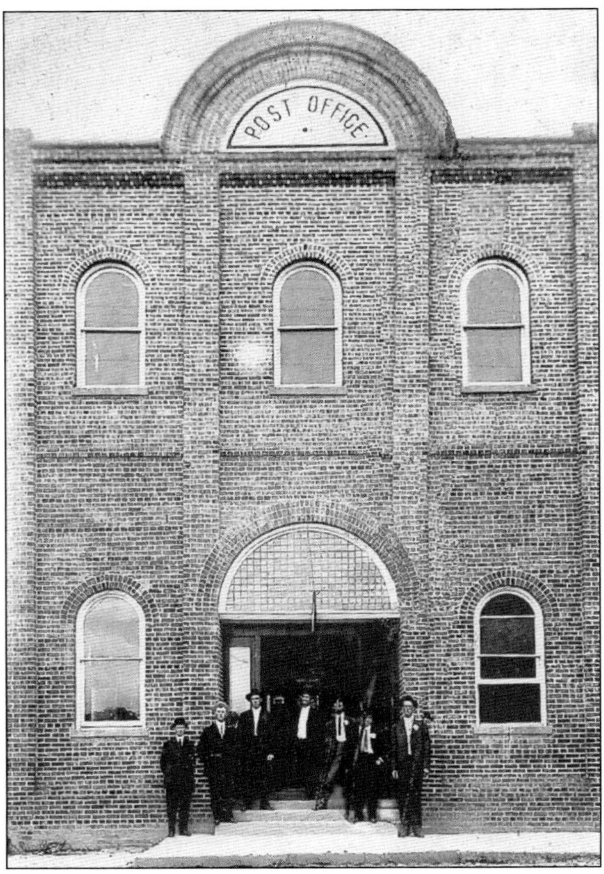

This photograph was taken in 1916 and shows the U.S. Post Office when it was located at 106 South Main Street. Later it became E. E. Lineberry's Jewelry Store, K&P Barbershop, and then Roy's Diamond Center. The first two men at left are Bill Todd and L. M. Todd. The other men are unidentified. (MM.)

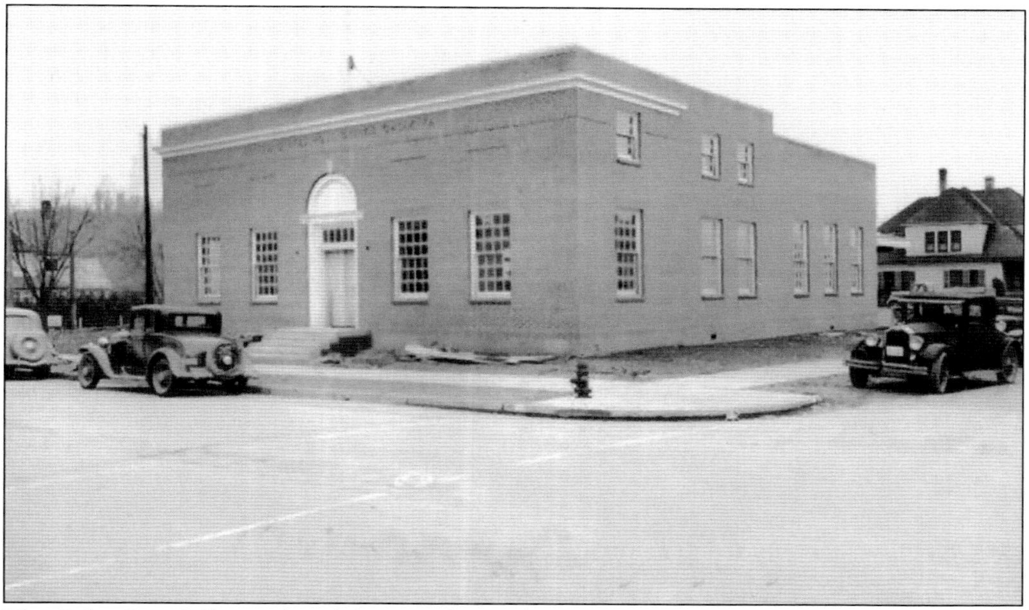

The Galax Post Office replaced the Waugh Hotel on the corner of North Main and East Center Streets in the mid-1930s. The U.S. government purchased the lots from E. B. Lenox on October 4, 1934, for $7,500. Lelia Waugh, the original owner of the site, had paid $2,900.75 for the five lots and the hotel in 1904. (GPL.)

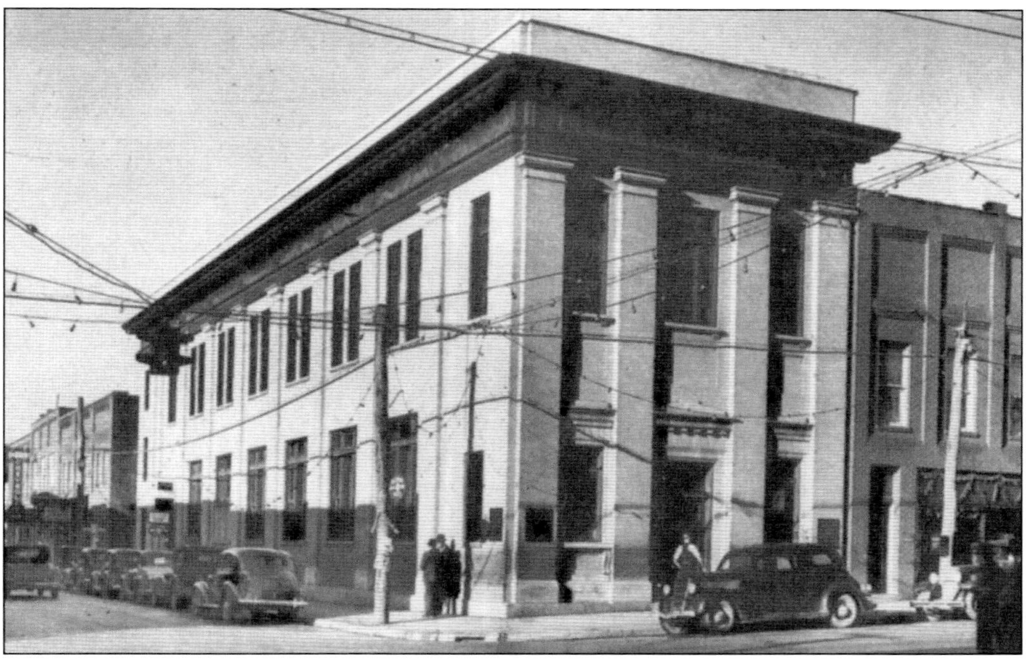

The First National Bank was one of the largest financial institutions in southwest Virginia when this photograph was taken in 1937. T. L. Felts and associates chartered the bank in July 1907, not long after Galax was founded. The board of directors included many of Galax's most influential citizens. (JJN.)

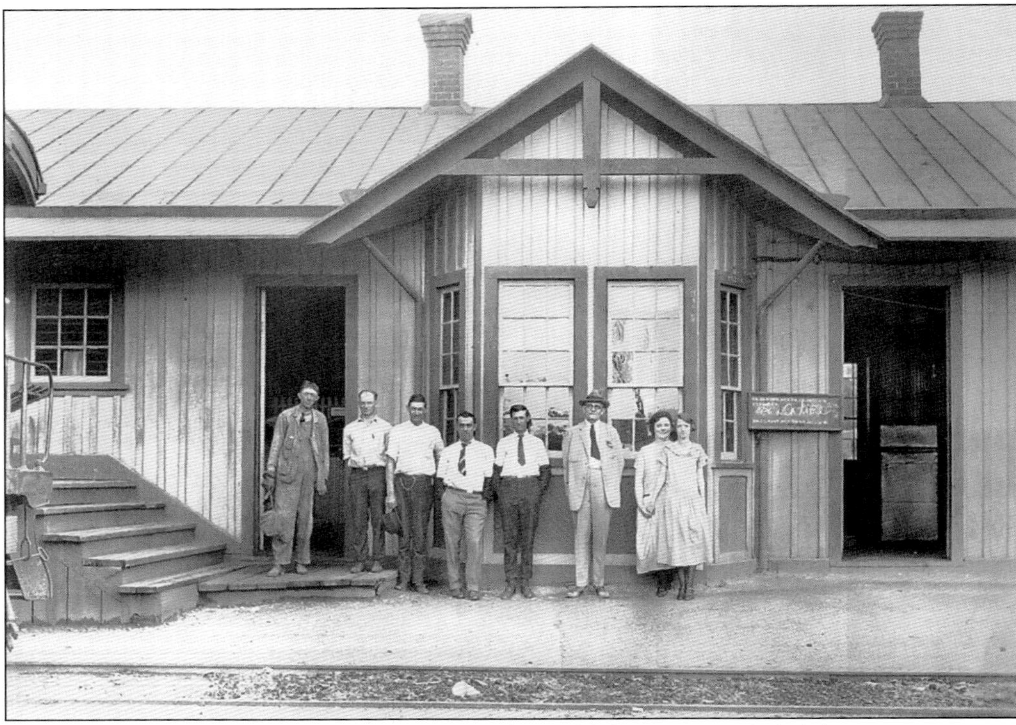

The railroad gave Galax the link to the outside world that was needed if the town was going to grow. Norfolk and Western Railway's business was booming in Galax when this photograph was taken at the local depot in 1923 or 1924. Pictured from left to right are Garnett Largin, Jeff Matthews, Albert Horton, Obie Dalton, Charlie Ballard, Charlie Baumgardner, Pearl Webb (who later married R. C. Bowie), and her niece, Bea Webb. (James Ballard.)

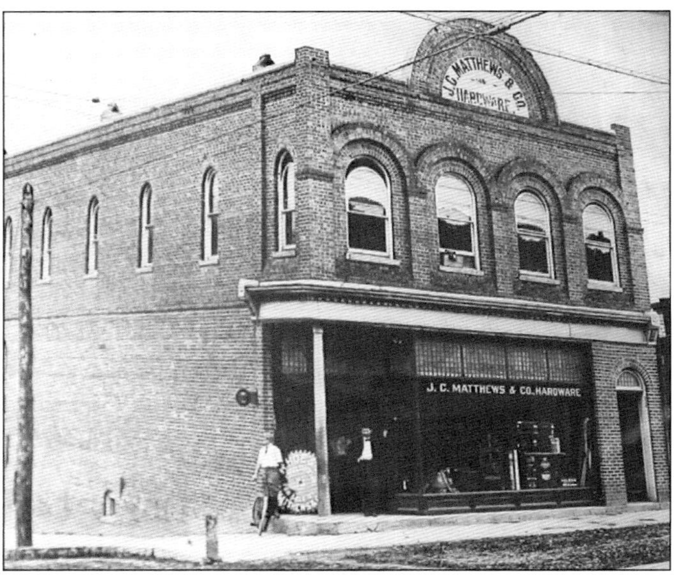

In 1911, the stockholders of the J. C. Matthews Hardware Company began construction of a modern brick building on the southwest corner of Main and Grayson Streets. When the store opened in 1912, the stockholders included J. C. Matthews, L. J. Todd, J. H. Faddis, Charlie Dobyns, and B. D. Beamer. J. H. Kapp sold his interest in the Galax Hardware Company in 1913 and joined J. F. Vass, J. H Vass, and J. C. Matthews in the J. C. Matthews Company. The business later became Vass-Kapp Hardware Company. (MM.)

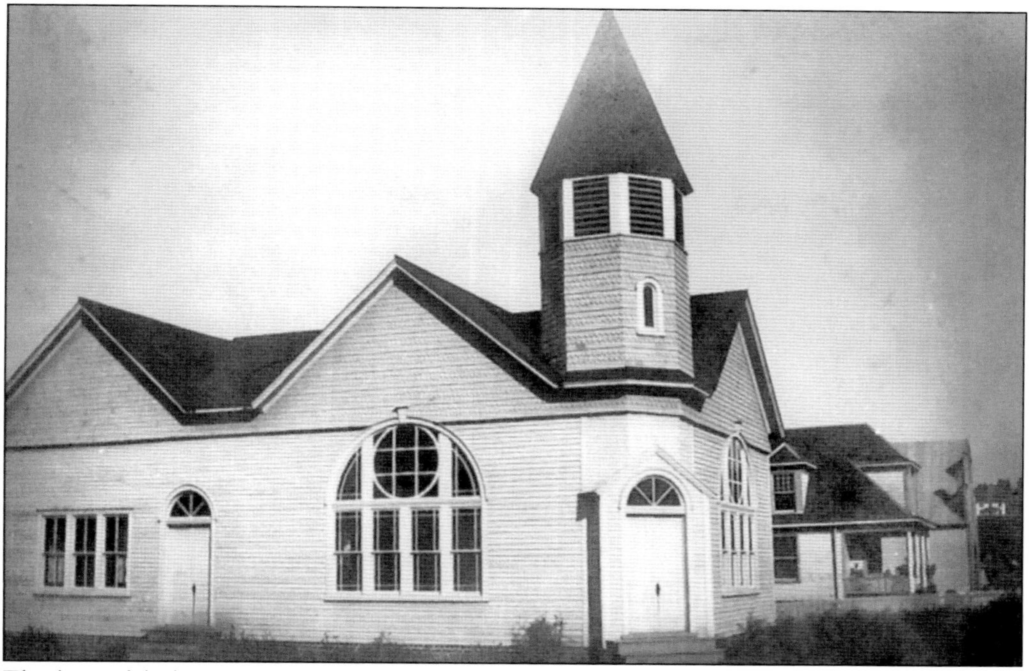

This beautiful white frame church was located on the corner of North Main and West Washington Streets. It would later be moved farther back on the property. Members of the Church of Christ worshiped here until they built a large brick church on Stuart Drive. (MM.)

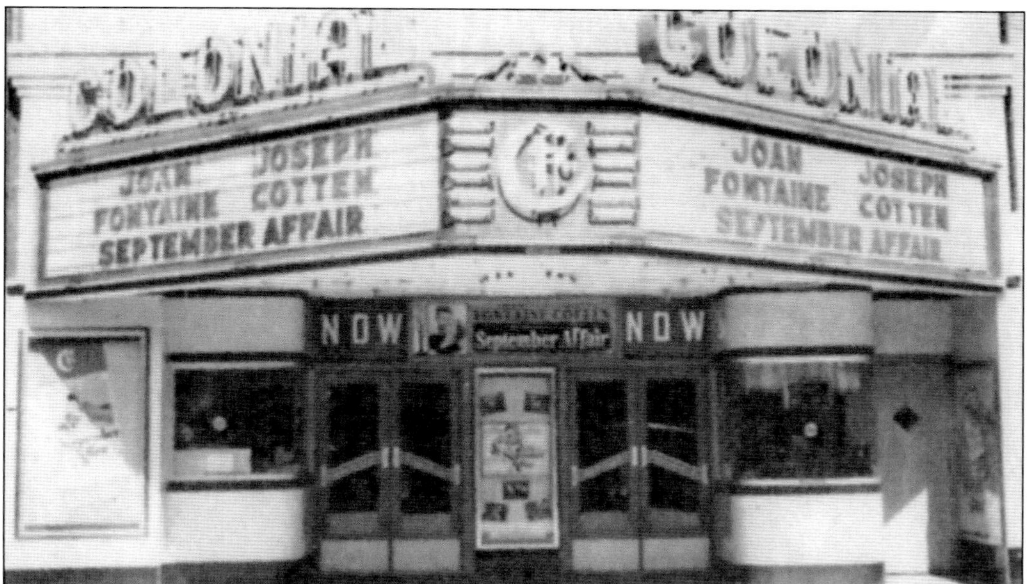

During the 1930s, the reels of movie film were shipped on the bus to Galax from the previous town. When the theater manager realized the film that was to be shown that night had not arrived, he called upon young Kenneth Messer to come to his rescue. Ken, an amateur pilot who flew to the town, picked up the tardy movie and brought it to Galax just in time for it to be shown that evening as scheduled. (JJN.)

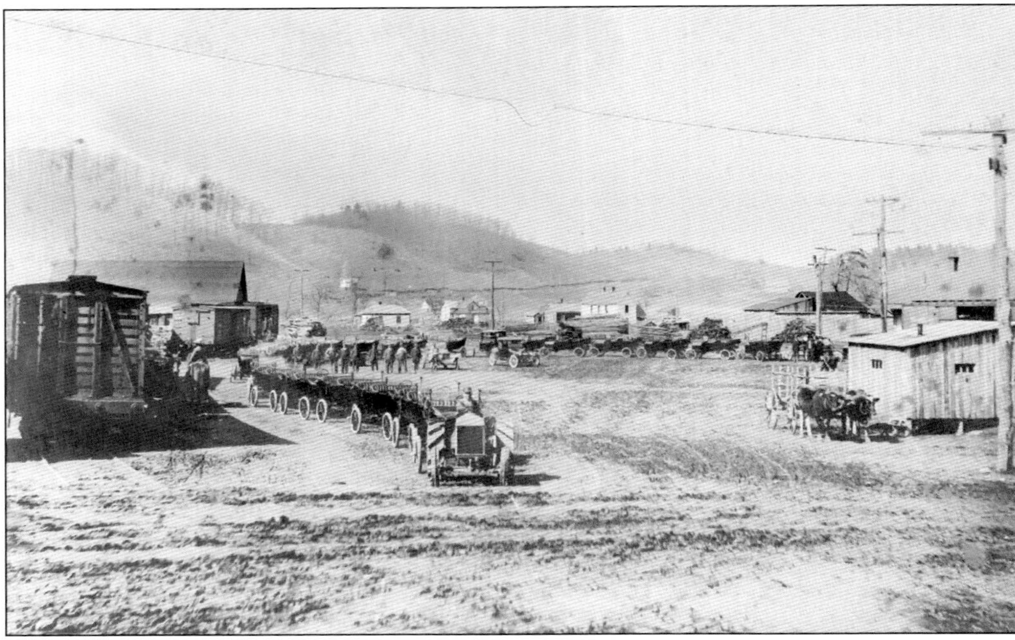

While most parades took place on Main Street, a special event took place at the train depot. When a large shipment of new Model T cars was unloaded at the depot on the west side of Chestnut Creek, they created their own parade. The date of this photograph and the identity of the owners of the new cars are unknown. (MM.)

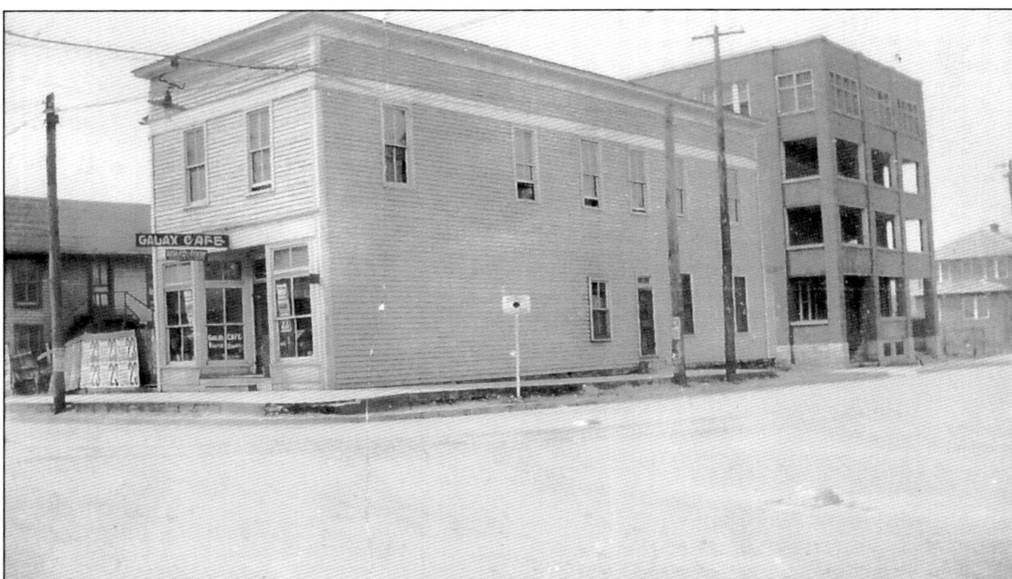

Dr. J. K. Caldwell, one of the pioneer citizens of Galax, opened his first medical practice in 1905. It was located in Dr. J. W. Bolen's boardinghouse in the southern part of town. He later purchased the lot on the southwest corner of Main and Center Streets and erected a building with several other men. The front part of the building was the site for several different businesses during the early years of Galax. The rest of the building was used for medical offices. (MM.)

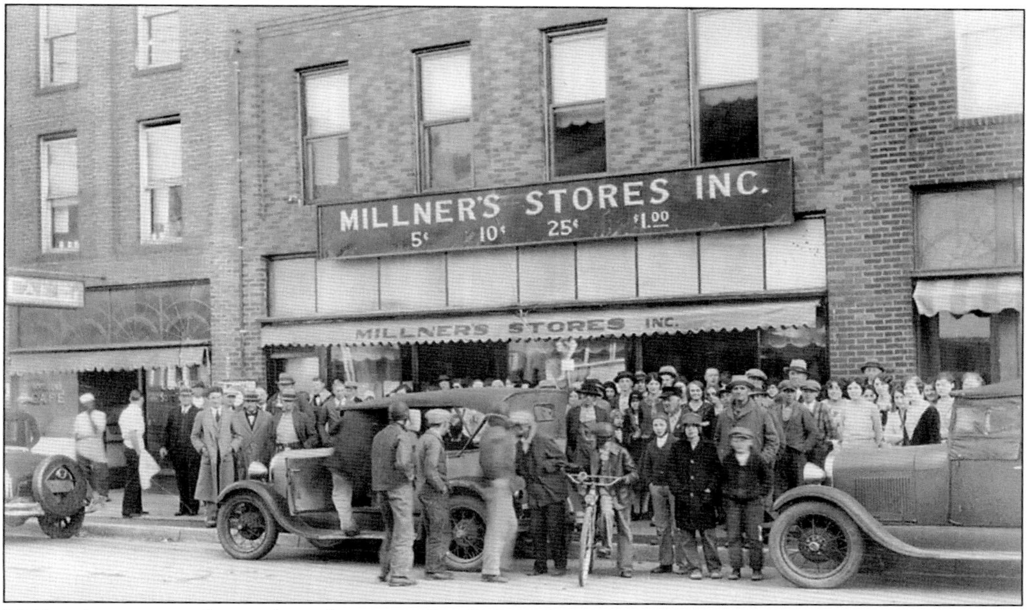

Millner's store was located on the east side of Main Street, across from Henderson's Jewelry Store. The date of this photograph is unknown, and none of the people are identified. Since most of the people are facing the street, could it have been a parade day? (MM.)

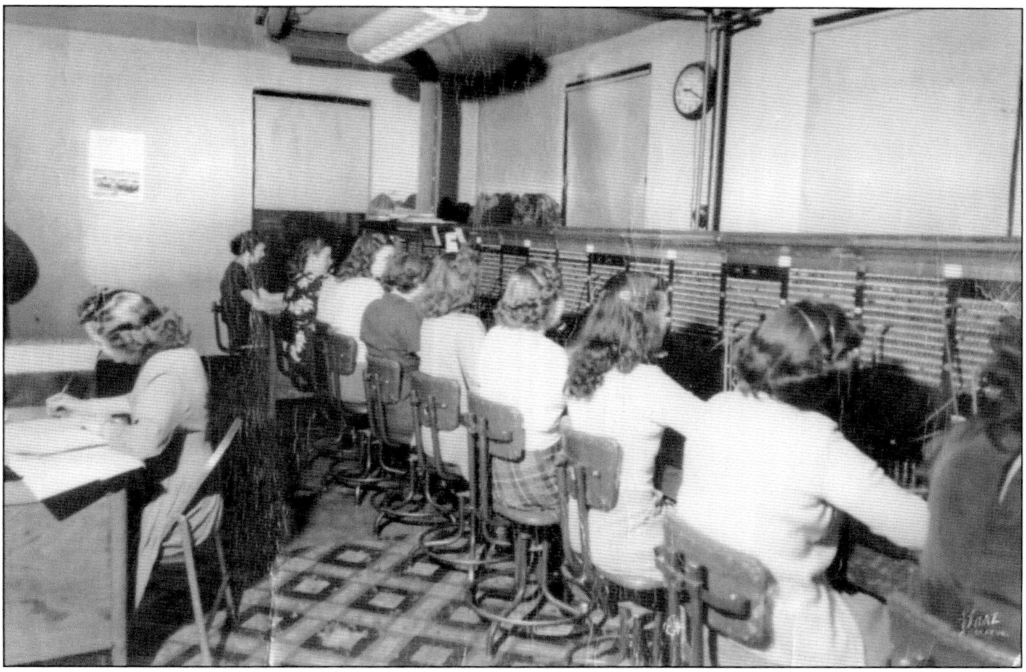

The Intermountain Telephone Company's switchboard was located on the second floor of the First National Bank building at the intersection of Main and Grayson Streets. Cathleen Brakens is seated at the desk (left). Switchboard operators include Juanita Smith (sixth from the left), Evagene Iroler (seventh from the left), and Helen Robinson (eighth from the left). The 1,000th telephone was installed in the home of Kenneth and Reba Messer on Academy Drive. (GPL.)

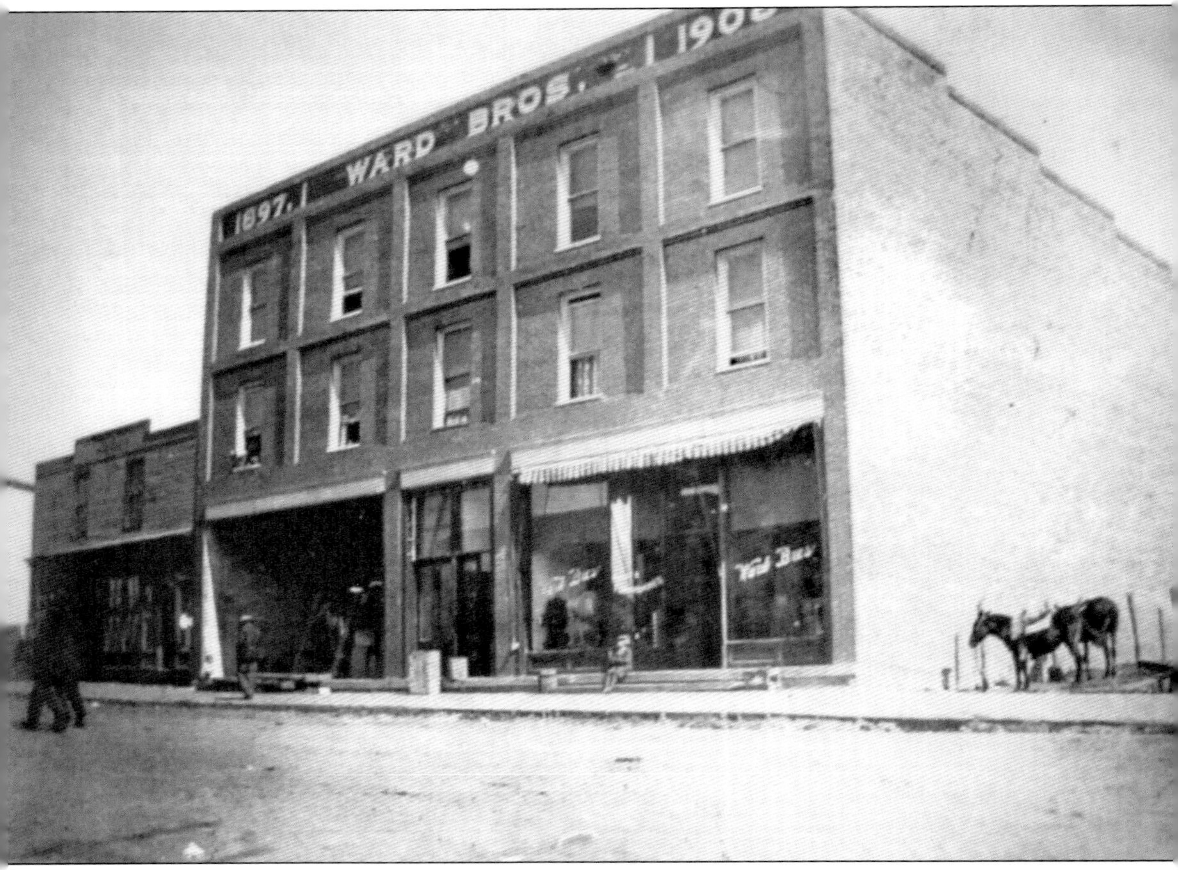

In 1903, the Ward brothers (Frazier, Marvin, and Monroe) purchased a lot on the east side of Main Street near the intersection of Main and Grayson Streets. They constructed a two-story frame building that burned to the ground the night before they were to open their gents furnishings and general merchandise store. The bucket brigade was called into service, and the entire stock of buckets from Blair Hardware, plus all the other buckets, blankets, and quilts were pressed into service. The line of men stretched from the well at the Waugh Hotel to the fire. While unable to save the Ward building, they were able to save the buildings on the west side of the block. The demand for brick became so great that the Ward brothers turned their attention to the construction of a brickyard on the east side of Chestnut Creek. They also replaced their two-story frame building with a three-story brick structure. Monroe Ward supervised the construction, while Marvin was in charge of manufacturing the brick. Ward brick can still be seen in abundance in buildings around town. (MM.)

Mabel Carpenter stands with her pet fox in front of the Boaz Studio. Herman Boaz founded Boaz Studio in 1922 and built his photographic studio on East Oldtown Street in 1927. He remained in this location until he retired. Boaz spent 65 years in his chosen profession and was recognized throughout the state as a photographer of exceptional accomplishments. (Jewell Melton.)

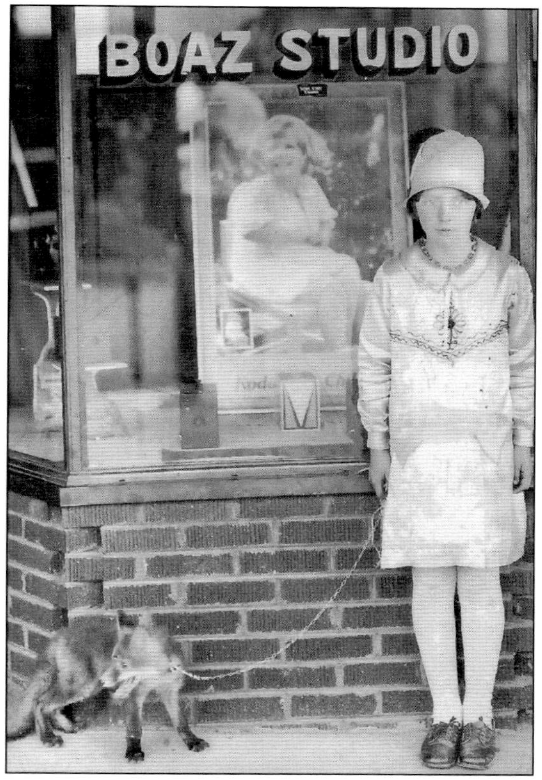

Dr. Robert Waddell came to Galax in 1945 and opened the Waddell Hospital. In the 1950s, the operating room staff included, from left to right, Louis Phipps (surgical assistant), Ruth Osborne (chief anesthetist), Joan McCarter (operating room supervisor), Georgia Crockett (assistant supervisor), and Helen Crockett (O. B. anesthetist). (JW.)

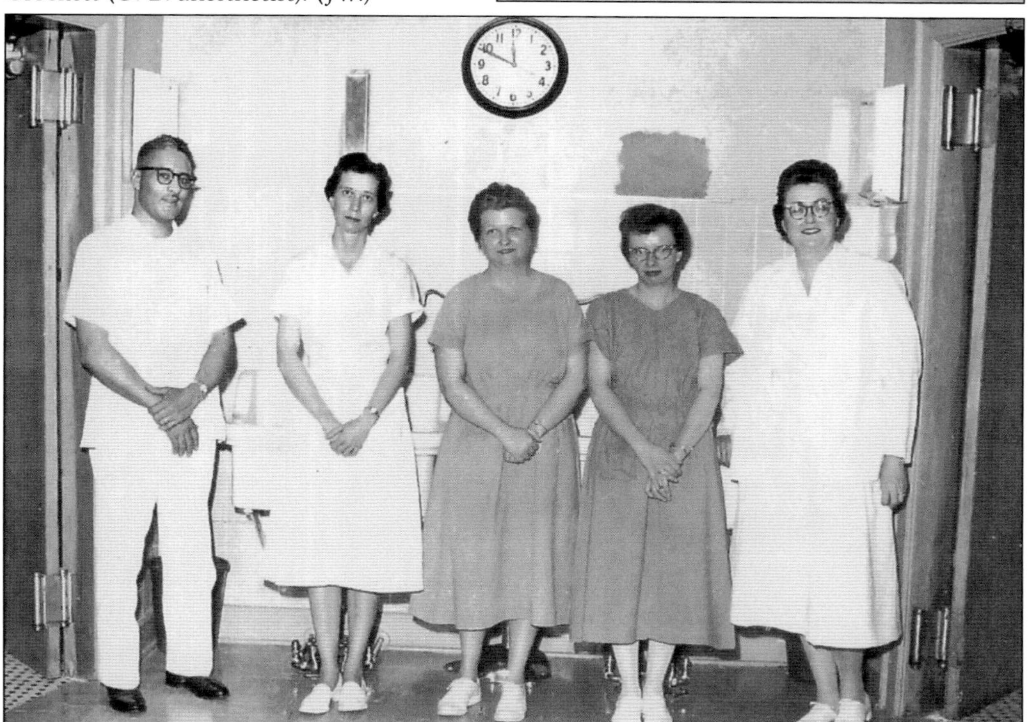

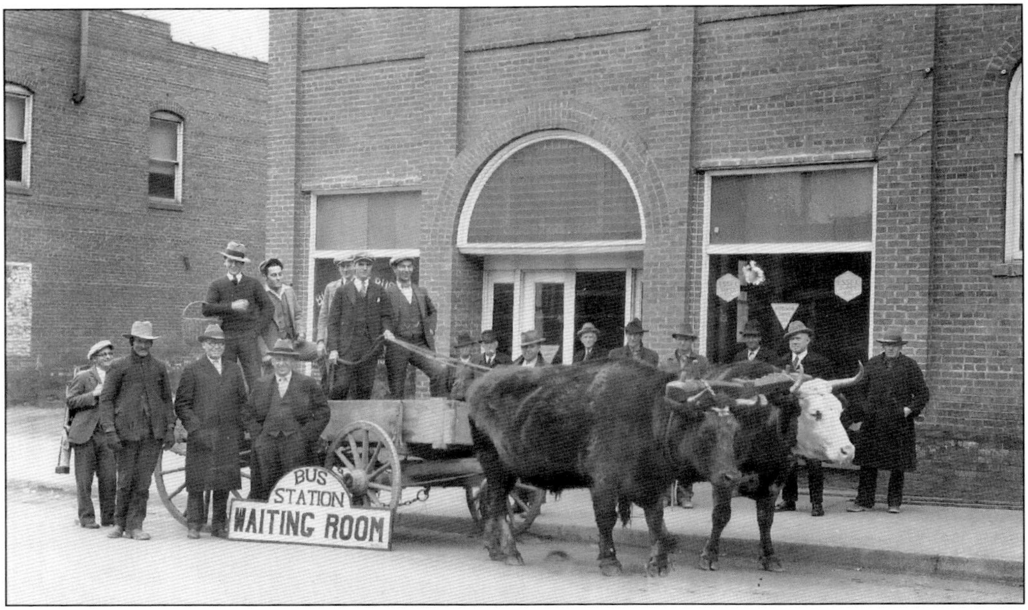

A team of oxen pulled early buses in Galax. This photograph was taken in front of the waiting room of the old bus station on South Main Street. The site would later become Lineberry Jewelry Store. The men in this undated photograph have not been identified, but one man was supposedly Shelby Vass, an early mayor of Galax. (Jack Pless.)

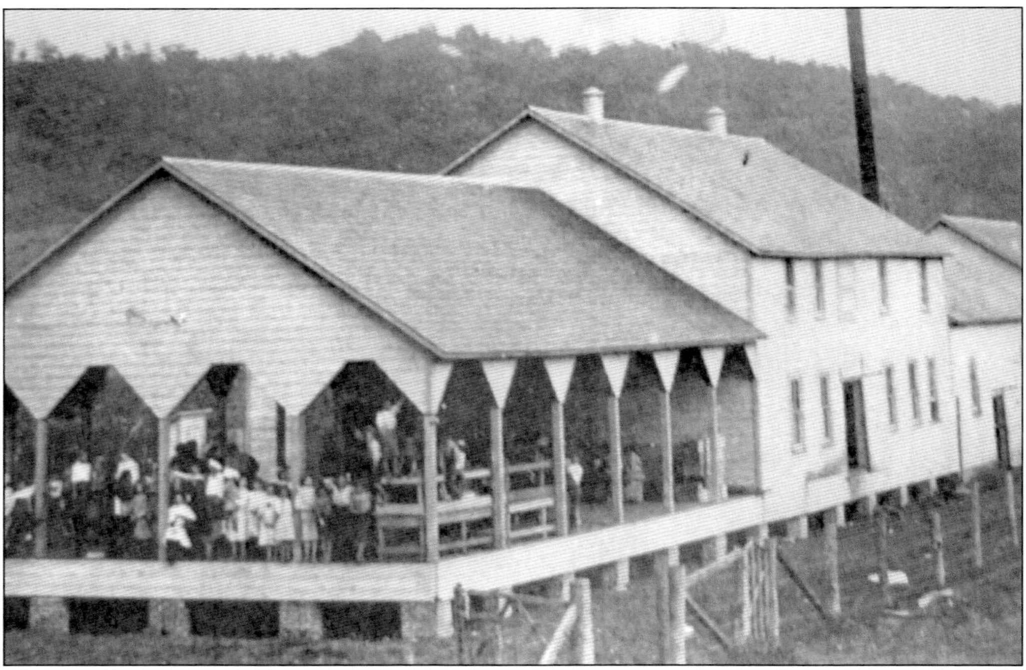

On August 1, 1906, a joint stock company was organized, and stock was issued to construct the Galax Canning Company on the west side of Chestnut Creek on Railroad Avenue. People from the surrounding counties purchased shares in the venture. C. A. Dickenson was president, and F. Williams served as secretary-treasurer. (MM.)

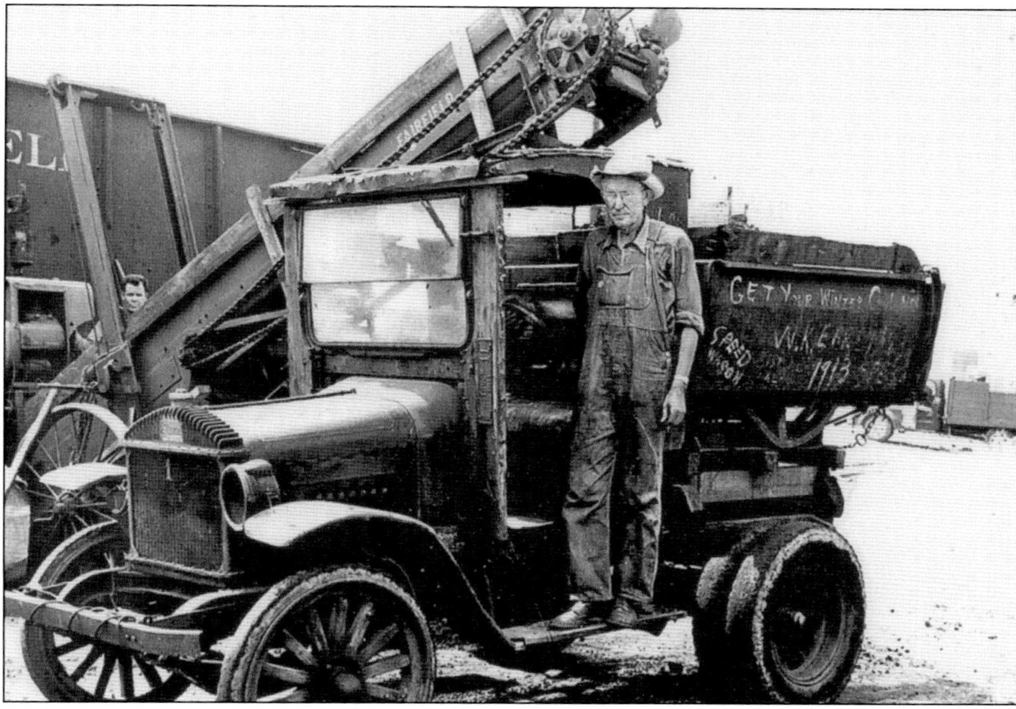

W. K. Early and Sons was established in Galax in 1906. The company sold everything from lumber and building supplies, to hardware and coal. Emmett Largen used the "speed wagon" to deliver coal. In this photograph, he is parked next to a boxcar as coal was being loaded into his truck. On the side of the truck is a sign that says, "Get your winter coal early." The sign is above the name of the company and the date, 1913. (MM.)

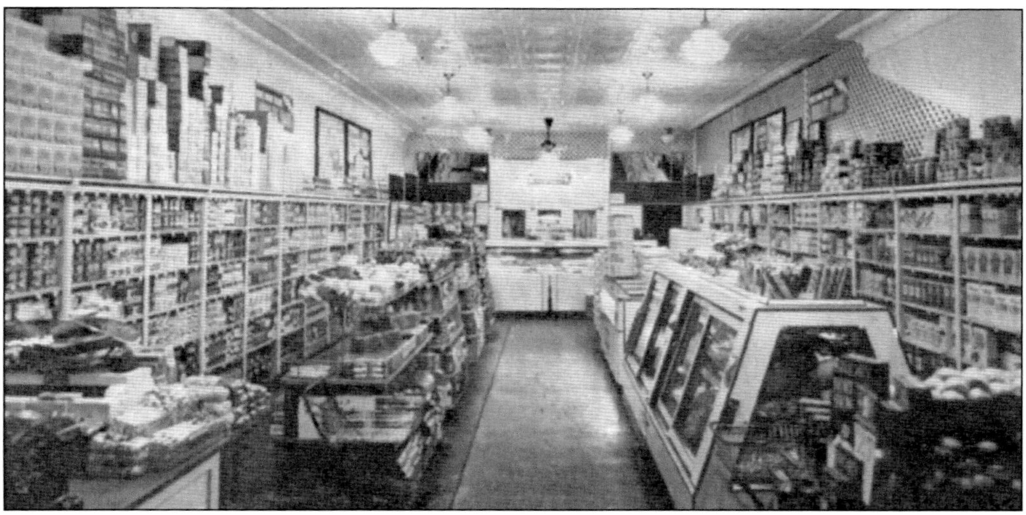

Mick or Mack was established in 1927. It was located in the Holder Building on Main Street, across from Ted's Market. G. A. Holder was the owner, and it was his policy to offer top-quality food at affordable prices. This photograph showed the interior of the store during the 1940s. The store featured a donut-making machine in the front window, which attracted all the children walking by on their way to school in the mornings. (JJN.)

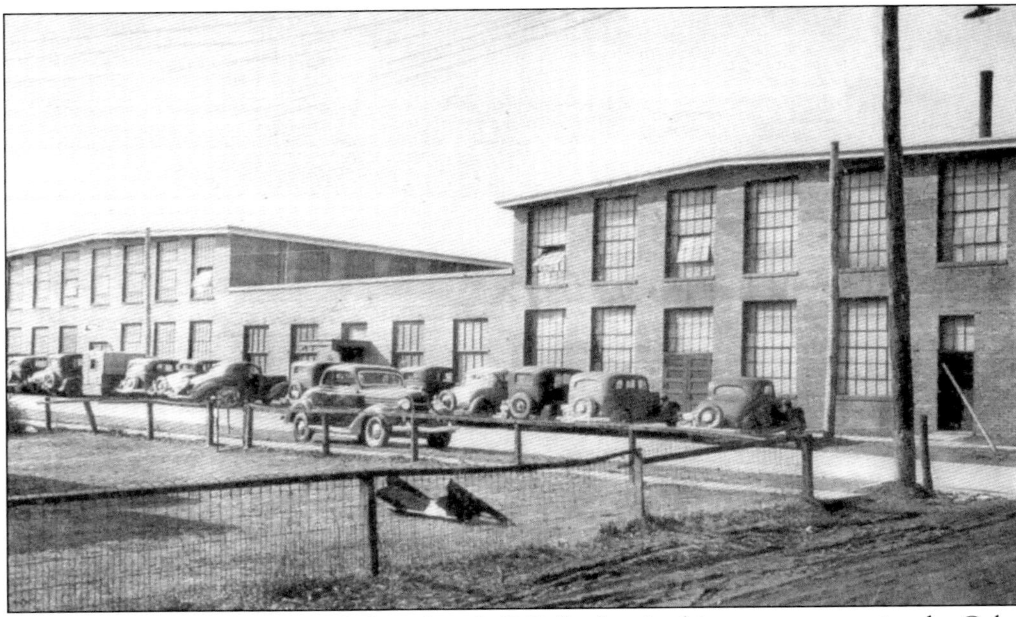

The textile industry began in Galax when J. T. Pollard arrived in town to organize the Galax Knitting Company. The citizens of Galax had agreed to underwrite the purchase of one third of the stock necessary to establish the hosiery mill. The plant, built on the original site of the Galax Furniture and Lumber Company, began operations in 1924. Later Tim Pollard served as president, and Rom Hawks was the secretary-treasurer. (JJN.)

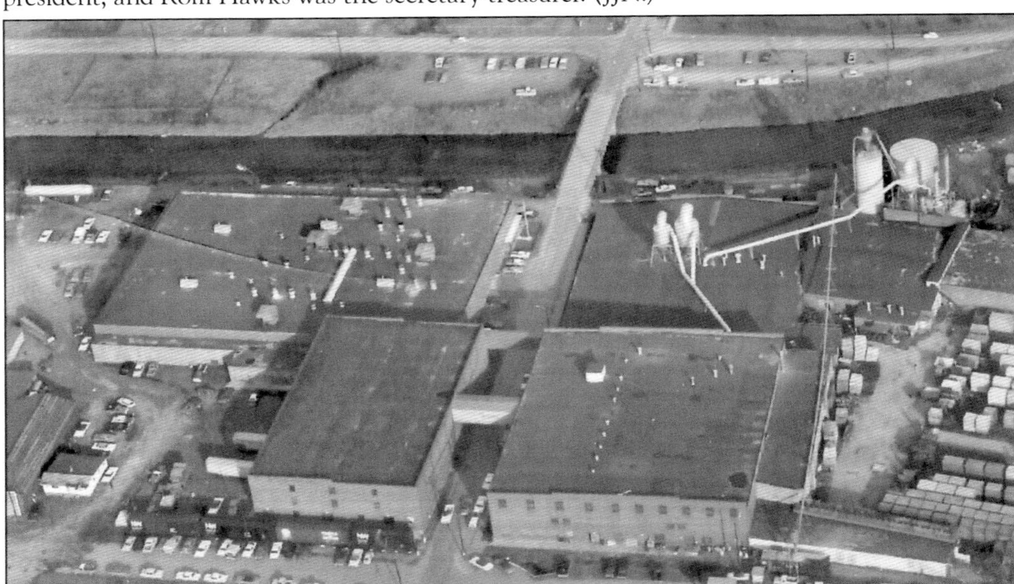

Soon after World War I came to a close, Galax civic leaders met with J. D. Bassett and B. C. Vaughan, noted industrialists from Henry County. The men, involved with furniture manufacturing, agreed to come to Galax and establish the Vaughan Bassett Furniture Company. B. C. Vaughan served as president, his brother, T. G. Vaughan, was in charge of sales, and E. B. Lennox was production manager when the company began production in 1919. (*Gazette Press.*)

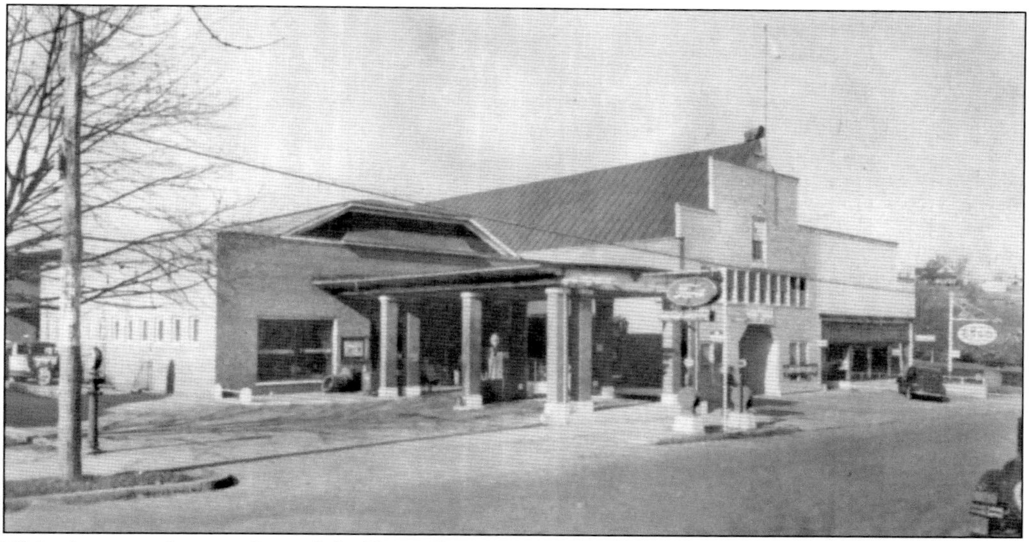

This photograph was taken of the Twin County Motor Company No. 1 on North Main Street at the intersection with Webster Street. T. L. Felts and E. L. Whitley established the company in 1915. The tall frame building was the original Twin County Livery Stable, owned by Felts. (JJN.)

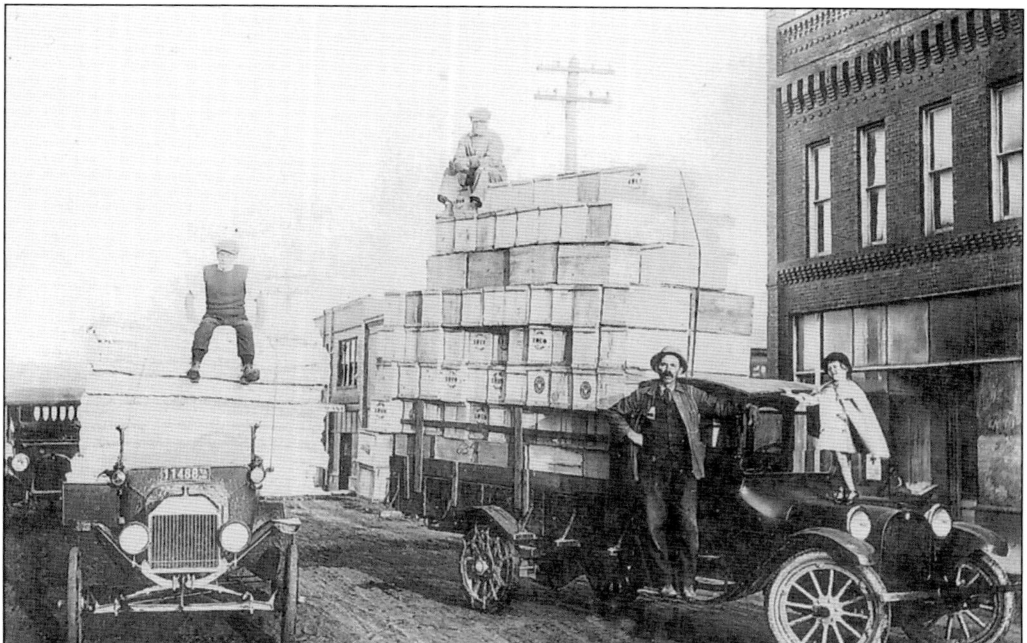

Manley McMillan and his daughter, Eugenia, posed for this picture in 1919 as they stood on his delivery truck while it was parked on Grayson Street. He was the owner of a successful produce business in Galax. The other two men in the photograph have not been identified. (Elaine Sexton.)

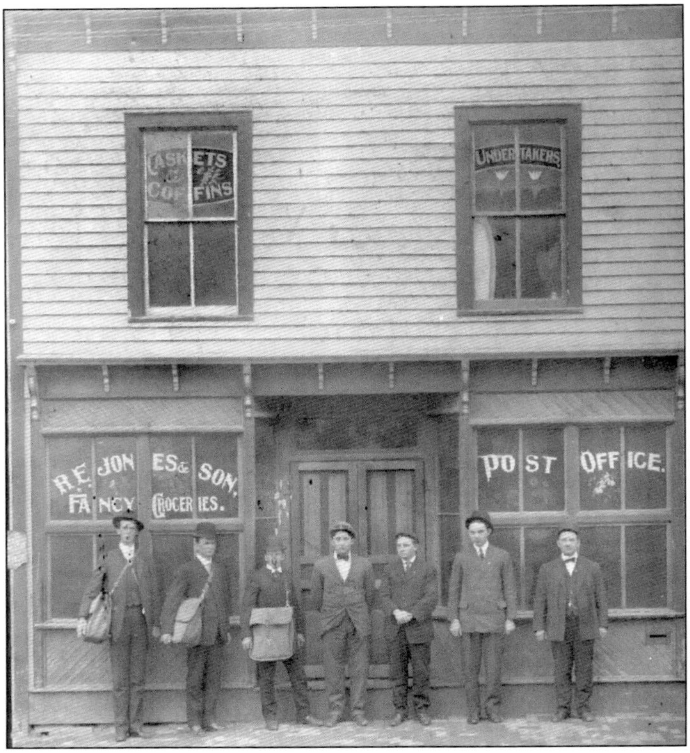

There was not much that could not be taken care of at R. E. Jones and Son on Main Street. It was the site of the first post office, the first school, a casket company, an undertaker's business, and a furniture store, and as the window indicates, Jones was also in the grocery business. Pictured ready for a day's work are, from left to right, Warrick F. Murphy, Benjamin Landreth, Elbert F. Ward, Nelson C. Jones, Samuel E. Jones, Walter M. Jones Sr., and Robert E. Jones. (MM.)

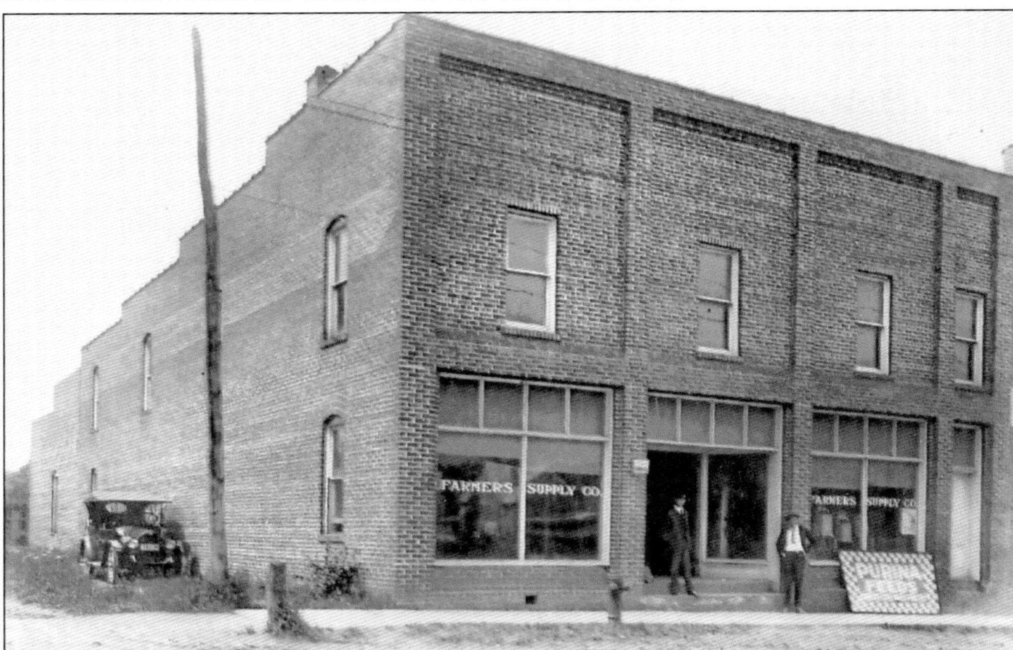

E. M. Todd (left) and Roosevelt Robertson stand in front of the Farmer's Supply Store in 1916. The building was located on the corner of West Grayson Street in Galax. This was only a block from Main Street, so it was an important business location in town. (MM.)

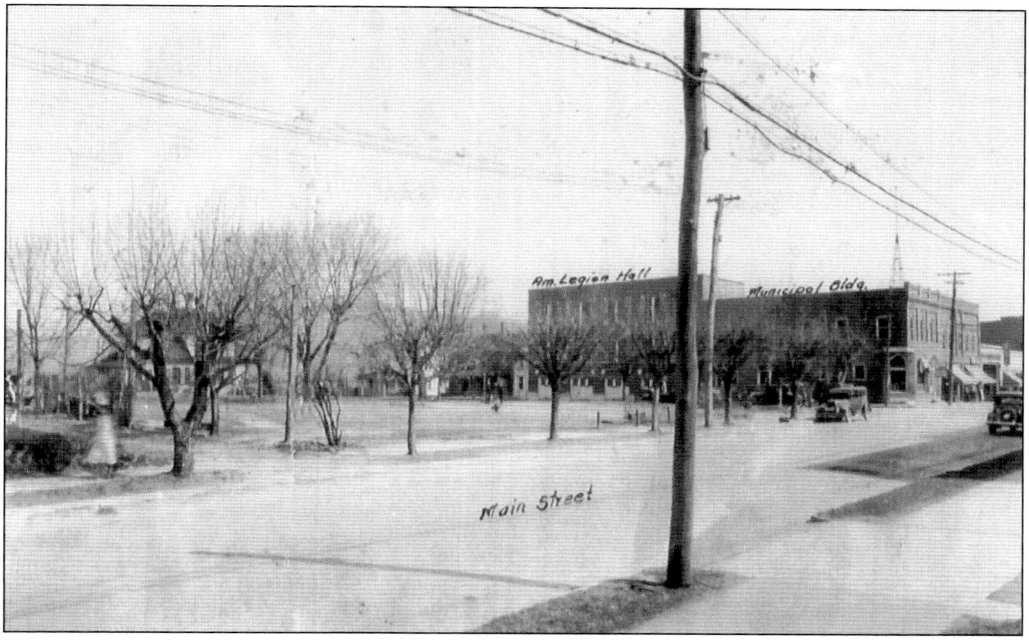

This photograph of the northeast corner of Main and Center Streets was made on April 7, 1934. It was the original site of the Waugh Hotel and the future site of the Galax Post Office. The house seen through the trees on the left was the home of Lelia Nuckolls Waugh, a pioneer citizen and the first owner of the Waugh Hotel. (JJN.)

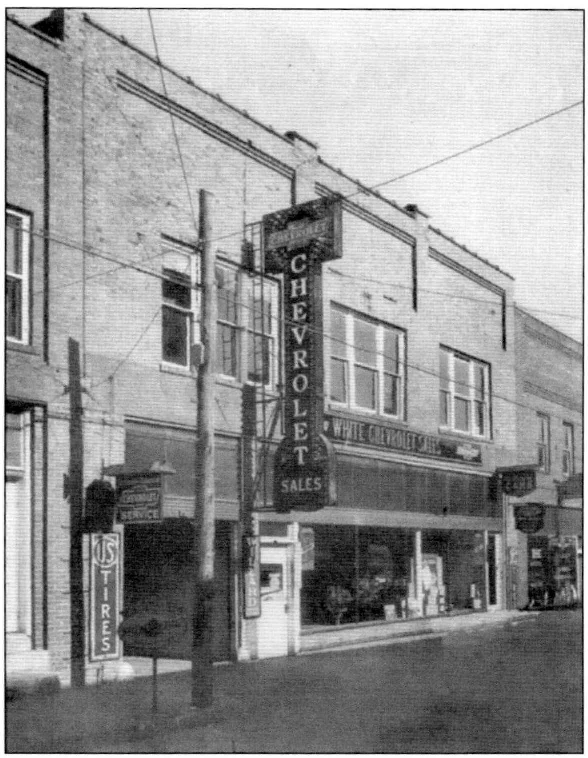

White Chevrolet Sales was established in Galax in 1931 by Hubert S. White Sr. The company's early location was on the north side of West Grayson Street between Main and Jefferson Streets. The company was the dealer for Chevrolet cars and trucks and Frigidaire products. The company also offered motor rewinding, house wiring, and general electrical construction. White later moved his business to the west side of South Main Street near the intersection with Calhoun Street. (JJN.)

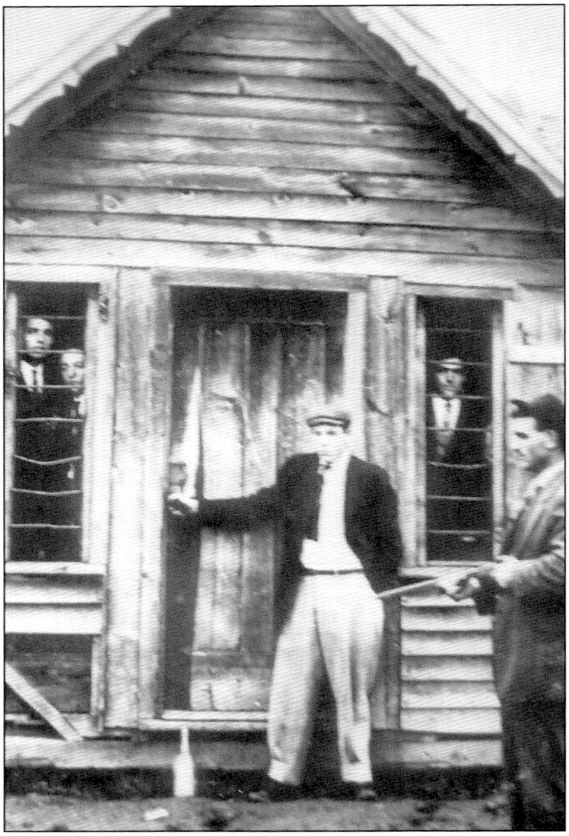

This photograph is supposedly the town's first jailhouse. It was located off North Main Street on an alley where the Merchants and Farmers Bank was located. The mayor's office faced the street in front of the jail. The man holding the rifle is Will Dotson. The other men in the photograph are unidentified. (MM.)

The exact location for these buildings has not been determined. The street has not been paved yet, and if one looks close at the sign advertising the Galax Fair, the date 1923 is visible. Work on the street must have begun after the fair was over. (GG.)

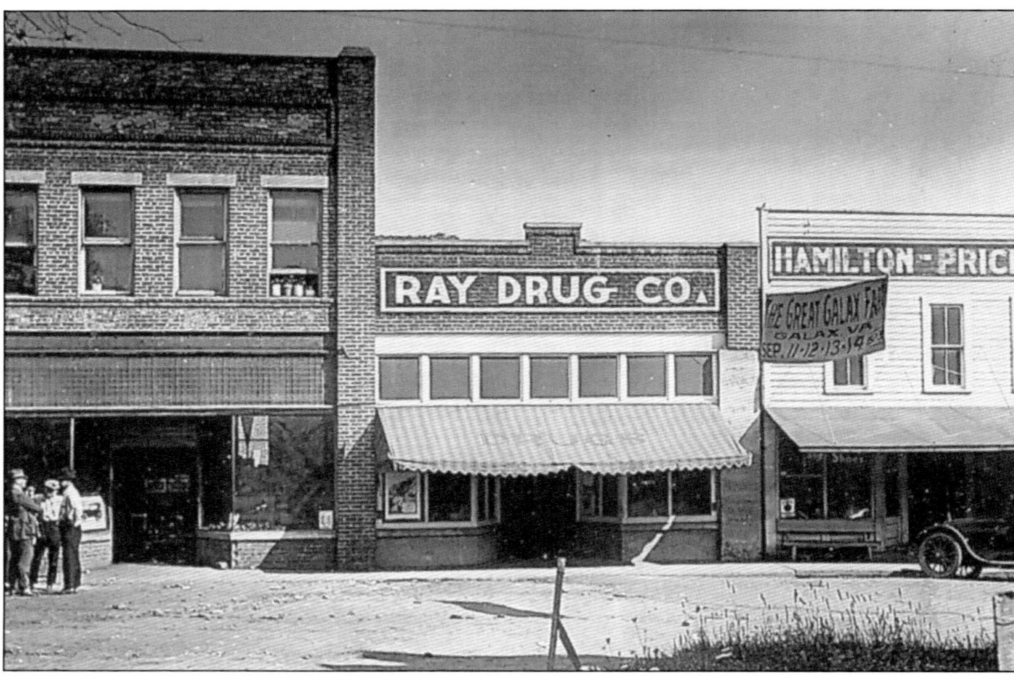

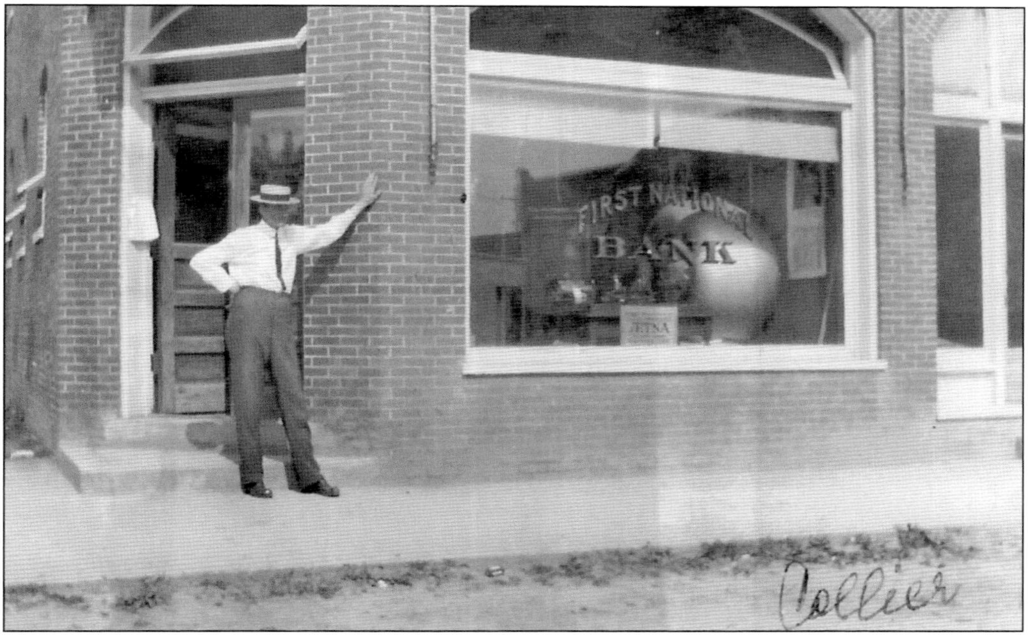

Charles Collier was standing in front of the First National Bank when this photograph was taken. At that time, the bank was located on the southeast corner of Main and Center Streets. The site became town hall when the bank moved to the northwest corner of Main and Grayson Streets. (PHB.)

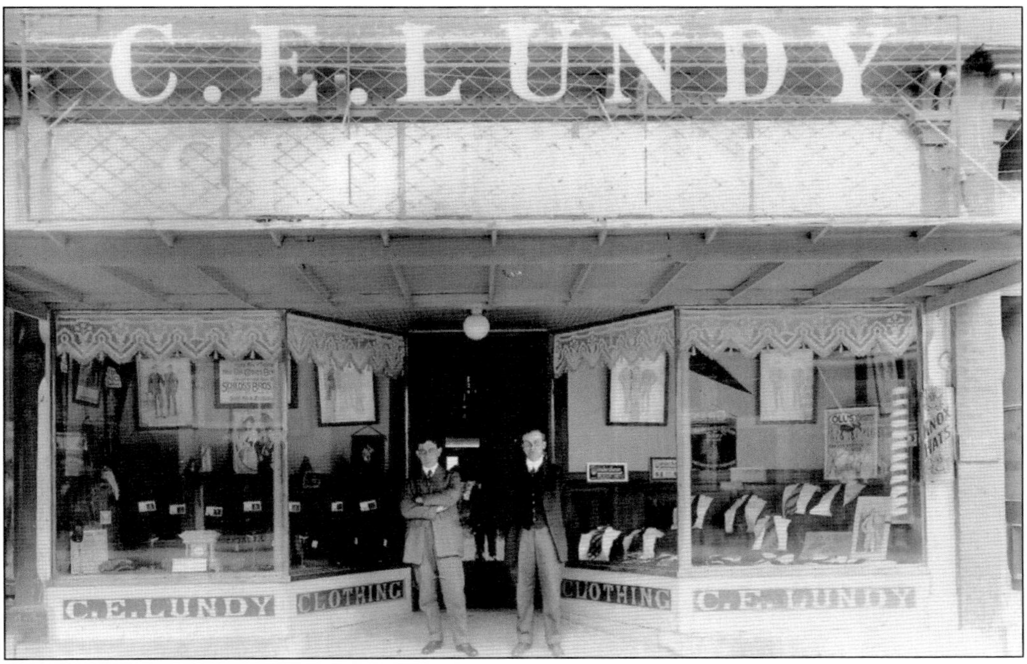

The exact location in Galax of the C. E. Lundy store has not been determined, and the men are unidentified. The merchandise on display in the windows indicates that it was a men's furnishing store. (MM.)

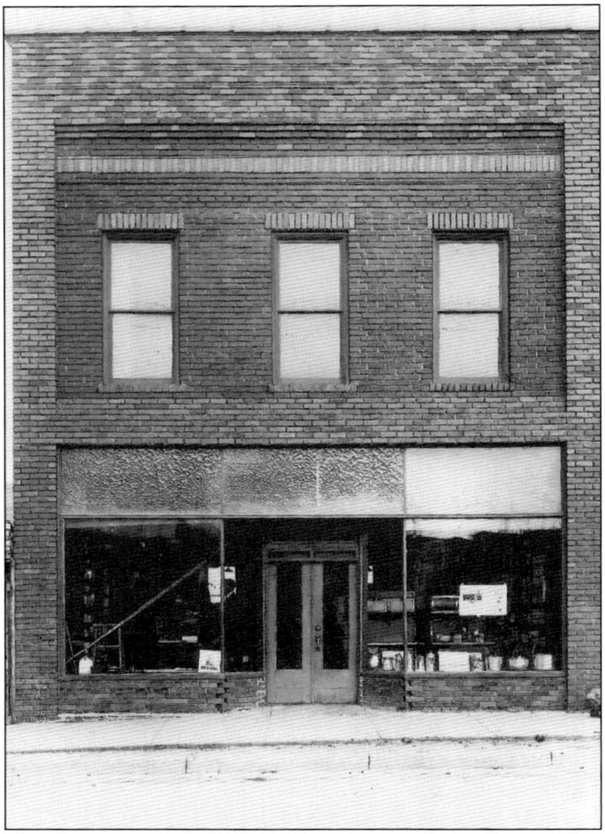

J. C. Matthews moved his family from Gap, Virginia, to Galax and established a successful hardware business in town. This is the third site of Matthews Hardware, with other locations on East Grayson Street in the old M. T. Blessing building and on the corner of Main and West Grayson Streets. (MM.)

The tall building was Adams Mill, operated by Fred Adams. It still stands on East Grayson Street. The small building to the right was the rear of the Galax Buggy Works, which would later become Galax Mirror Company, owned by John Messer Sr. To the left was the Galax Icehouse, owned by William Adonijsh "Nige" Alderman. The walls of the room were lined with cork for added insulation. (GPL.)

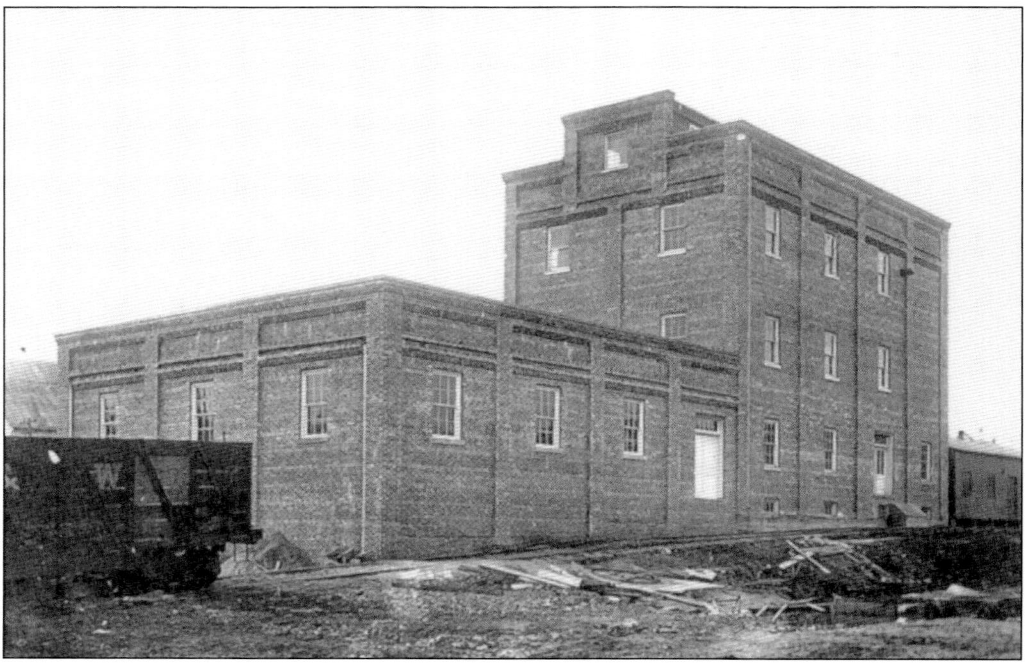

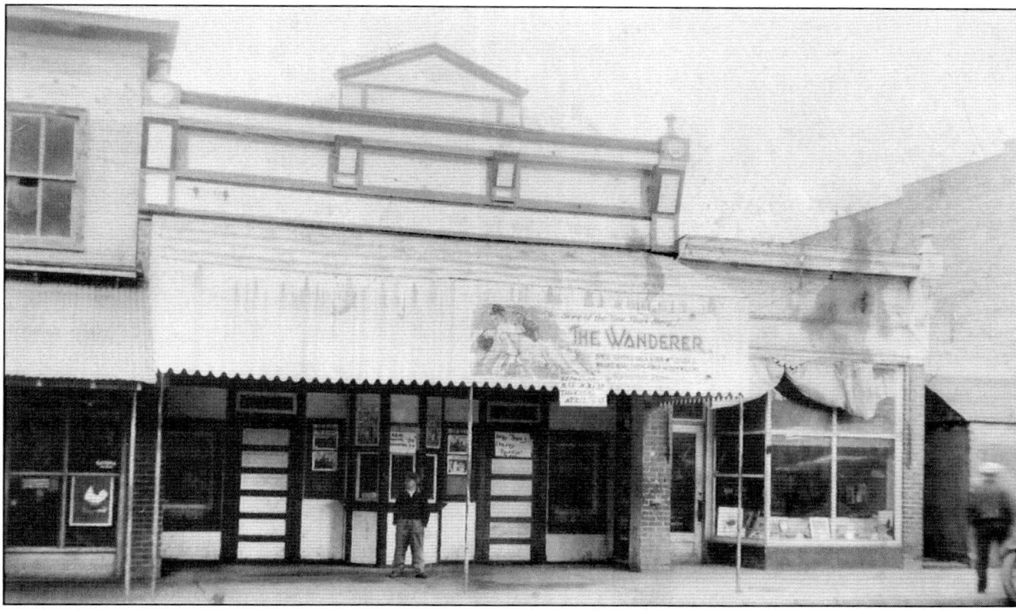

Going to the movies has always been high on the priority list of social activities. Monroe Ward's attempt to open a theater was met with disaster when the Ward building burned on the eve of the grand opening. Claud Hackler built and operated one of the movie theaters in town. He later built the Colonial Theater. One resident recalled not only seeing silent movies at the theater, but also watching his first talkie movie there as well. (EN.)

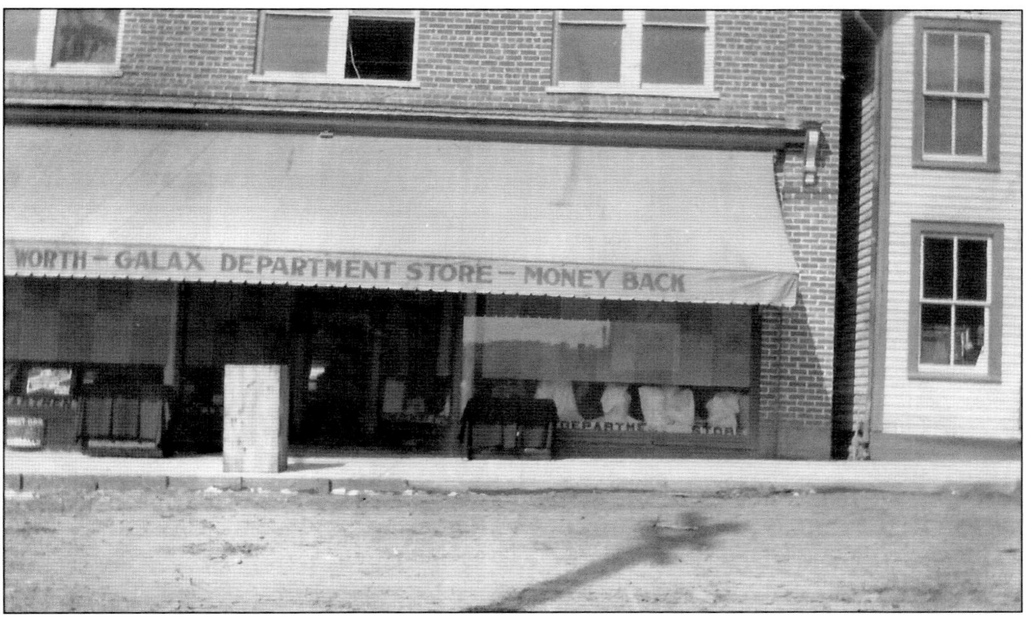

Two men from Bristol, Virginia, opened the Galax Department Store in 1910. Even though it was located on the west side of North Main Street, they were forced to file for bankruptcy in 1913. The store was closed to invoice the merchandise, and then a court-ordered sale was held. In 1914, Dan B. Waugh purchased the store and remaining stock, and renamed the business Dan B. Waugh Fashion Shop. (PHB.)

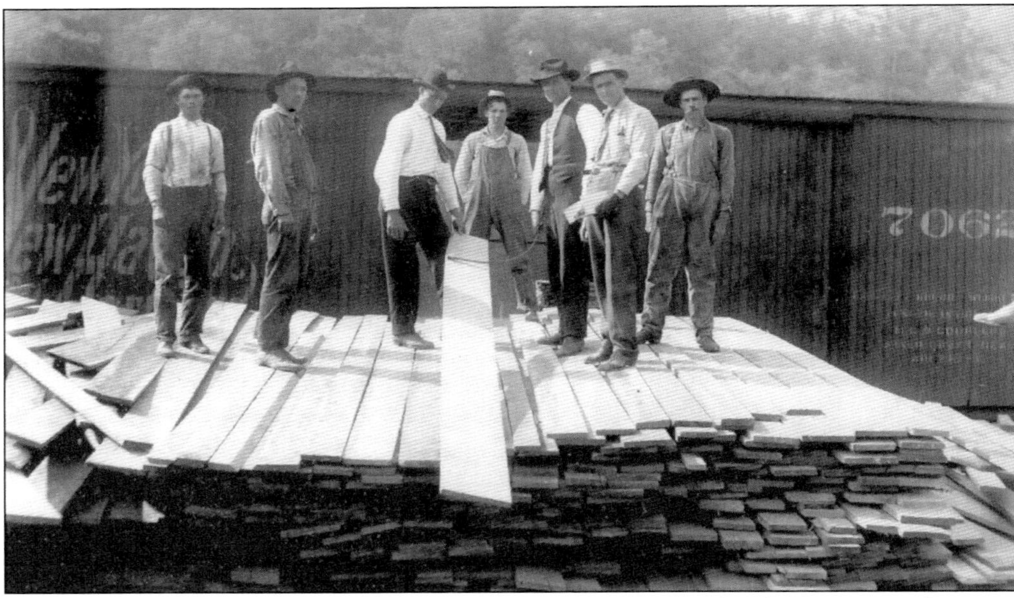

Lumber was an important commodity in Galax. Not only was it used in furniture manufacturing, but in the building industry as well. The area had a large virgin timber resource, including oak, pine, chestnut, maple, poplar, ash, and birch. In 1905, there were at least five lumber businesses in town. (MM.)

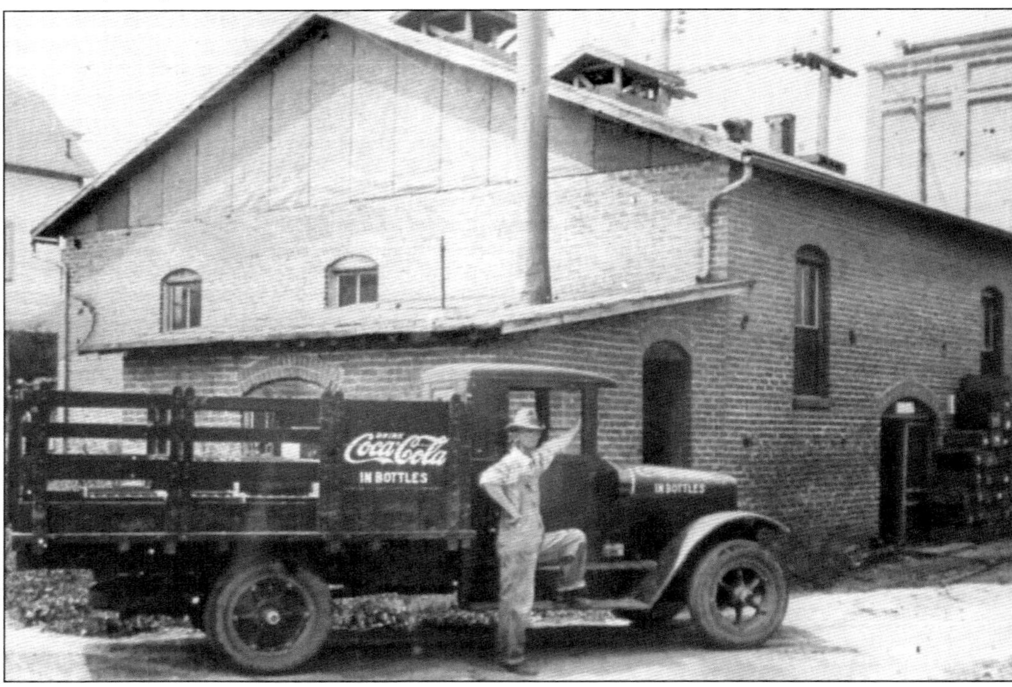

The Galax Coca-Cola Company was established in Galax in 1929 with R. J. Knisley as manager. The volume of sales proved that Southerners drink other beverages as well as sweet tea. The local plant met the most exacting requirements in sanitation and automatic equipment, and provided efficient daily delivery service. The man in the photograph is unidentified. (JW.)

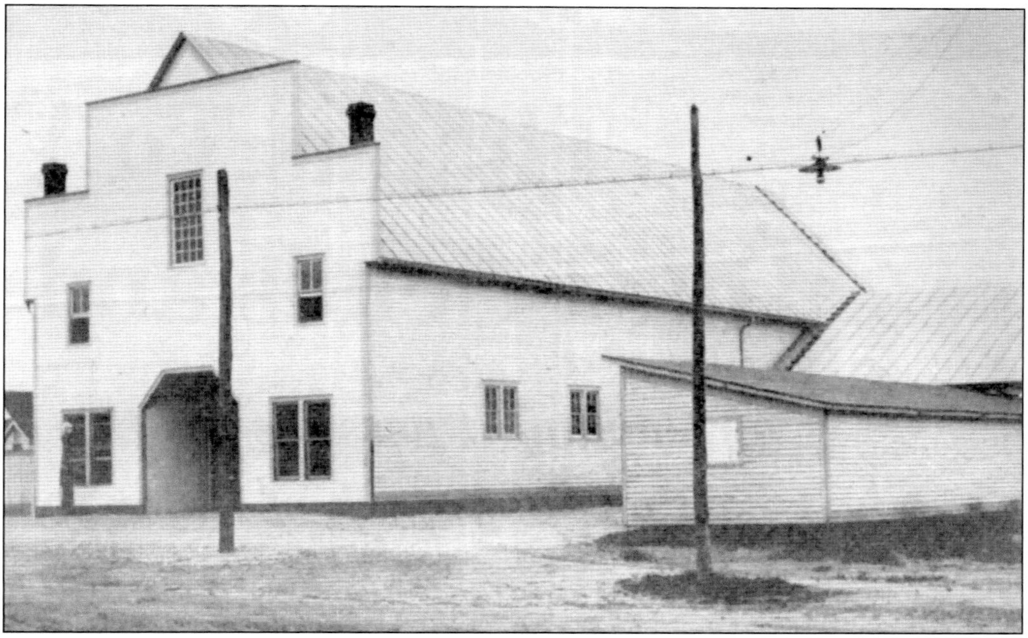

During the early days when passengers arrived at the train depot in Galax and needed transportation, they could choose the M. L. Bishop Livery Stables on South Main Street, the Dobyns Livery Stable on West Grayson Street, or the Felts Livery Stable on North Main Street. Felts would later convert his livery business into the Twin County Motor Company. (JJN.)

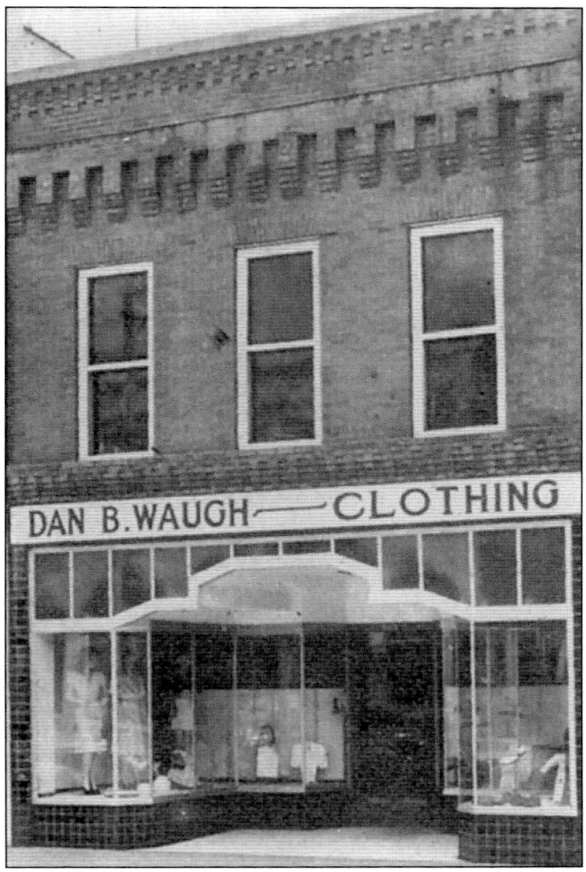

Dan B. Waugh, son of John Blair Waugh, purchased the Galax Department store in 1914 and renamed it as the Dan. B. Waugh Fashion Shop. He later moved the business to East Grayson Street, next door to the original J. B. Waugh location. Dan was married to the former Hazel Phipps, and they were the parents of two sons, Blair and Charles, both of whom followed their father and grandfather in the retail business. (JJN.)

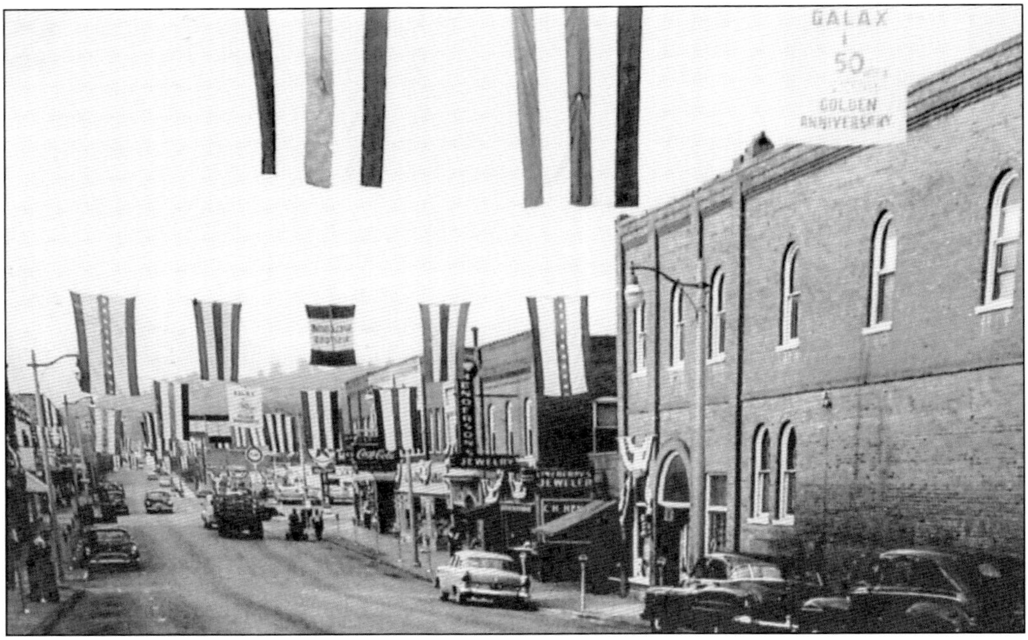

During the summer of 1956, Galax was the scene of reunions, parades, pageants, contests, and other forms of celebration in honor of the town's Golden Jubilee. This is a view of South Main Street, with Vass-Kapp Hardware at right. Note the parking meters that were installed in the business section of town. (MM.)

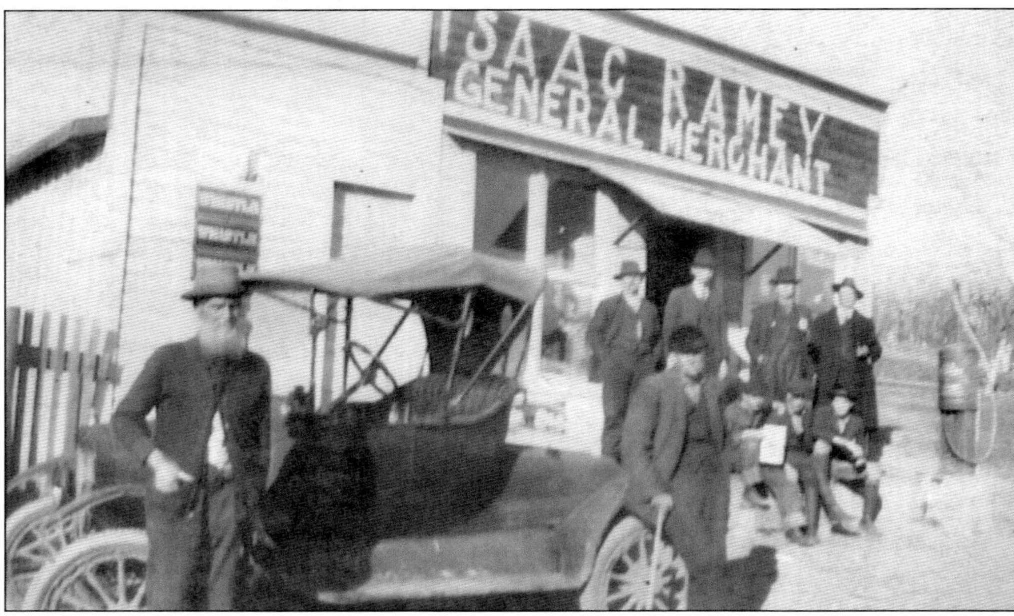

In 1910, Isaac Ramey was owner of a wallpaper and paint store on West Stuart Drive in Galax. None of the gentlemen in the photograph have been identified, but the car dates from 1914. Isaac was living in town with his second wife, Jennie, their daughter, Gertrude, and his sister-in-law, Emma Lundy. He was born in North Carolina, Jennie was born in Missouri, and their daughter was born in Virginia. (EN.)

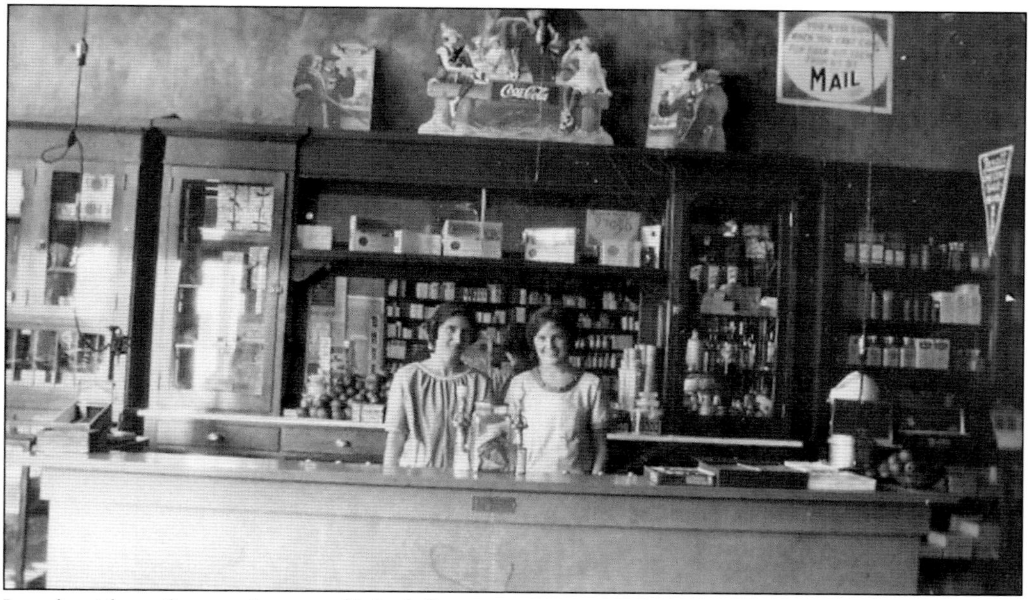

Local residents frequently met at Bolen's Drugstore to visit and enjoy a treat from the soda fountain or to chat while they shopped in the store. Greeting customers from behind the counter were best friends and coworkers Izetta Weaver (left) and Zelle Matthews. (Margaret Thomason.)

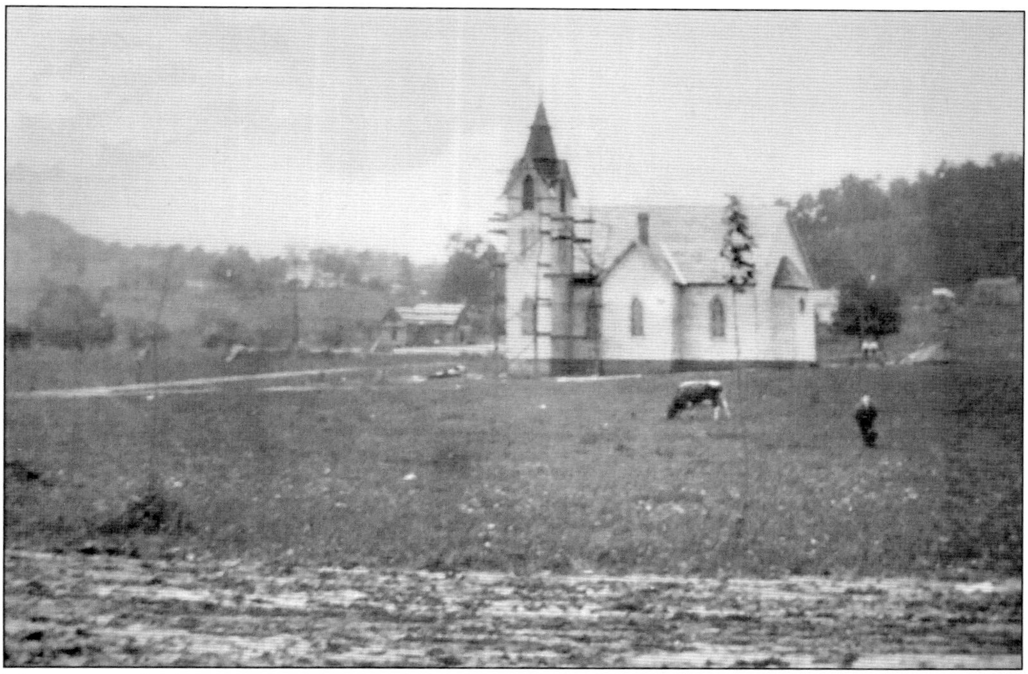

This is an early photograph of Galax. The First Presbyterian Church of Galax is under construction, and cows are grazing where homes will be built. The muddy path in front became Main Street. The path running past the church is Center Street. The church paid $1 for the lots, and the building was dedicated on August 7, 1905, a year before the town was incorporated. Rev. R. D. Carson was the first resident pastor. (MM.)

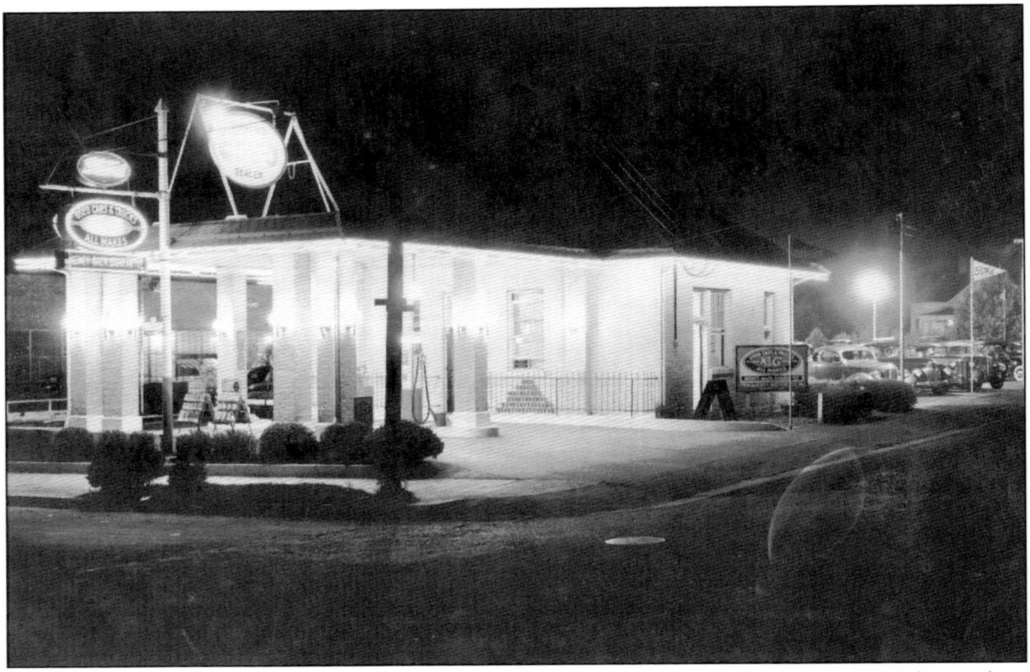

This photograph was taken in the 1940s of the Twin County Motor Company No. 2, located on South Main Street in Galax. The large sign hanging in front of the building is advertising the sale of used cars and trucks, which can be seen behind the building. (EN.)

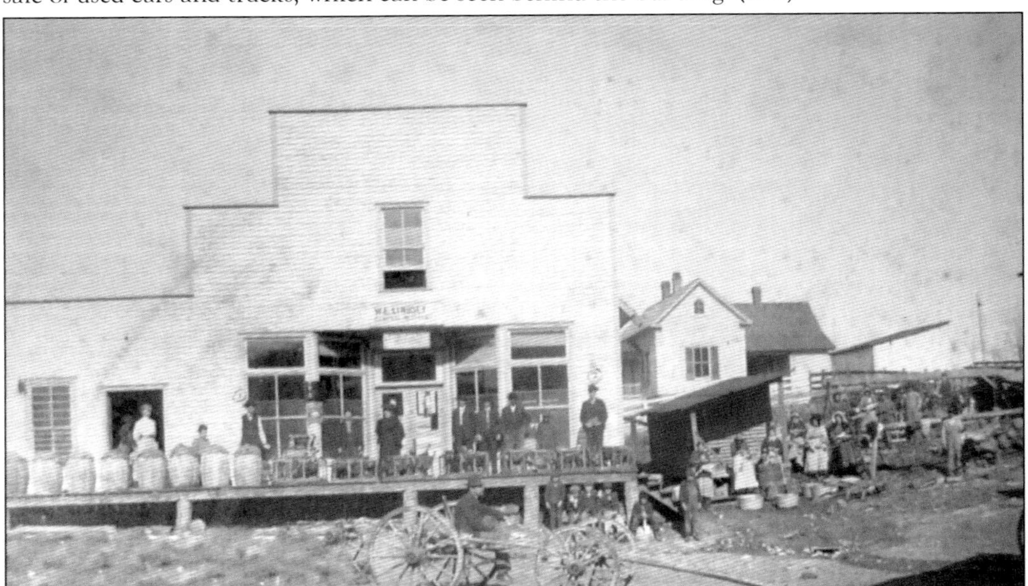

W. E. Lindsey came from Blair and opened his general merchandise store on East Grayson Street near Railroad Avenue. He was also a cross-tie and tanning bark dealer. Many of the merchants would buy eggs, ham, butter, live turkeys, poultry, and livestock from the local residents. They also purchased chestnuts, chinquapins, animal hides, beeswax, feathers, ginseng, Seneca roots, and tallow for shipping to larger markets via the Norfolk and Western Railway. (MM.)

Dr. J. K. Caldwell was one of the first doctors in town. It was his dream that the citizens of Galax should have the best medical treatment possible. In 1924, Dr. W. P. Davis, Dr. John Phipps, Dr. Z. G. Phipps, and Dr. Robert Kyle joined Dr. Caldwell to form a joint stock company to construct the Galax Hospital. The building, located on West Center Street, was completed on July 1, 1925. The hospital had 30 beds, complete x-ray equipment, a chemical lab, and a diet kitchen. The hospital's ambulance is parked in front. (NF.)

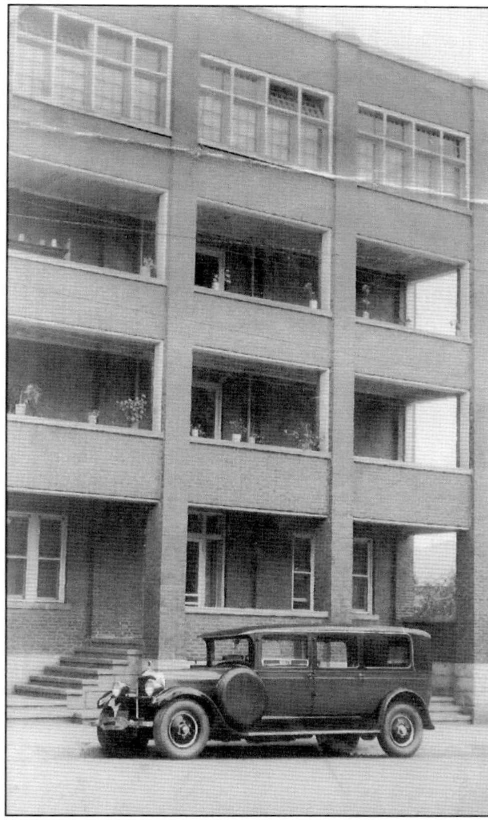

This is a later photograph of the Galax Hospital on West Center Street. Mary Brintle was the first head nurse, Bertha Muse was the first nurse, and there were 10 nurses in training. These doctors and nurses were engaged in one of the highest of all callings, the tending and healing of the sick. Local babies were now being born in the hospital instead of via home deliveries. (NF.)

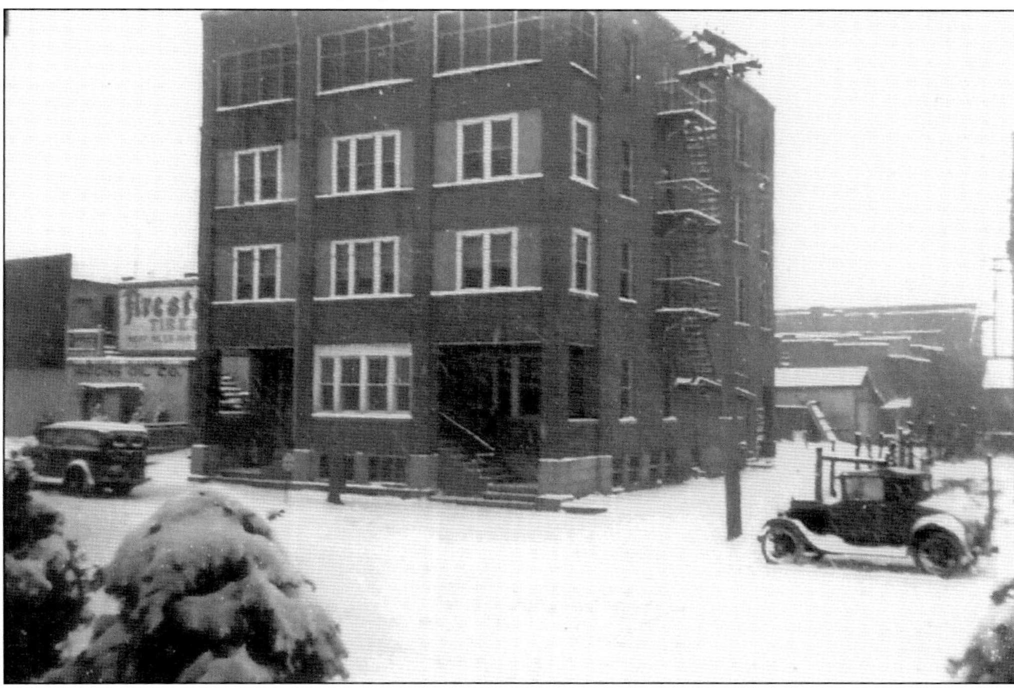

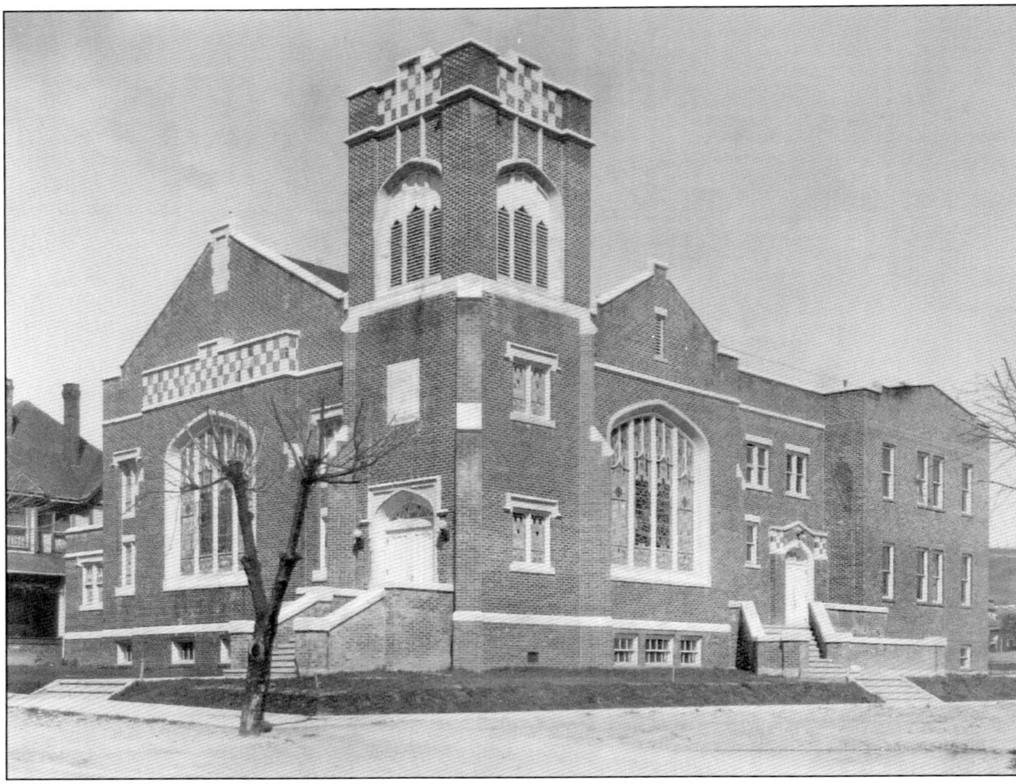

On October 8, 1904, the Methodist Episcopal Church South paid $1 for two lots on the corner of West Center and Monroe Streets. Members of the board of trustees whose names were on the deed were J. B. Waugh, J. P. Carico, A. C. Painter, S. N. Nuckolls, B. F. Nuckolls, M. L. Bishop, S. H. Jackson, B. A. Anderson, and C. W. Caldwell. (JJN.)

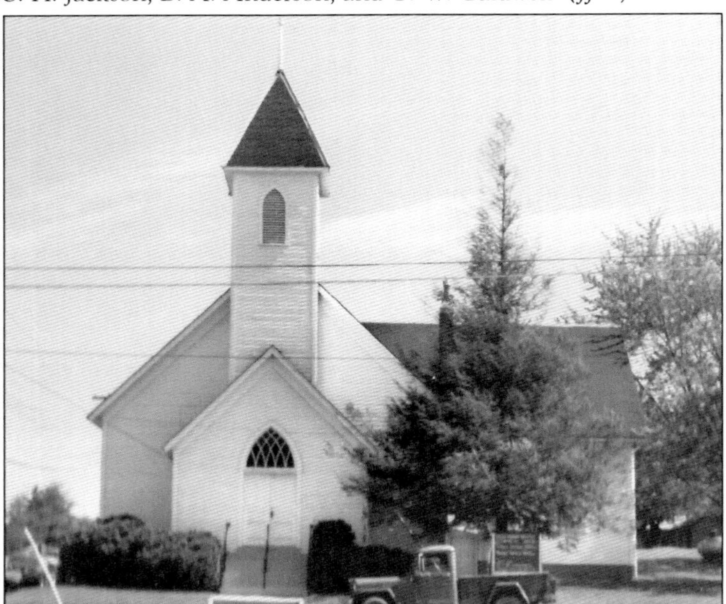

The Missionary Baptist Church purchased the two lots on the corner of Oldtown and Jefferson Streets in 1907 for the sum of $1. The congregation completed their new brick church on North Main Street in 1926 and turned the old white frame church building over to members of the Quaker faith, who established the Friends church. This beautiful church still maintains its simple design and offers peace to those who enter its doors. (MM.)

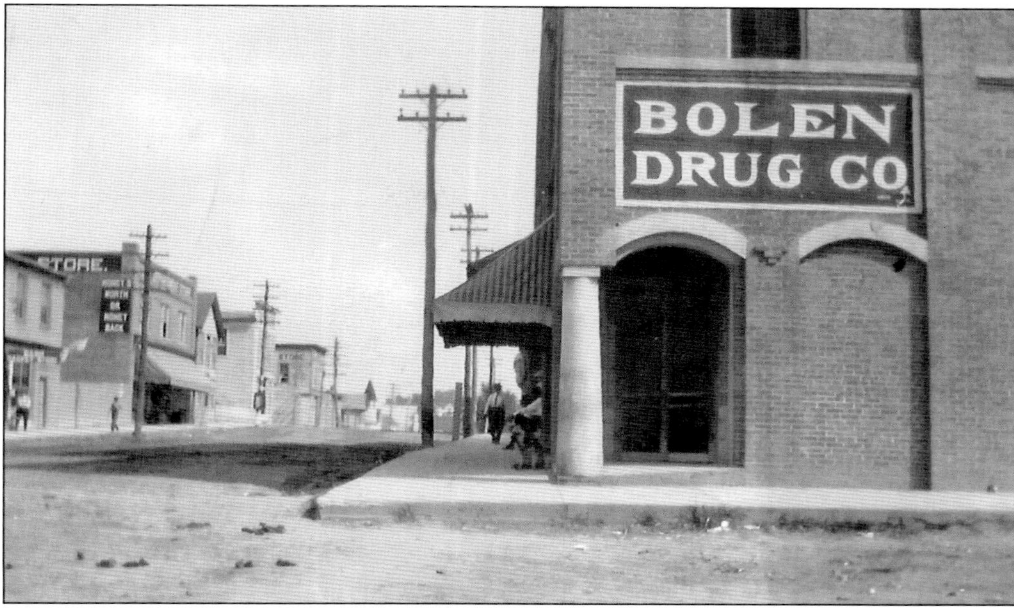

An unidentified man and his dog sit in front of the Bolen Drug Company in this early photograph. The street is unpaved, and many of the stores have not been rebuilt with brick. Note that casual attire for men meant that they only removed their suit coats but were still wearing ties and white shirts. (PHB.)

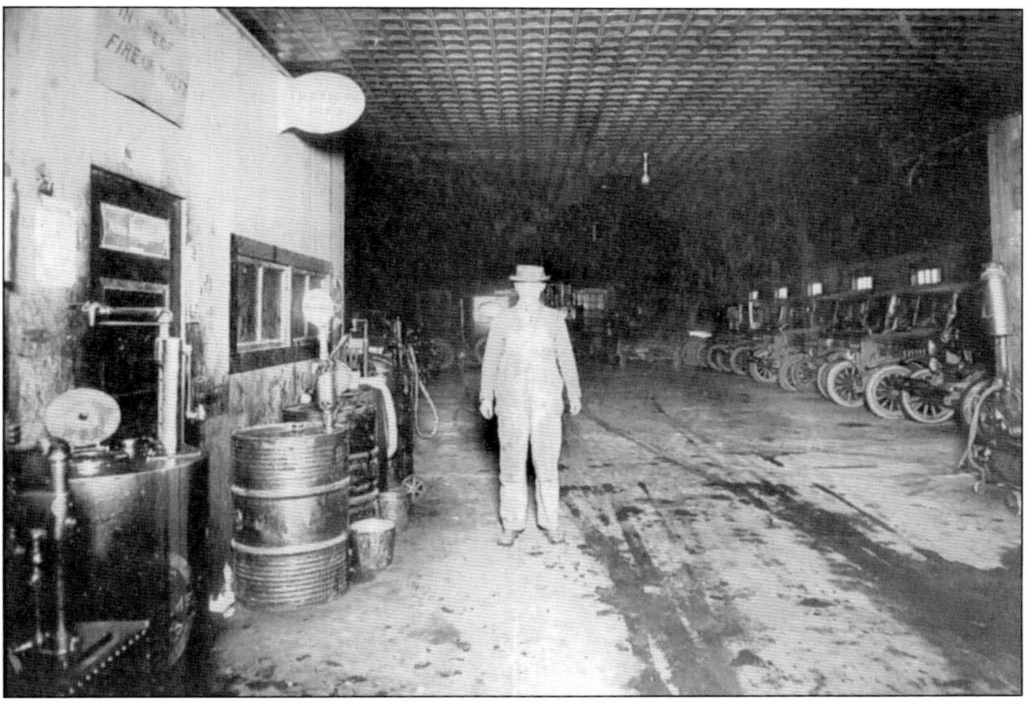

Twin County Livery Stables was converted to Twin County Motor Company by T. L. Felts and his partner, E. L. Whitley. A row of Ford cars in the garage can be seen at right. Willy Lindamood is checking out the cars. (RB.)

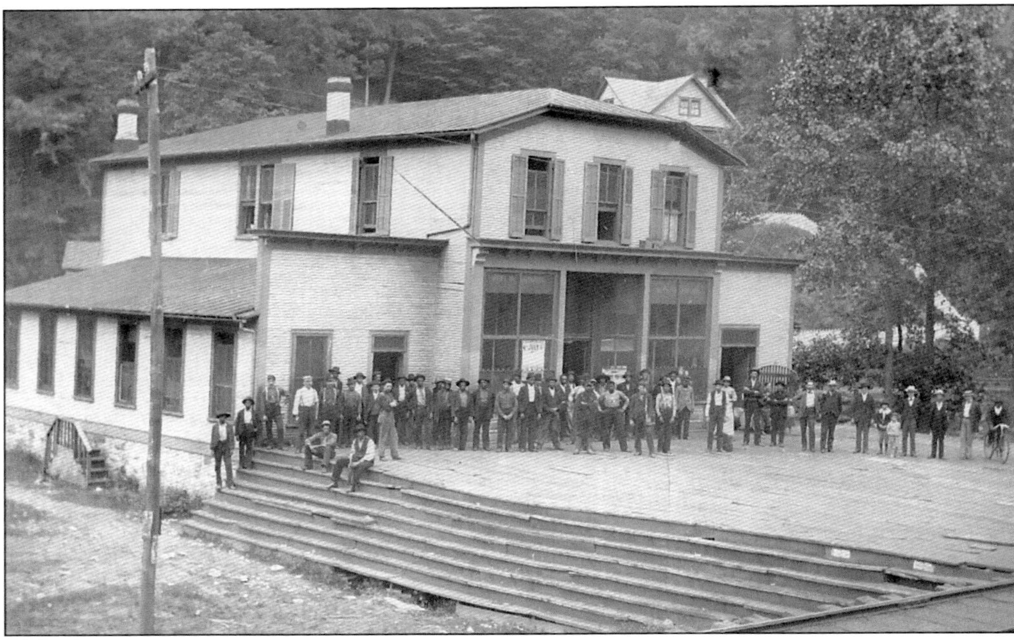

When J. B. Waugh returned from the Civil War, he took over his father's general mercantile business in Blair, Virginia. As one can see by its size, it was one of the main business establishments in Blair. The sign in the window indicated the store was holding a Fourth of July sale, so the unidentified people may have been waiting for the store to open its doors for business. (MM.)

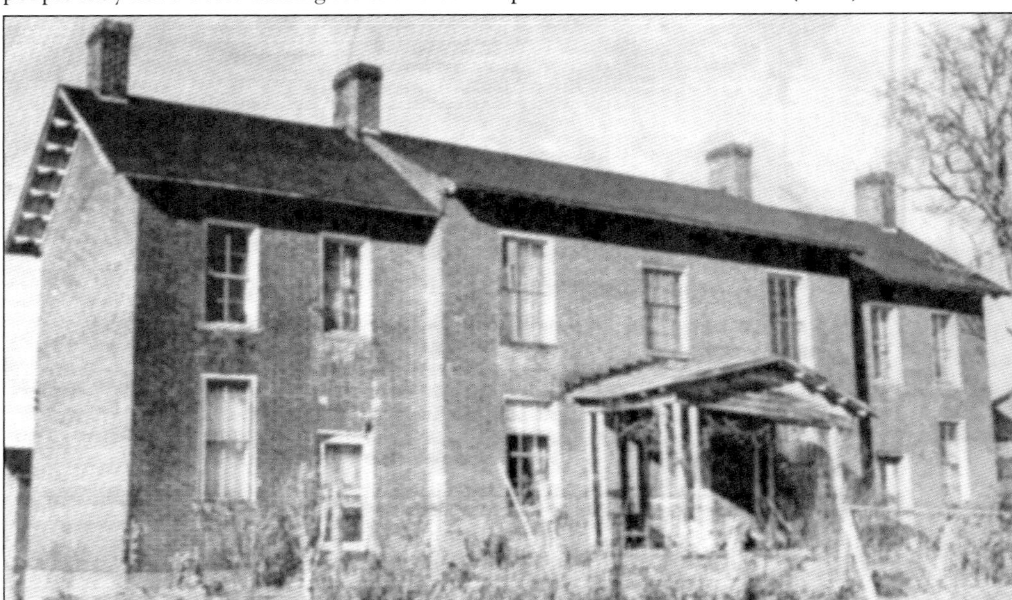

The Grayson County Courthouse was located in the village of Greenville, but as the area expanded, the residents realized the courthouse needed to be more centrally located. After a debate between two factions, it was finally decided to move the Grayson County Courthouse to Independence. The Village of Greenville became Nuckollsville and then Oldtown. The old, brick courthouse building is still standing in Oldtown and is now a private residence. (MM.)

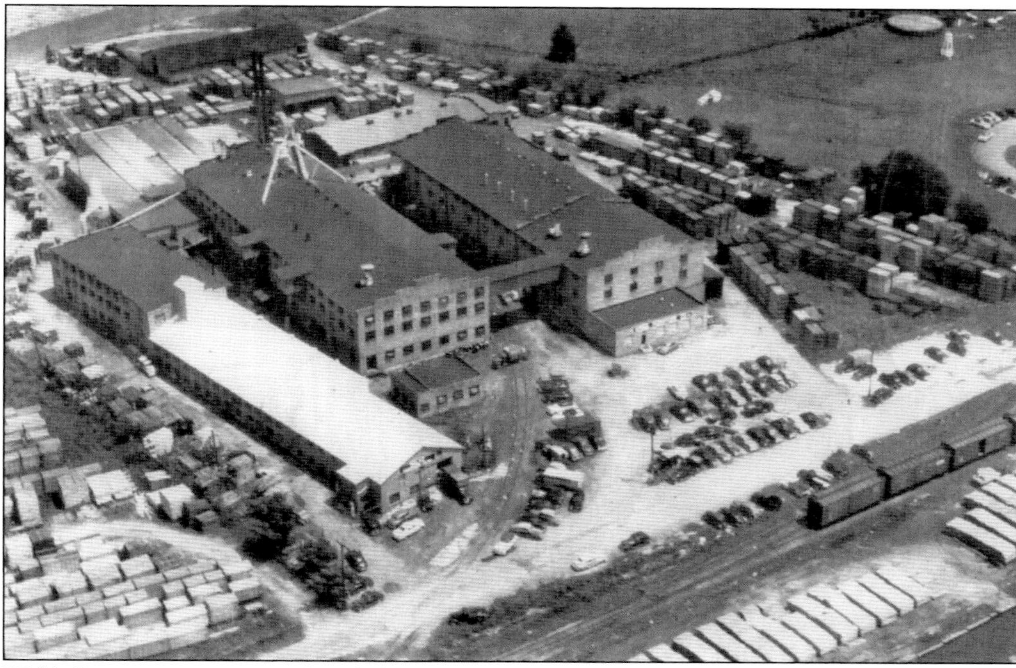

Webb Furniture Company, founded by J. V. Webb, began production of medium-priced dining and bedroom furniture in 1923. John A. Messer Sr. took over ownership of the plant in 1932 and made it a part of Messer Industries. By the 1950s, Webb Furniture had become one of the largest furniture factories in the United States and was shipping its products to every state in the union. Messer served as chairman of the board, and Duane E. Ward Sr. served as president. (JJN.)

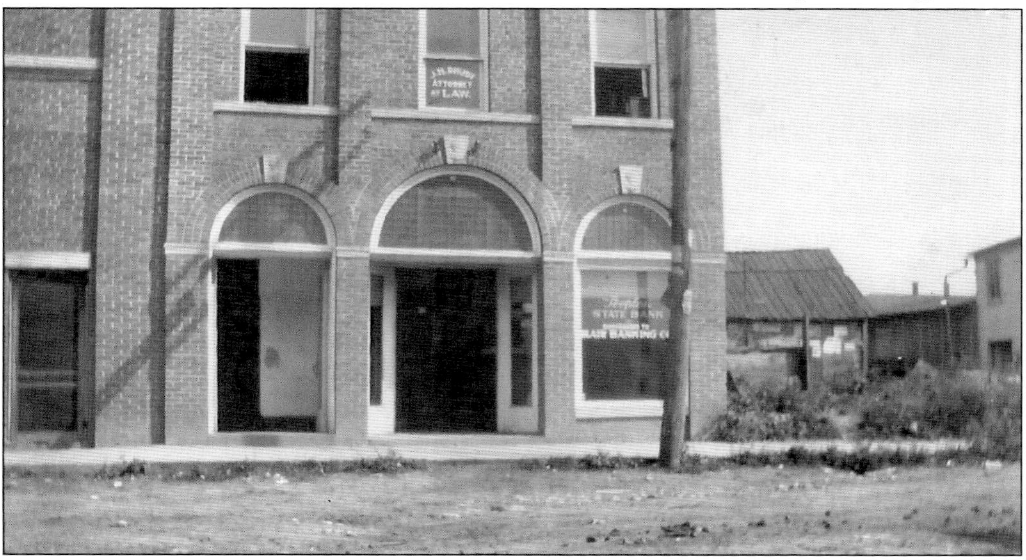

The People's State Bank was organized in 1912 and was located in a brick building on East Grayson Street behind Bolen Drugstore. It was the successor to the Blair Banking Company, established in Blair in 1904. Galax attorney J. H. Rhudy maintained his law offices upstairs. The People's State Bank defaulted during the 1929 Depression and was reorganized in 1934 as the Merchants and Farmers Bank, with Fred Adams as president. (PHB.)

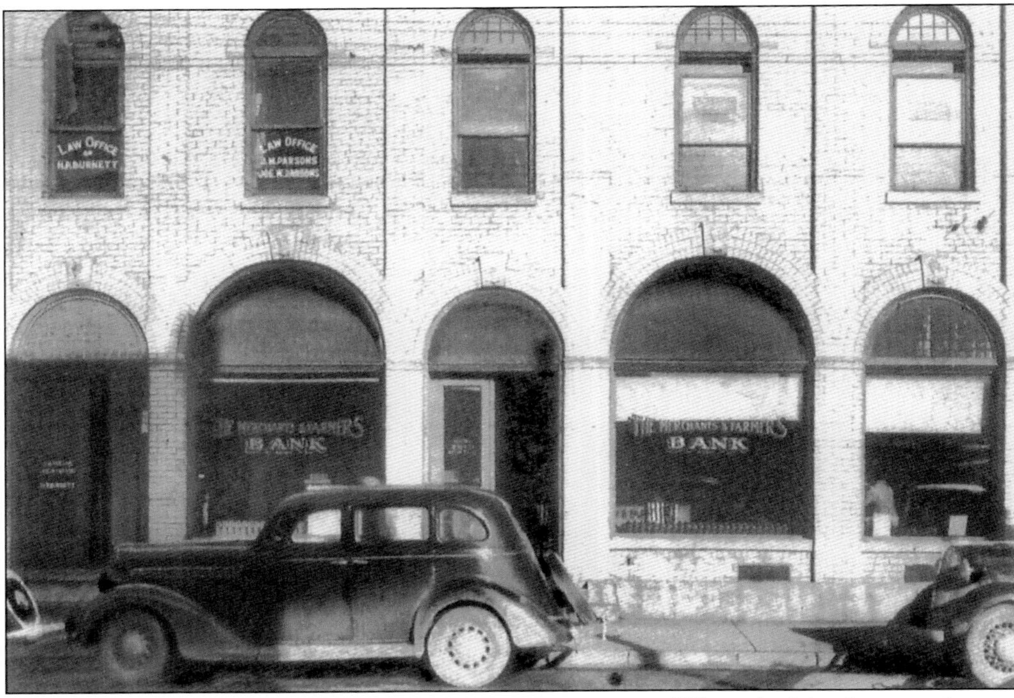

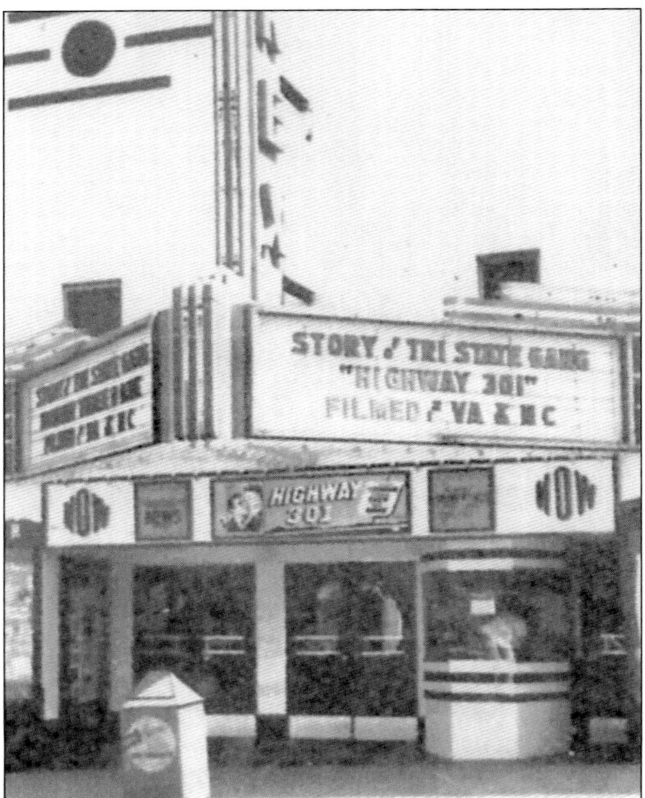

When the Merchants and Farmers Bank was established in 1934, Fred Adams served as president, and Collin Webb was active vice president. The board of directors included Adams, I. L. Gray, B. D. Beamer, Paul Dalton, and T. N. Woodruff. The law offices of H. Prince Burnette, J. M. Parsons, and Joe W. Parsons were maintained on the second floor. (JJN.)

Cecil Curtis, manager of the Rex Theater, endeared himself to all the parents of young children in town. He made Saturday afternoons children's day at the theater. He opened the Rex at noon and ran a variety of suitable cartoons, serials, and movies until dinner time. Children did not have to worry about having something to eat, because the concessions offered hot dogs, sodas, popcorn, candy, and their favorite ice cream and Popsicles. (JJN.)

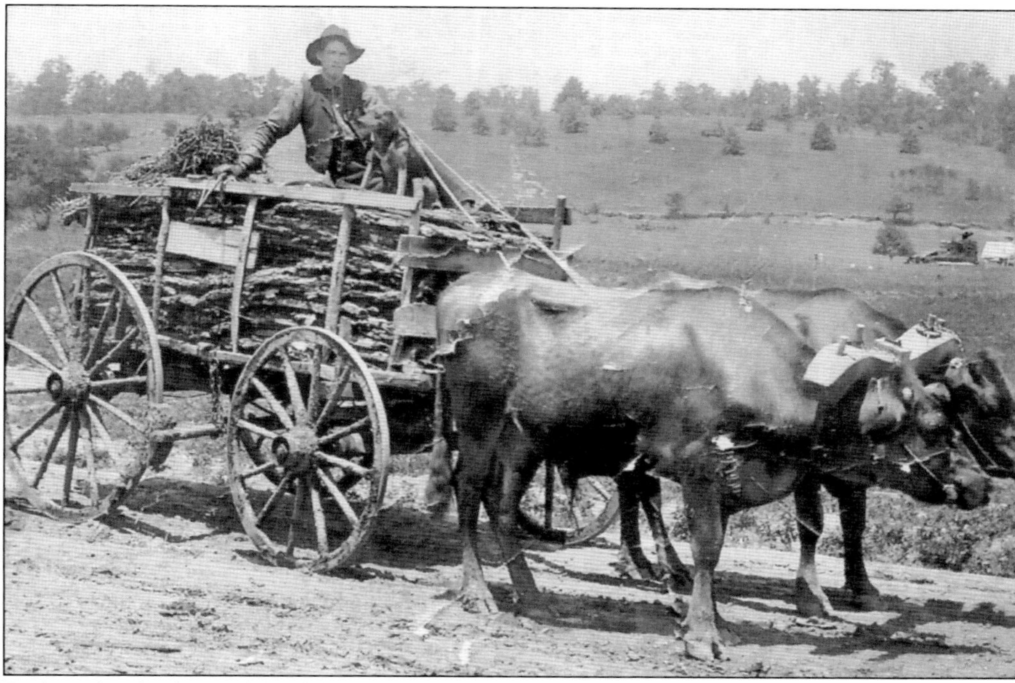

Early Galax had a wealth of chestnut trees, which provided lumber for construction. The trees were stripped of their bark, which was a separate commodity. The bark produced tannic acid that was used in the process of tanning leather. Tanning bark dealers in town included B. D. Beamer, W. E. Lindsey, C. H. South, and Charlie P. Waugh. This unidentified man sits on top of his oxcart loaded with tanning bark. (MM.)

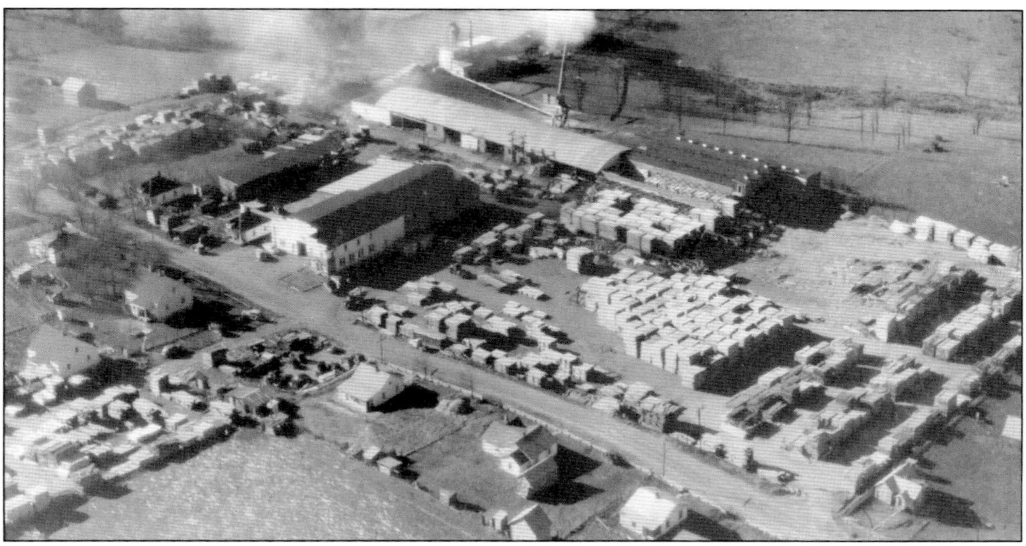

S. R. Dixon established a sawmill business with six employees in the early 1920s. In 1938, the name was changed to S. R. Dixon Lumber Shop. By 1941, the company expanded to include a sawmill, planting mill, and retail lumber supply. Following World War II, hardwood flooring and a dimension plant were added. It was incorporated into Dixon Lumber Company, Inc., in 1949. Following Dixon's death, his son, Glenn, became president of the company. (Glenn Dixon family.)

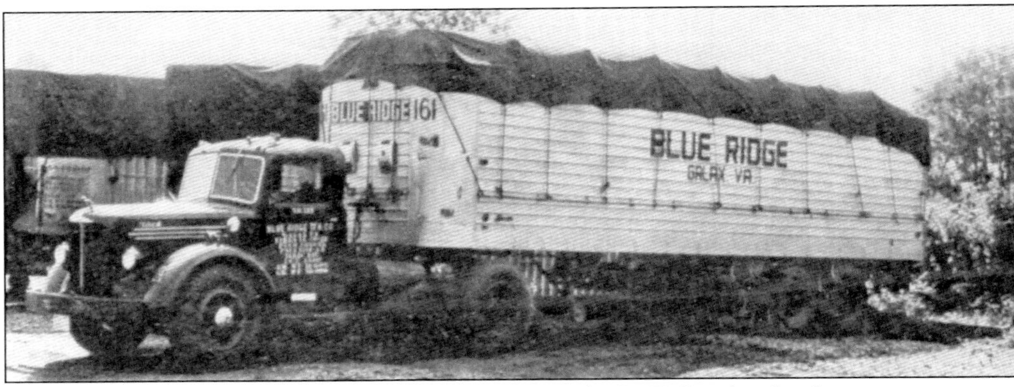

Blue Ridge Transfer Company was organized in 1932 by J. W. Stanley for the primary purpose of serving the furniture industry in Galax. The large volume of sales produced by furniture manufacturers Vaughan, Vaughan-Bassett, Webb, Galax Furniture, and Carroll Furniture made it necessary to have an efficient method of shipment. Galax remained the headquarters when Stanley established terminals in Roanoke and Henry County. He provided a delivery service to the furniture trade in 14 states. (JJN.)

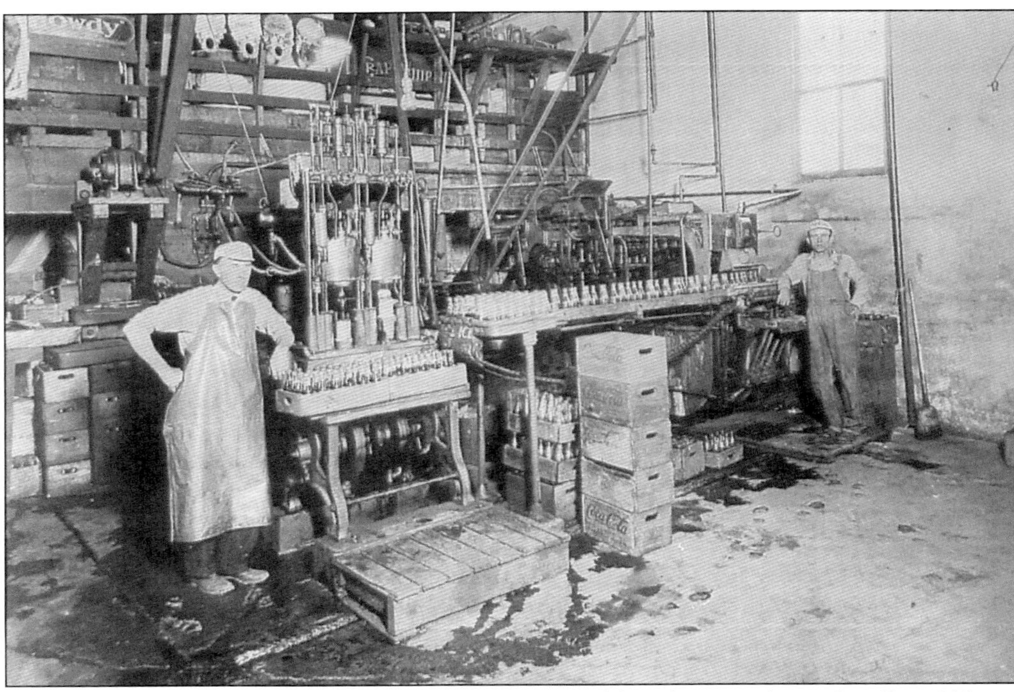

The Galax Coca-Cola Bottling Company, a locally owned franchise, was located on East Oldtown Street across from the Adams Mill and the Galax Mirror Company. The beverage was presented in glass bottles and delivered in wood crates painted in the company's colors. Randall Knisely, manager of the plant, lived with his wife, Georgia, on West Stuart Drive. (JW.)

Four

Houses

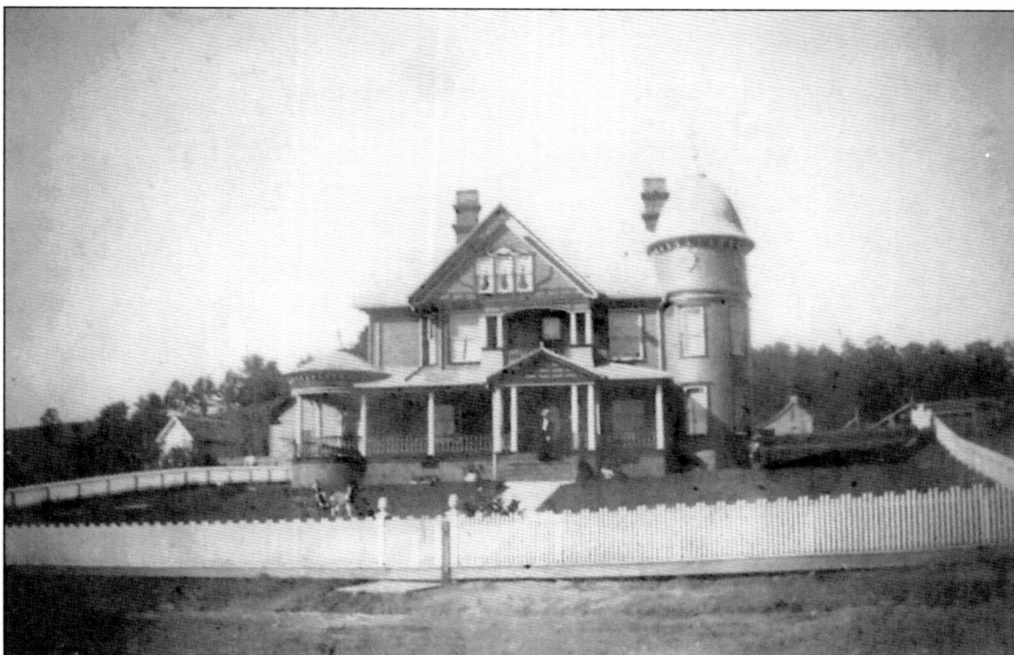

Dr. James Henry and Josephine Witherow built their family home on West Stuart Drive. Dr. Witherow owned a pharmacy on the corner of Main and West Grayson Streets. When the First National Bank purchased this lot for a new brick bank building, Dr. Witherow and his partner, H. C. Cox, decided to erect a brick building at 115 South Main Street and open Witherow's Clothing Store for men. A large antique safe with "J. H. Witherow" lettered across the front is still in the building. (MM.)

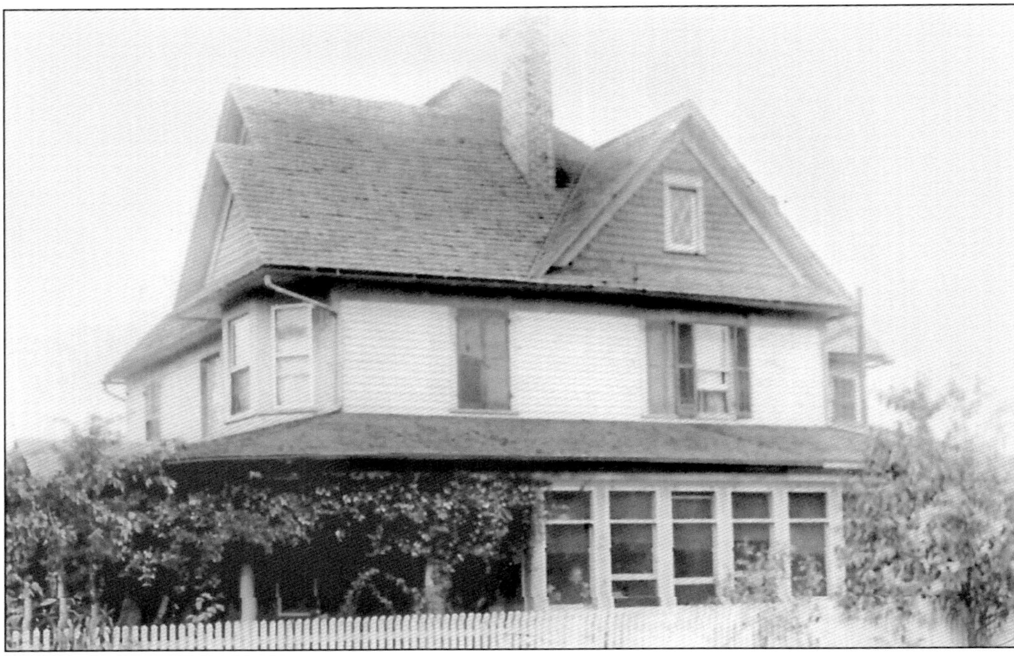

William Kenny and Mary Early built this beautiful white frame house on North Main Street. It was later the home of the Earlys' son, George, and his wife, Sarah. Following George's death in 1951, Sarah continued to manage W. K. Early and Sons. (MM.)

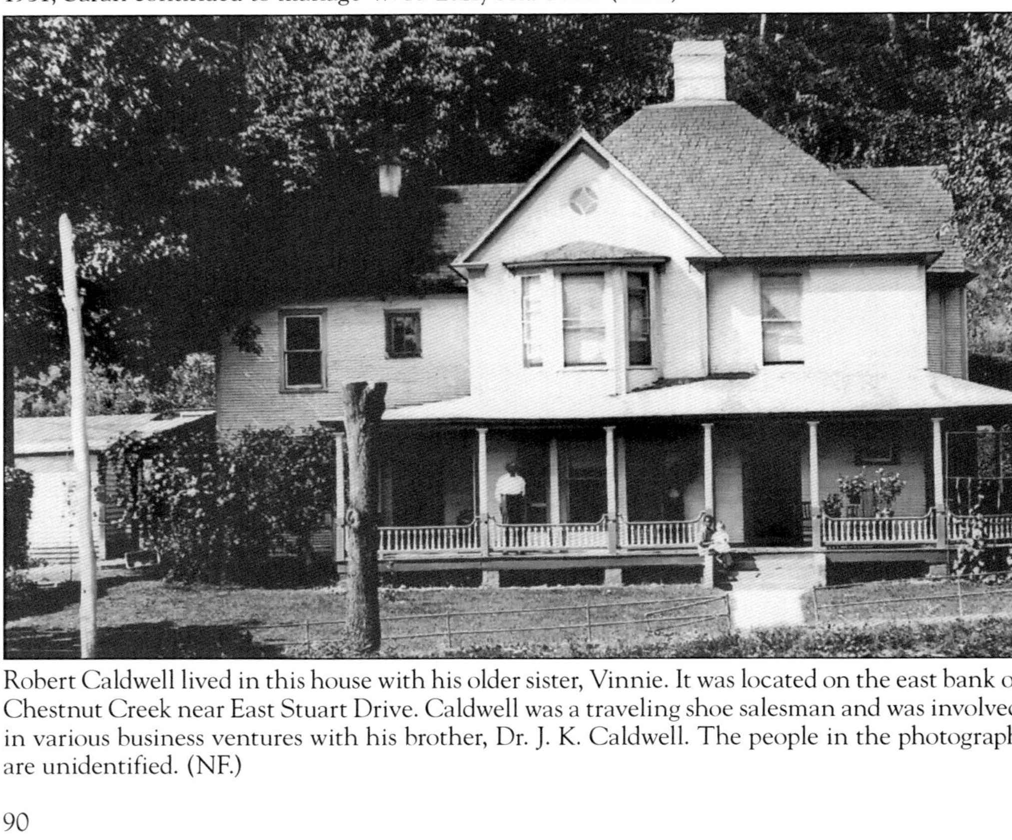

Robert Caldwell lived in this house with his older sister, Vinnie. It was located on the east bank of Chestnut Creek near East Stuart Drive. Caldwell was a traveling shoe salesman and was involved in various business ventures with his brother, Dr. J. K. Caldwell. The people in the photograph are unidentified. (NF.)

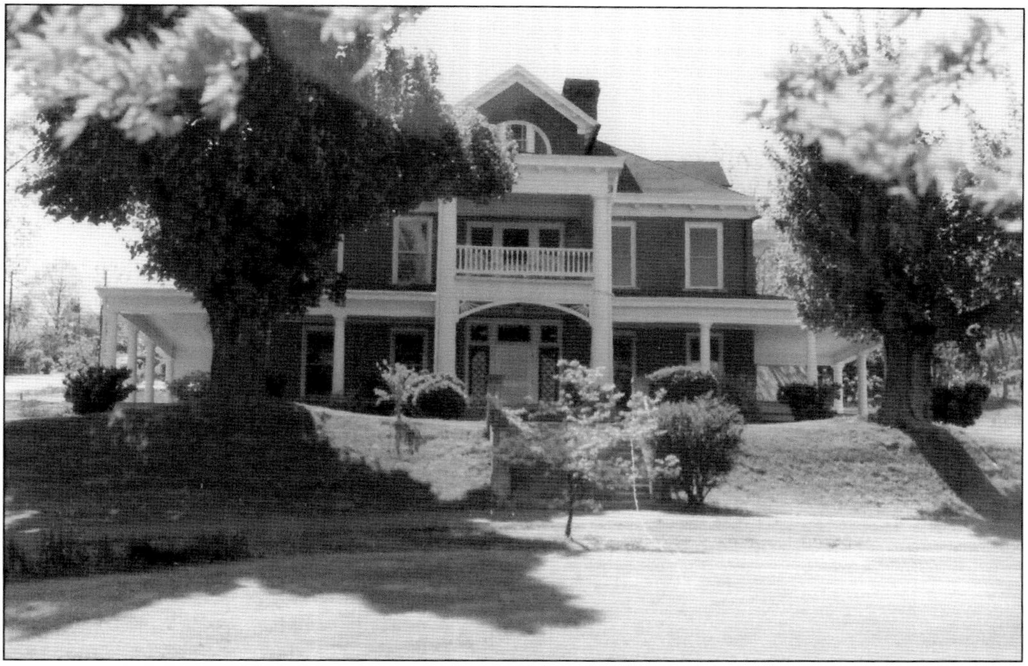

Galax pioneer Capt. John Blair Waugh built this stately home on West Stuart Drive for his wife, Jennie, and their children. The location provided the family with a magnificent view of Galax. Their son, Charles, moved his family into the home following the death of John Waugh in 1934. (MM.)

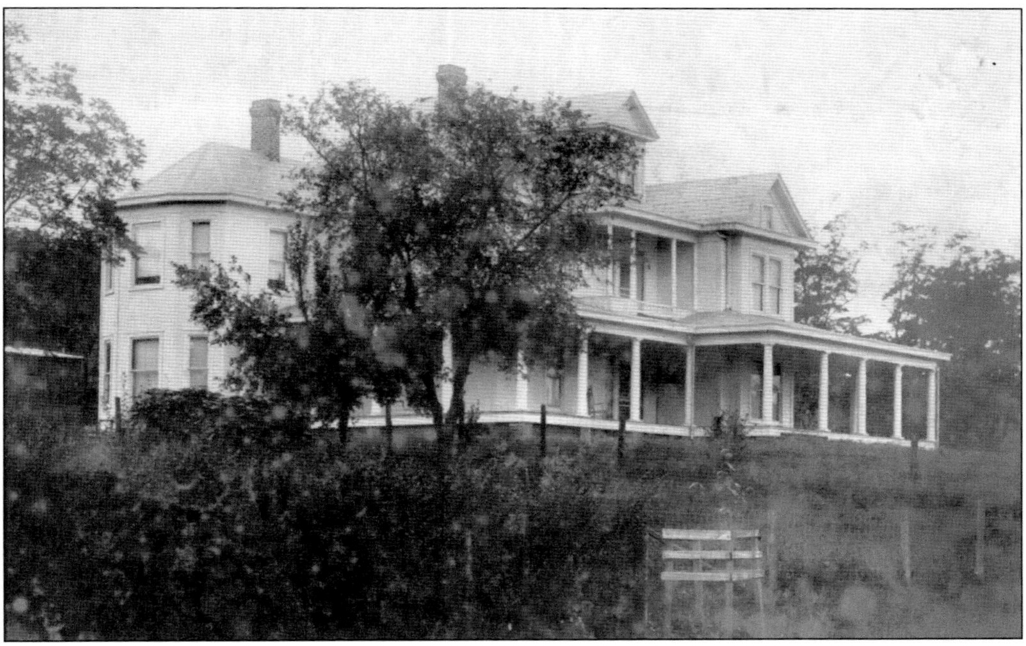

This beautiful home was built on West Stuart Drive by Ed Cox. However, it will always be known as the home of Dr. Virgil Cox, a well-known and highly respected doctor. Dr. Cox purchased the 20-room home from his uncle for $8,000 in the 1930s. (Jim Carico.)

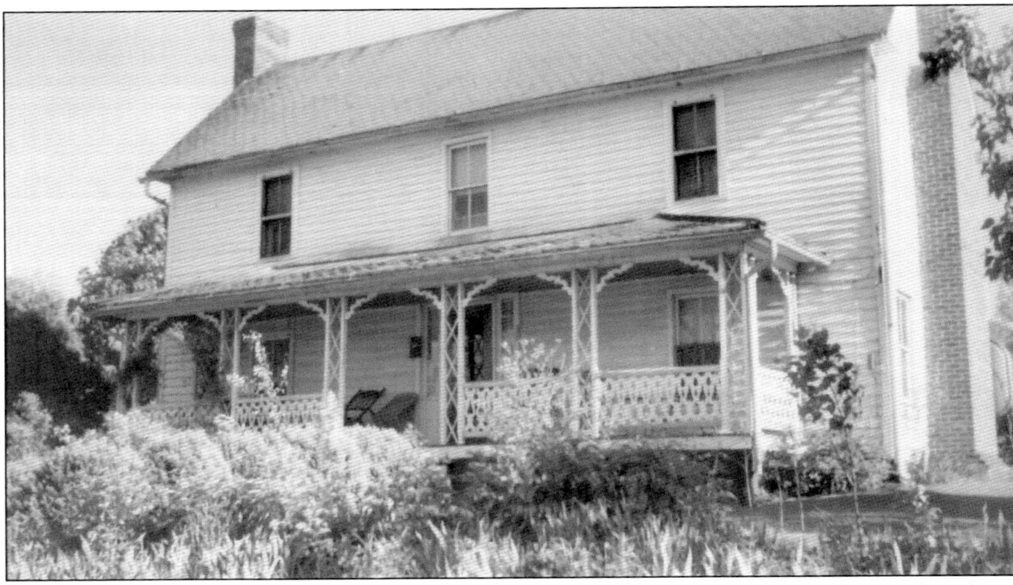

Alexander Chapman Anderson married Ada May Cooper in 1895. He built this large white frame house on Anderson Road about seven years after they were married. They were the parents of seven children, so the two-story home provided ample space to raise a large family. A springhouse, a smokehouse, and a privy were located behind the house. Three of the children, Ned, Dan, and Virginia Anderson Lundy, resided there following the death of their parents. (Barbara Eanes.)

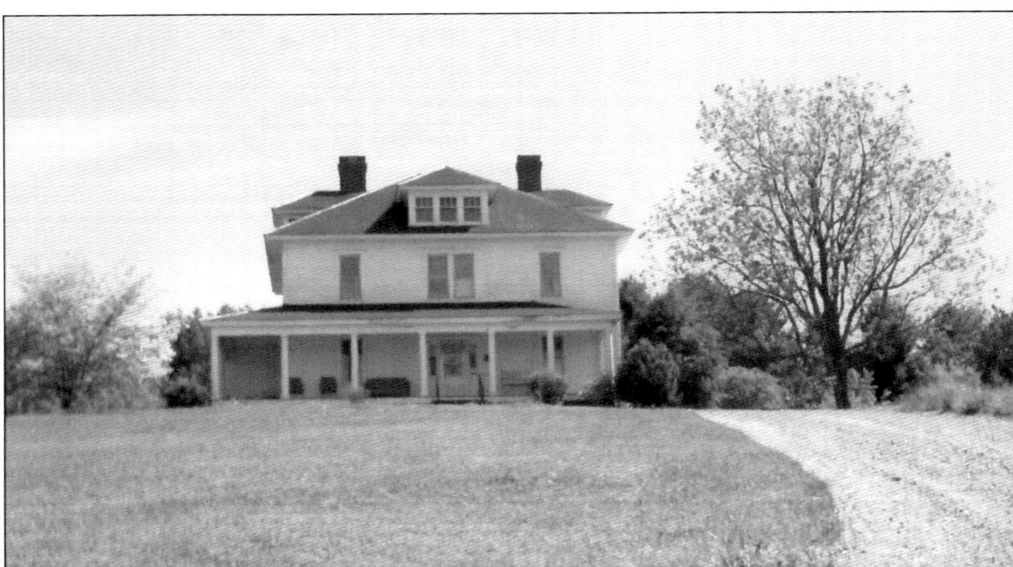

Alexander C. Painter built this home on Anderson Road for his wife, Amanda, and son, James Orville. It was rebuilt on the site following a fire in 1923. Following the death of his parents, James lived there with his wife, Lettie. (MM.)

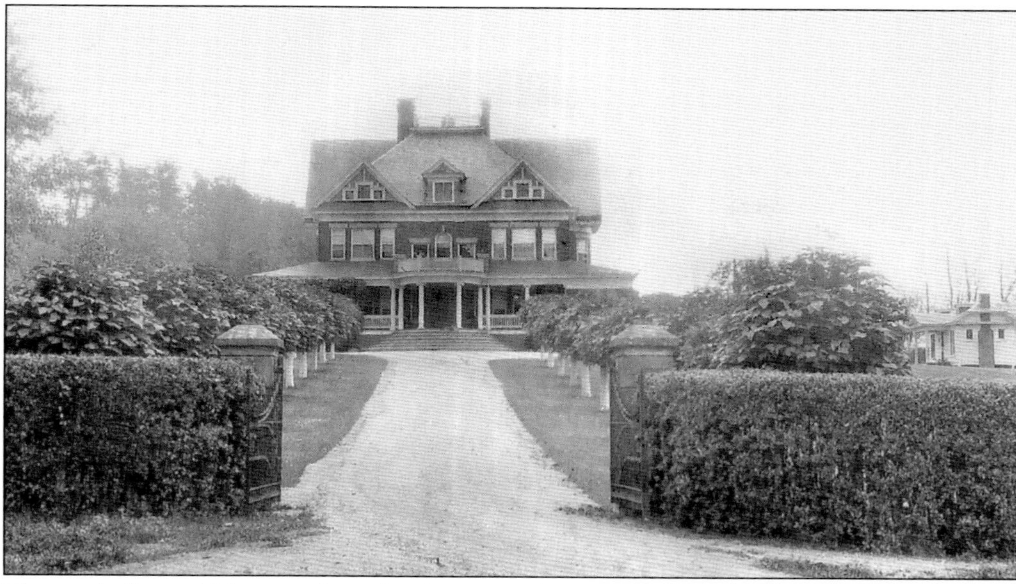

Thomas Lafayette Felts was a large landowner in the area. He built this grand home in Blair for his wife, Ethel, and son, Gordon. The magnificent estate included a summerhouse, barns, office buildings, servant quarters, and a well house. The home featured a grand double staircase and an oval dining room. There were additional bedrooms and a ballroom on the third floor that were reached by a separate, indoor staircase at the back of the home. Following the death of the Felts, their son, Gordon, and grandson, Frank, occupied the home. (MM.)

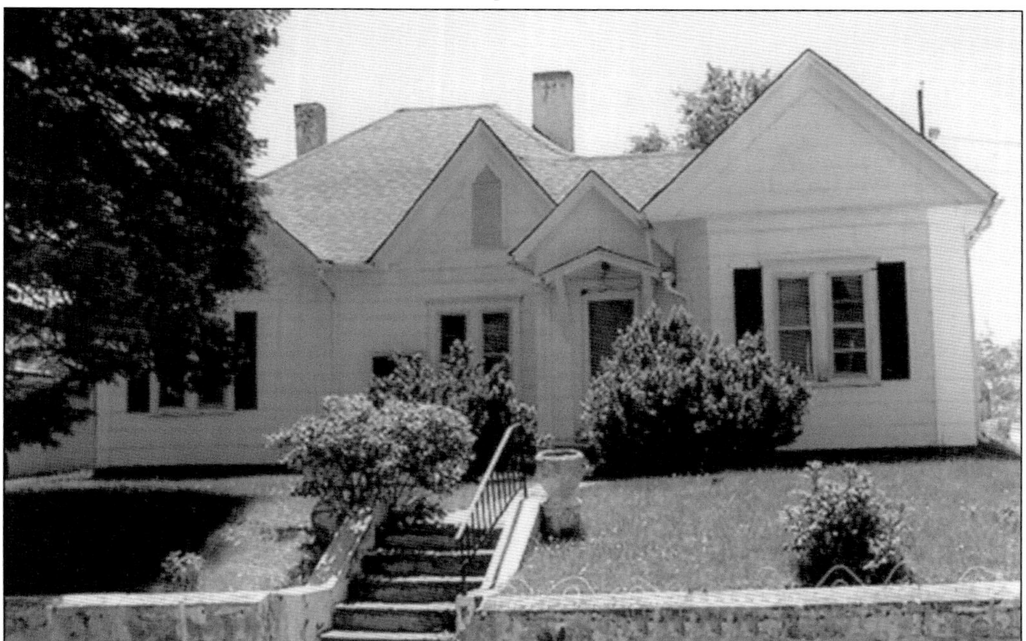

Louis and Ray Perelman built this home on West Oldtown Street, where they raised their three children, Bessie, Mildred, and Casper. It was conveniently located just around the corner from the family's clothing store on the west side of South Main Street. (JJN.)

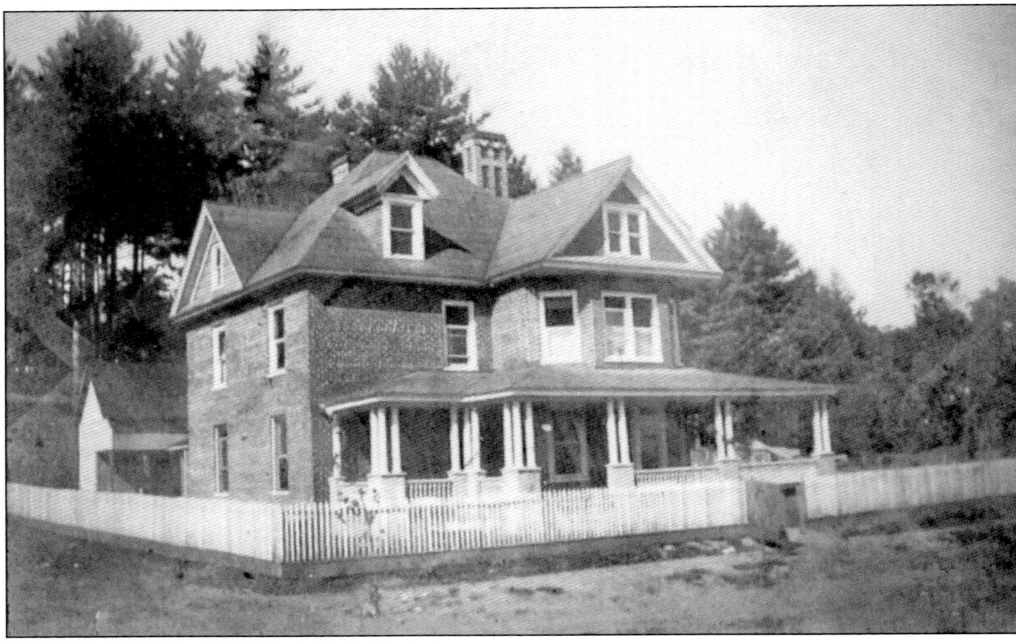

Pioneer resident Hardin H. Todd built this house on the west side of South Main Street for his wife and four children. The home did not have indoor plumbing and contained very small closets. When his brother J. J. Todd died, Hardin assumed his position on the board of the Grayson Real Estate Company and helped to direct the early development of the town. (MM.)

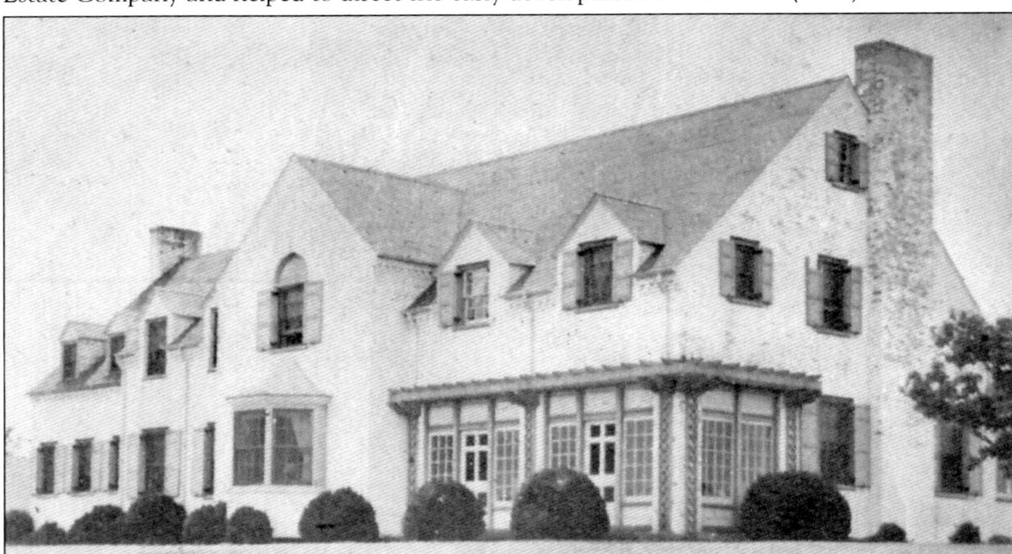

John and Augusta Messer arrived in Galax in December 1927 with their four children, Beatrice, Gertrude, Kenneth, and John. The family resided in a brick home on the corner of West Oldtown and Adams Street while this grand home was being constructed on the old Hillsville Highway, east of Galax. The 9,000-square-foot, three-story home was situated on 70 acres of lawn and beautiful gardens, all enclosed by white fencing. The house featured a grand staircase and the only elevator in town. It was completed in 1935 for only $35,000. (JJN, JNA.)

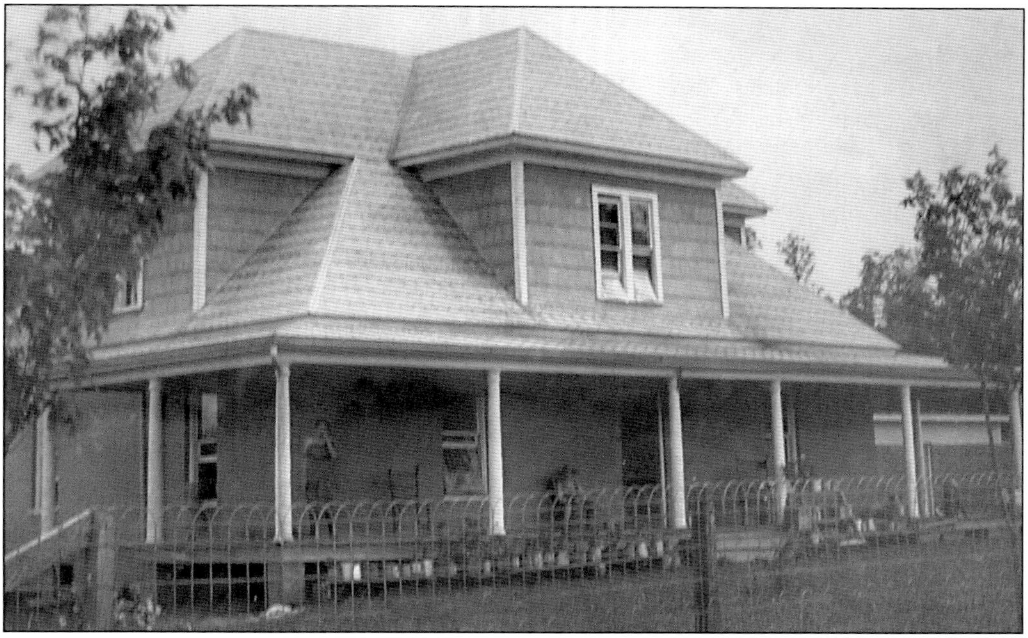

When John Creed and Cora Cox Matthews moved from Gap, Virginia, to Galax, they resided in this home on the east side of Chestnut Creek in the area known as Anderson's Bottom. Matthews had been an employee of the Blair Hardware Company in Blair. When the family moved to Galax, he established the J. C. Matthews Hardware Store and warehouse on East Grayson Street. (MM.)

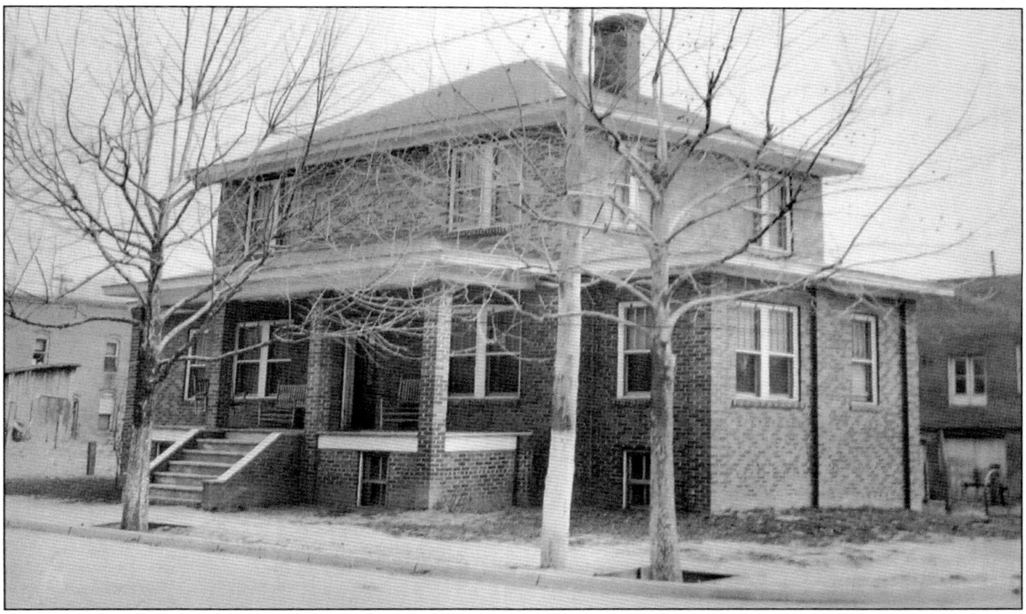

John Creed and Cora Cox Matthews built this home on the corner of West Center and Jefferson Streets, next door to the site of the future Galax Hospital. Matthews was a member of the Galax High School Corporation in 1907. The group's goal was to finance and construct a new brick school building in town. This was just the beginning of the entire Matthews family's dedicated involvement in local civic affairs. (MM.)

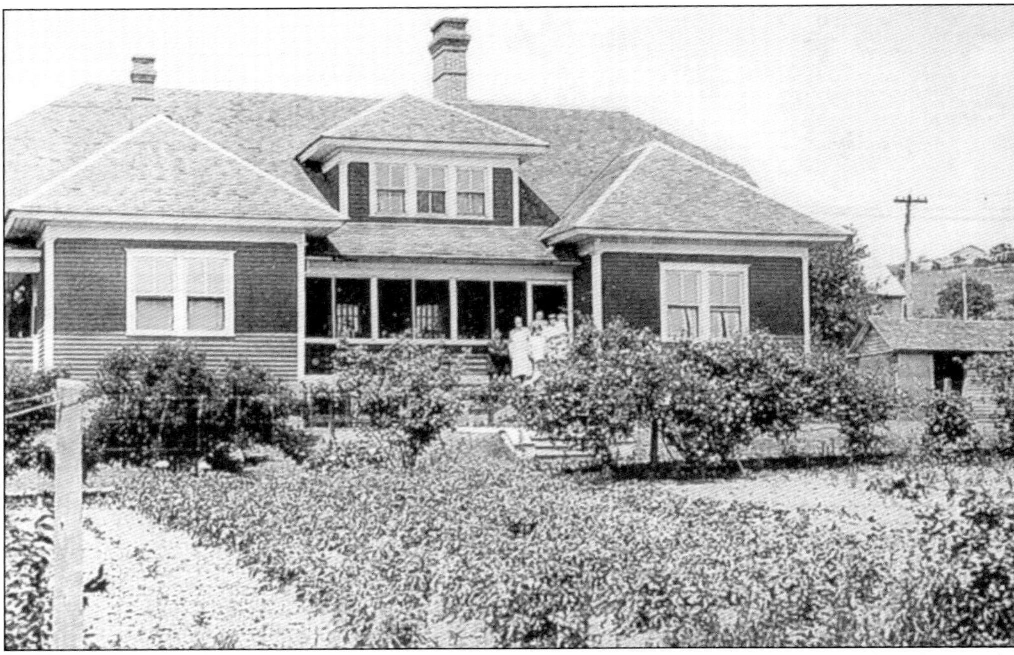

This undated photograph shows a house at 408 West Grayson Street in Galax. Ed Perkins, who later moved to Roanoke, built the house. It was sold to Will and Dell Warren of Independence. Their daughter, Hattie Warren Fulton, lived there until her death. (MM.)

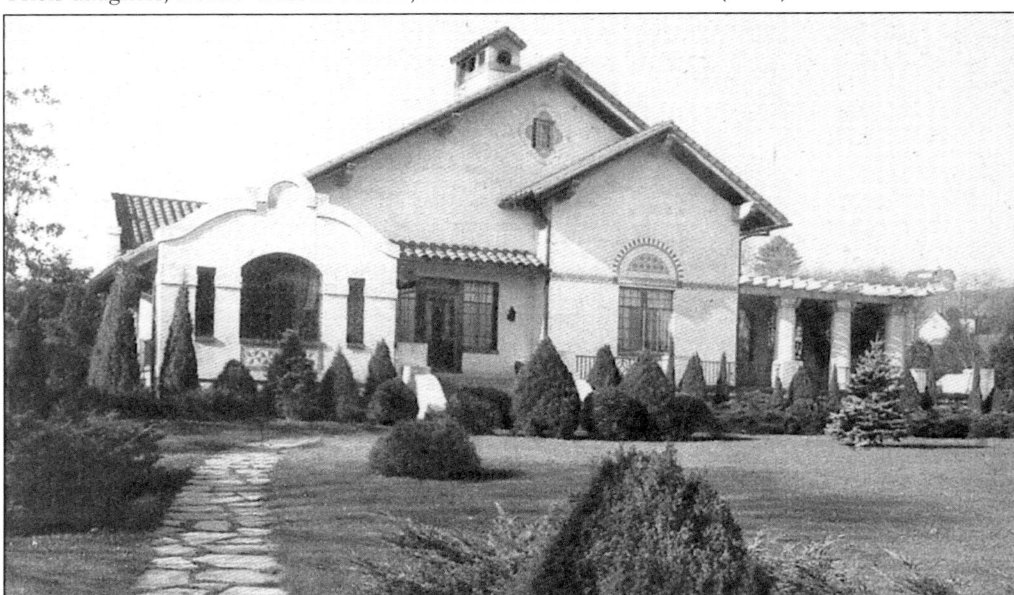

This stately home on the west side of North Main and Webster Streets belonged to Gordon and Alice Felts. Gordon Felts was president of Twin County Motor Company, so he only had to walk across the street to go to his office. Not only did his company handle cars, but they also sold Ford tractors, Dearborn implements, and a wide variety of tillage tools. Gordon was the son of Thomas L. Felts, one of the pioneer citizens of Galax. (GG.)

Dr. J. K. Caldwell built this beautiful, large frame two-story home on West Center Street next to the First Presbyterian Church of Galax, about a block from the Old Galax Hospital and the site where he would later build a brick home. (JJN.)

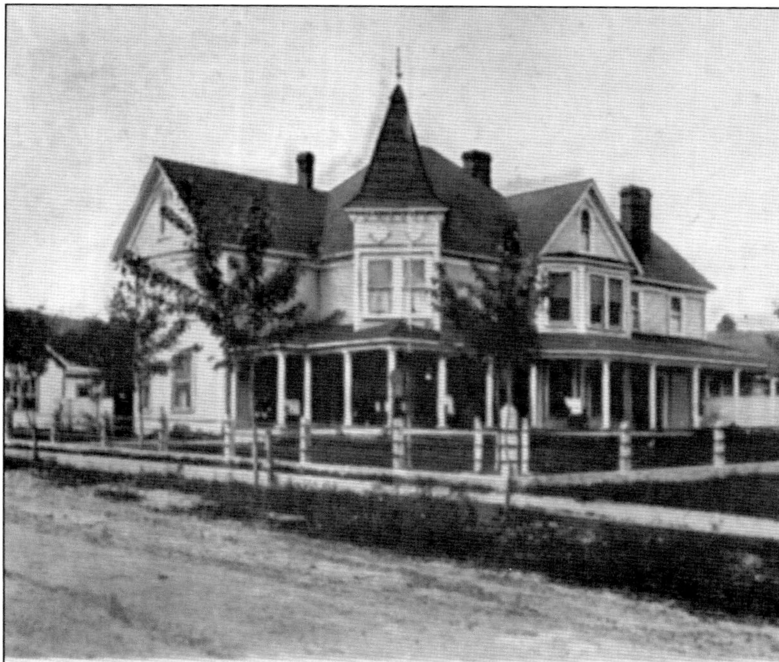

Dr. J. K. Caldwell

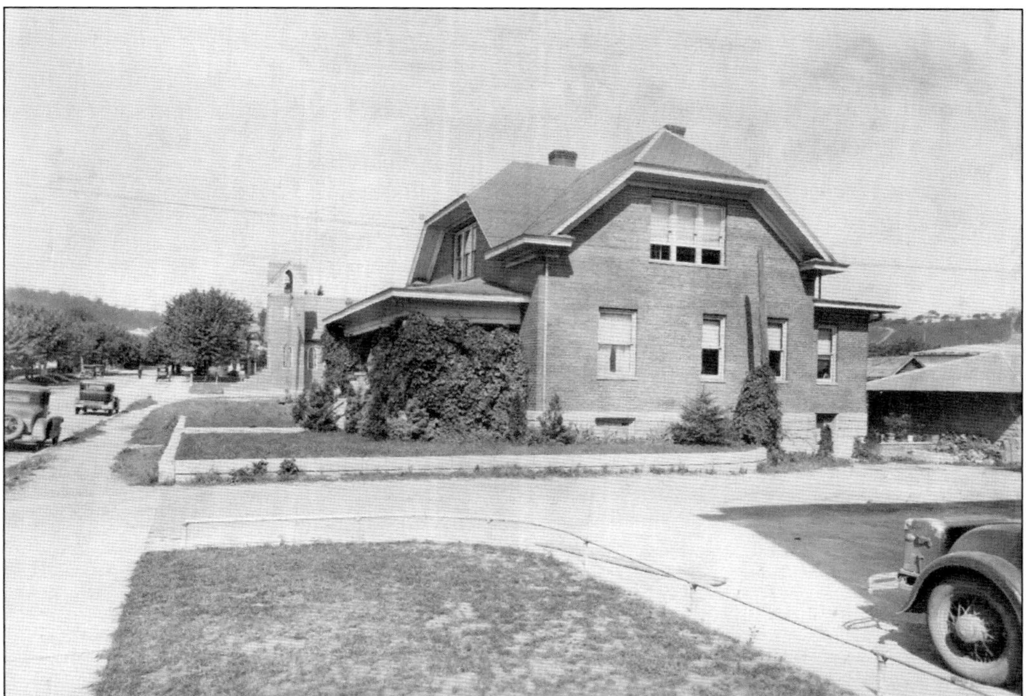

This brick home was built later by Dr. J. K. Caldwell. It is located on West Center Street across from the old Galax Hospital. The Bluemont Hotel would later be built next door, on the northwest corner of Center and Main Streets. (NF.)

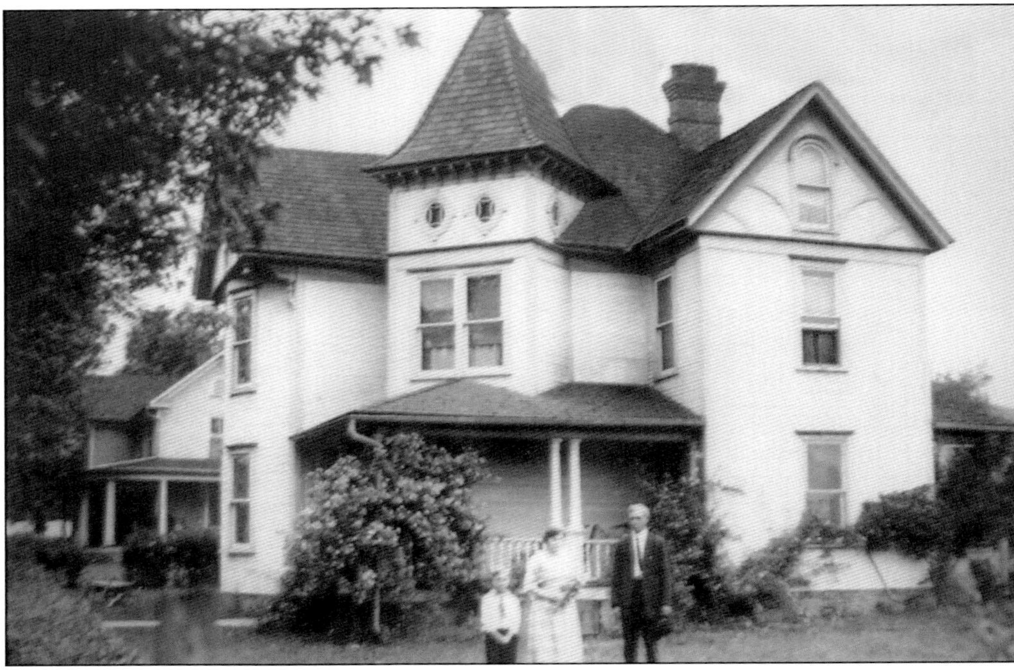

The E. Lane Whitley home was visible in several early photographs of West Grayson Street in town. In this undated photograph, the house is now surrounded by fully grown trees, hedges, and flowers, instead of sheep running in front of the house on the way to market. Note the interesting detail in the third story of the home. The people are unidentified. (MM.)

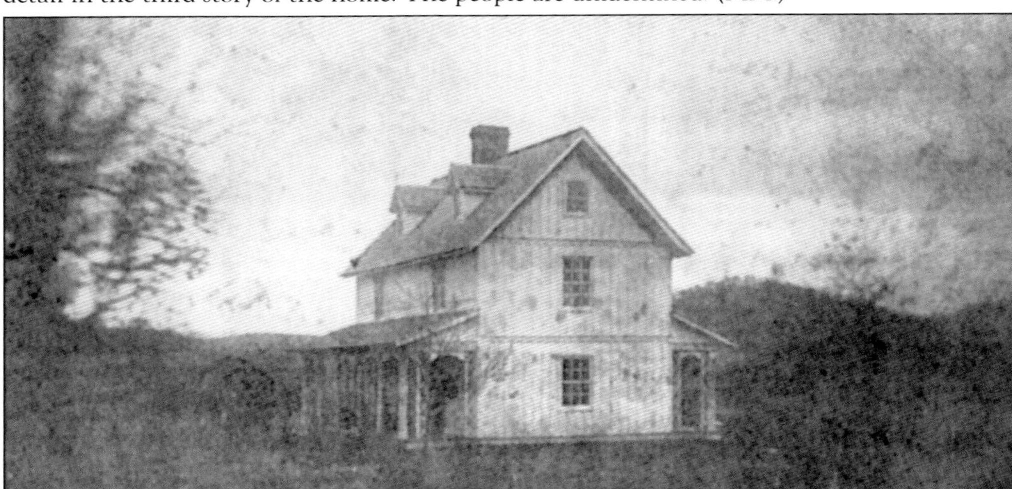

J. Badger Caldwell purchased land in Carroll County in the 1880s. Little did he realize that his investment was going to be located on the east side of a new community. Badger and his wife, Fannie, were the parents of nine children, living as of 1900. All but two of the family members were buried in the Caldwell-Givens Cemetery in East Galax. Upon Barger's death, his son Archie sold his share of the inheritance to his siblings. They had the land surveyed and divided into lots and blocks, and began to auction them off in April 1913. In June 1913, each sibling purchased lots, blocks, and plots of land from the family group. The area became known as the Sunnyside addition. The exact location and date of this photograph is unknown. (NF.)

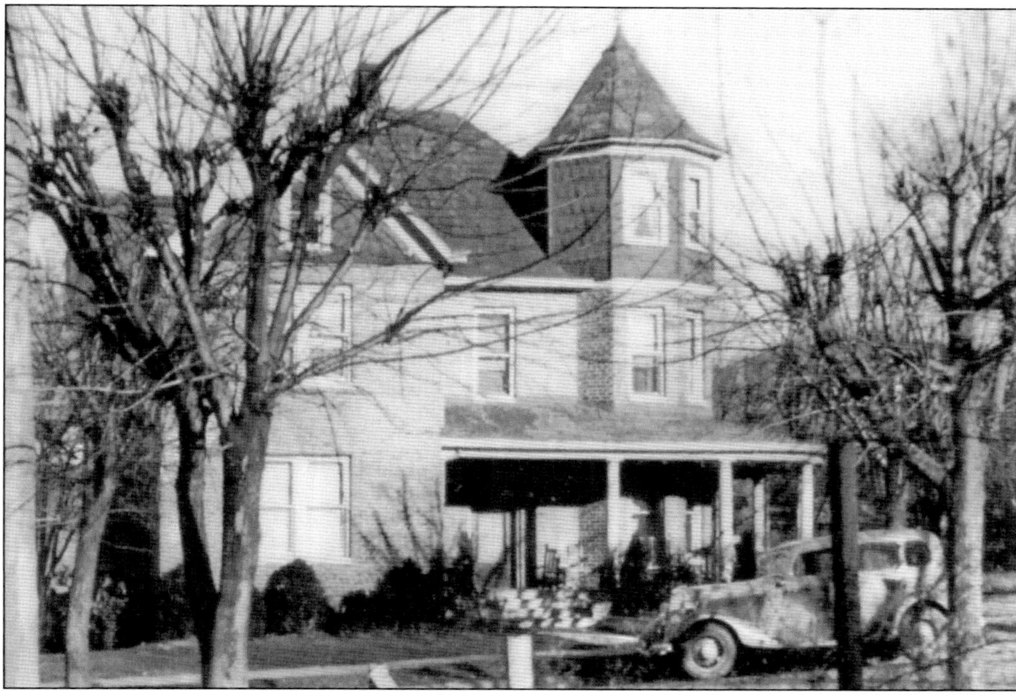

Elbert Frazier and Josie Williams Ward built this large brick home on the east side of South Main Street. They resided there with their children until 1919, when they moved to Danville, Virginia. Ward was one of the first rural mail carriers in Galax. He was a brother of Monroe and Marvin Ward, who were also pioneer citizens of Galax. The James P. Carico family was the next family to occupy the house. (Jim Carico.)

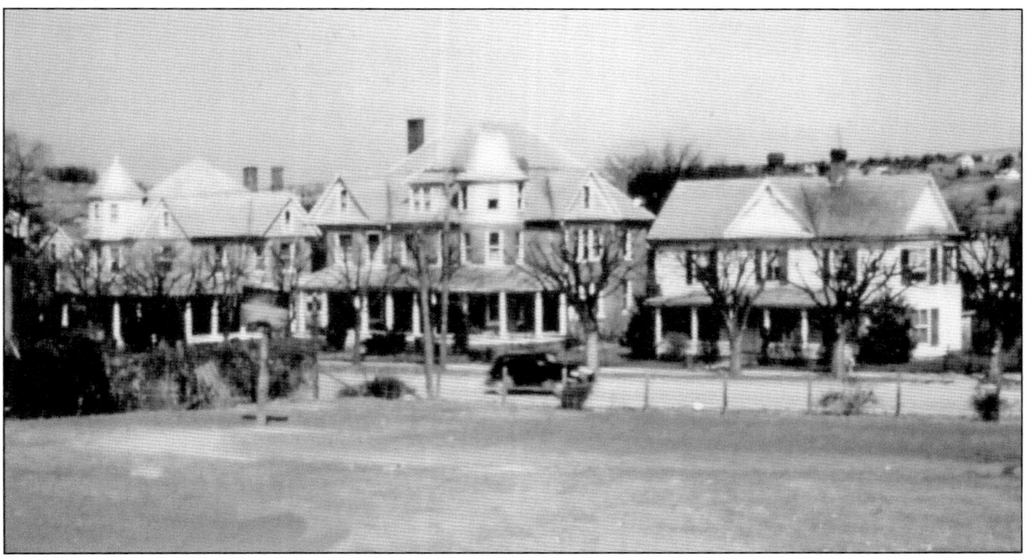

This undated photograph was taken from Academy Drive looking across South Main Street toward the homes of Marvin Ward, Monroe Ward, and Martin Luther Bishop. All three men were pioneer residents and leaders of the community. The Ward brothers owned a brick company, and Bishop owned a livery stable. (MM.)

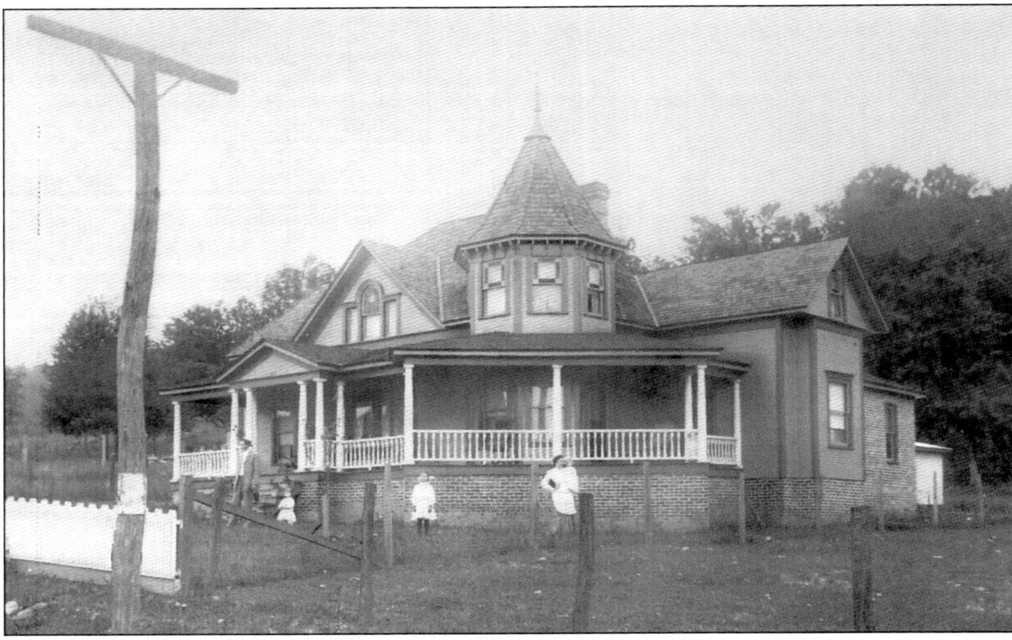

This is another home that can be seen in early photographs of Galax. Charles Collier resided there with his wife, Roberta, and their three daughters, Opal, Stella, and Thelma. In 1930, Stella's husband, Marcus Dalton, and Thelma's husband, Sam Hampton, were also living with the family. Opal would later marry Bernard Webb. (PHB.)

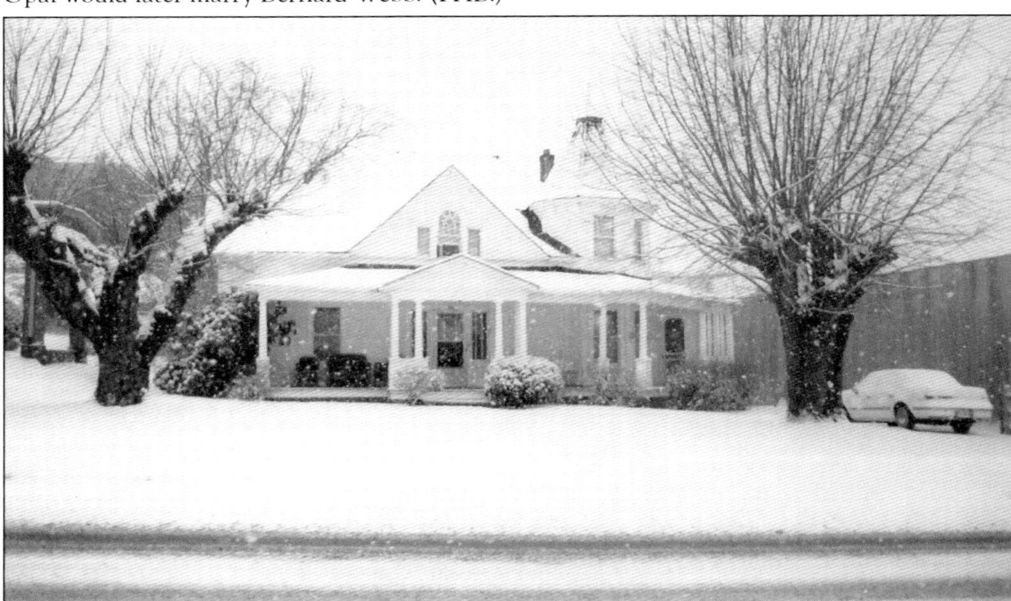

This is an undated photograph of the Charles and Roberta Collier home, located on the west side of South Main Street. This would be an excellent selection for a Currier and Ives Christmas card. The wide porch on the two-story frame house provided an excellent view of the parades that passed by. After the death of her parents, it became the home of Opal and Bernard Webb and their children. (PHB.)

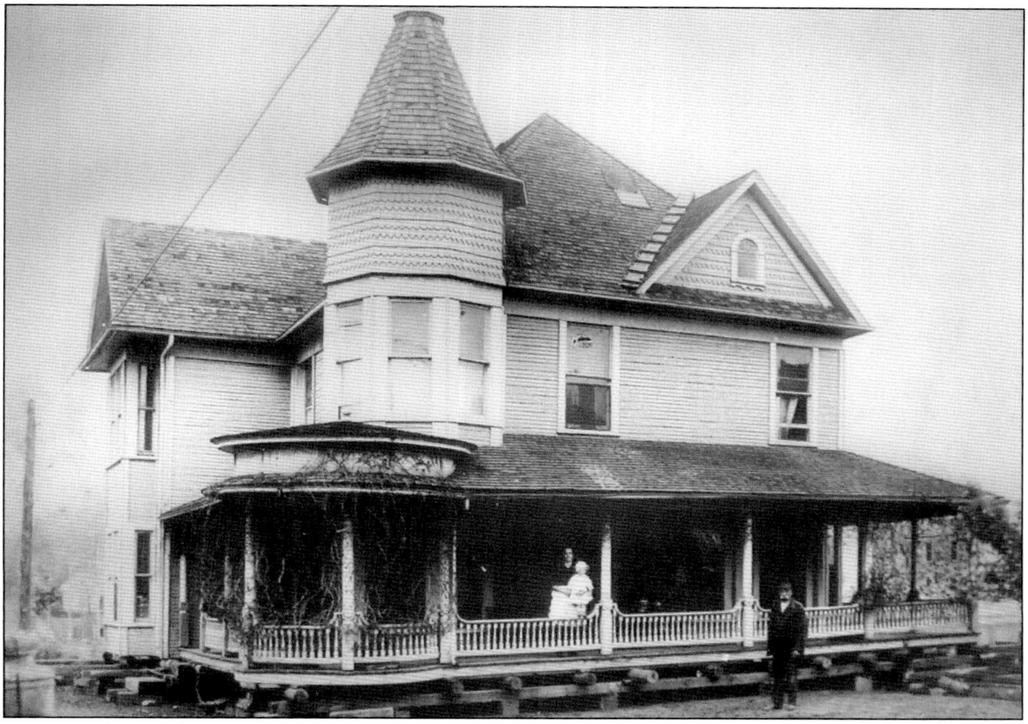

Dr. A. Glenn Pless moved from Haywood County, North Carolina, to Carroll County before 1910. He was a 35-year-old widower with his young son, Glenn, and a housekeeper when he built this home. He soon met and married Wirt Shelton, and they were the parents of two children, James and Mary. This house was originally located on the east side of North Main Street, but as the photograph reveals, the house was being prepared to move to Washington Street. The people in the photograph are unidentified. (MM.)

The A. G. Pless house has been moved to its new location on Washington Street. Dr. Pless was the father of Glenn Pless, a well-known and highly respected citizen of Galax. (RL)

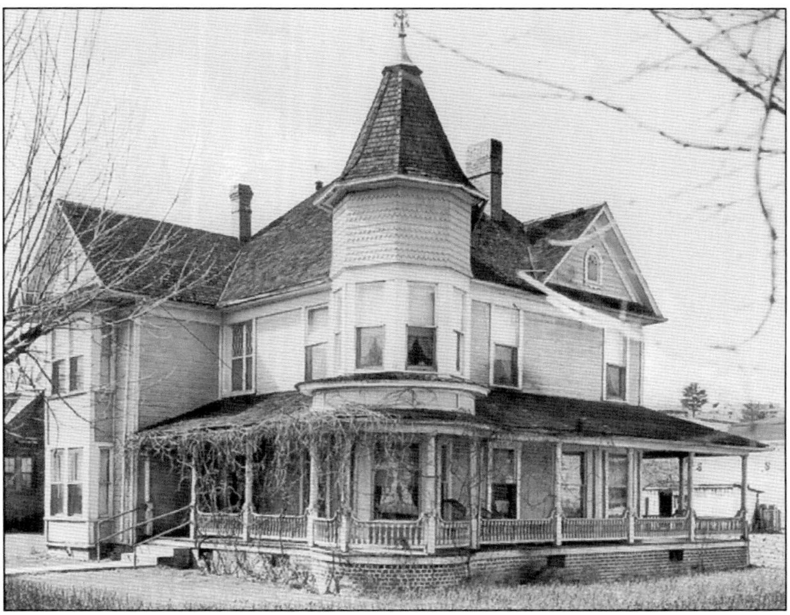

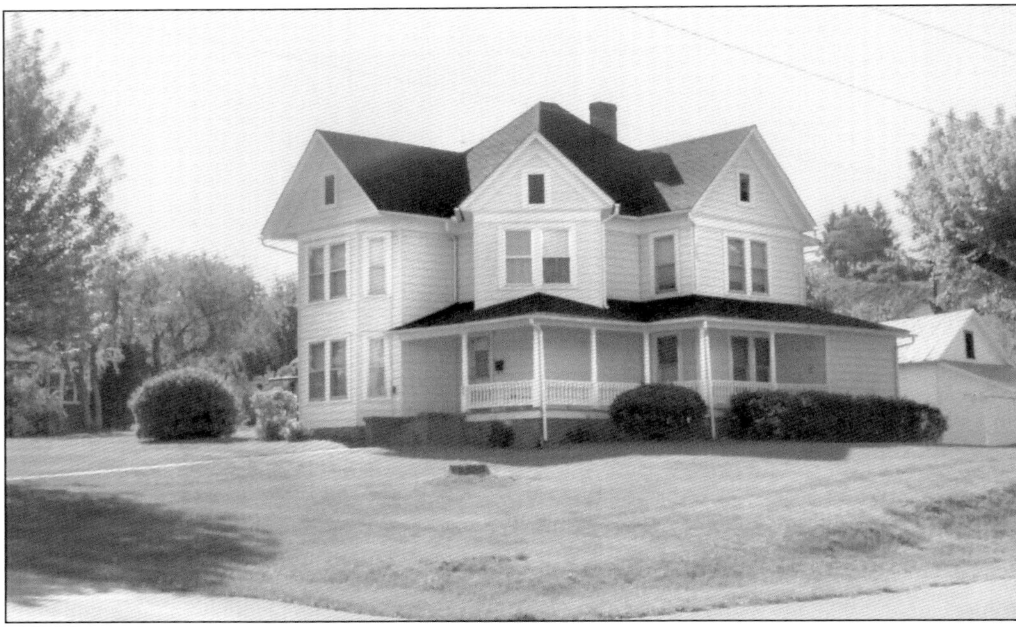

This undated photograph is of the Posey Lester Vass home, which was built on Washington Street around 1910. In the pantry of the house, there was a small stone trough, which was called the "dairy" and was used to keep eggs and milk cold. Bruce and Patty Robertson purchased the house in 1941. (MM.)

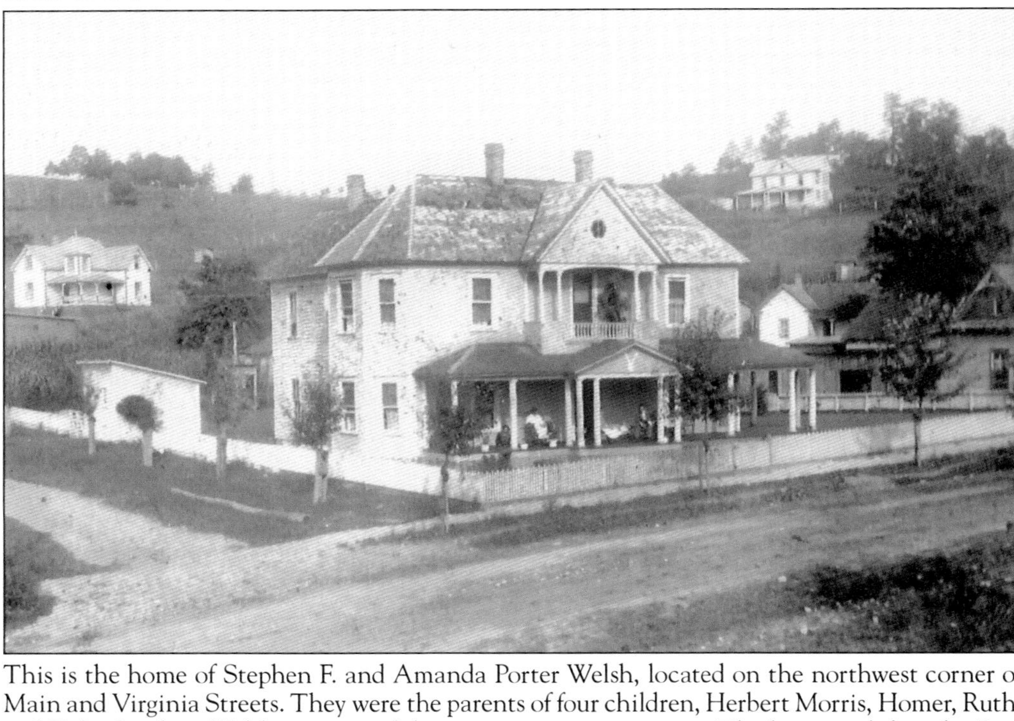

This is the home of Stephen F. and Amanda Porter Welsh, located on the northwest corner of Main and Virginia Streets. They were the parents of four children, Herbert Morris, Homer, Ruth, and Eula. Stephen Welsh was one of the pioneer citizens in town. The house at left is the Bert Alred home, and the Kinzer home is on the hill to the right. (JJN.)

Five

Events and Favorites

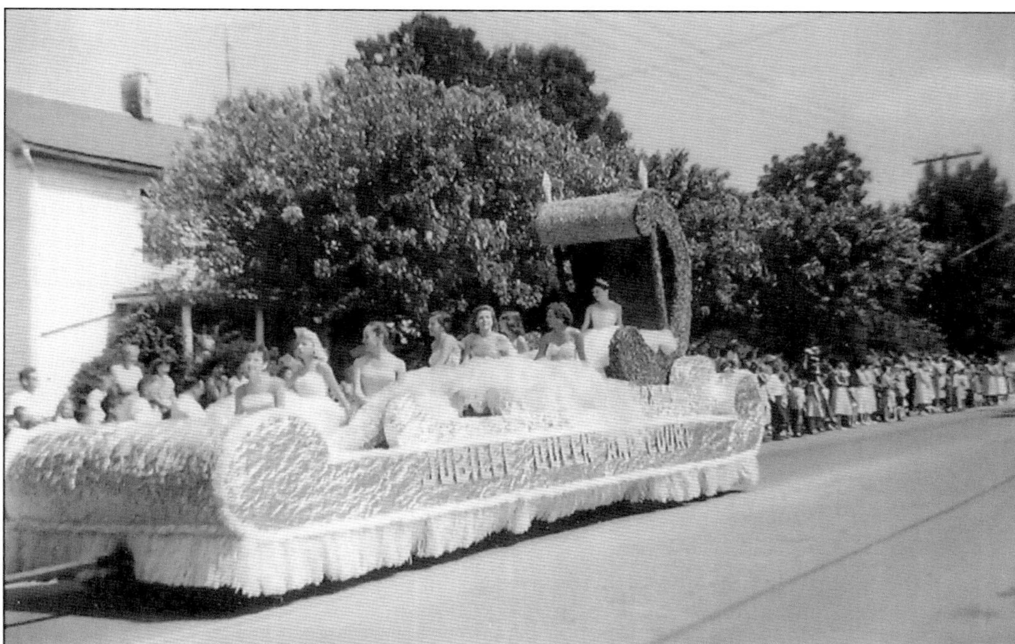

Queen Judy Nunn and her court led the Golden Jubilee Celebration's parade on August 6, 1956. Pictured from left to right on the float are Margaret Ward, Elizabeth Ann Todd, Phyllis Cox, Carolyn Hankley, Jane Eller, Libba Hawks, Janice Hurd, and Judy Nunn. The event attracted major political and civic leaders from around the state, including Virginia governor Thomas B. Stanley. (GPL.)

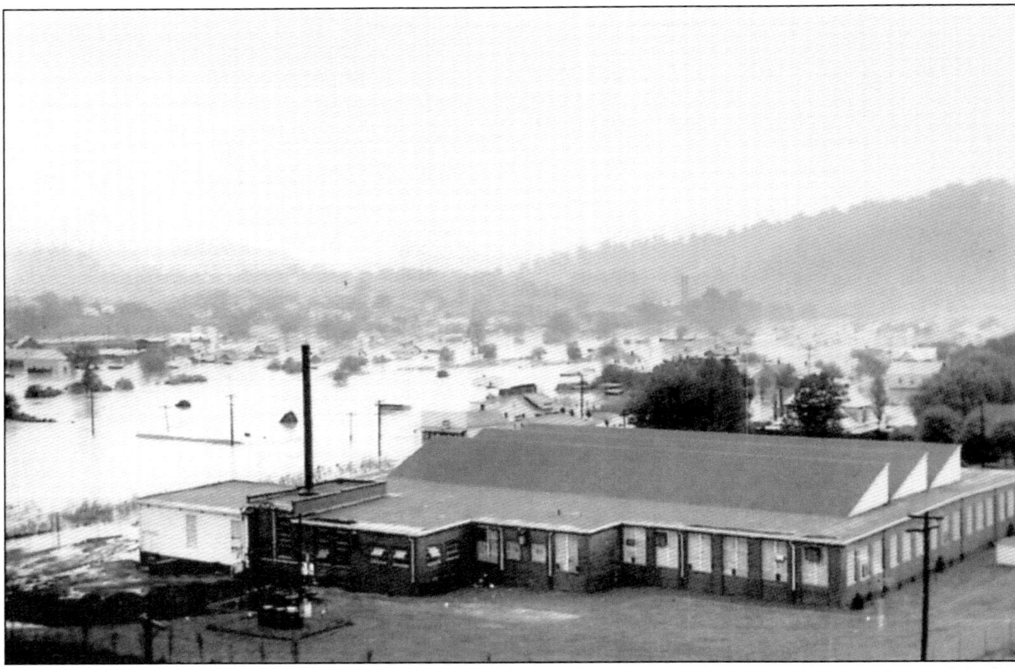

This photograph provides an excellent view of the devastation caused in the east section of Galax when Chestnut Creek overflowed its banks in 1941. (MM.)

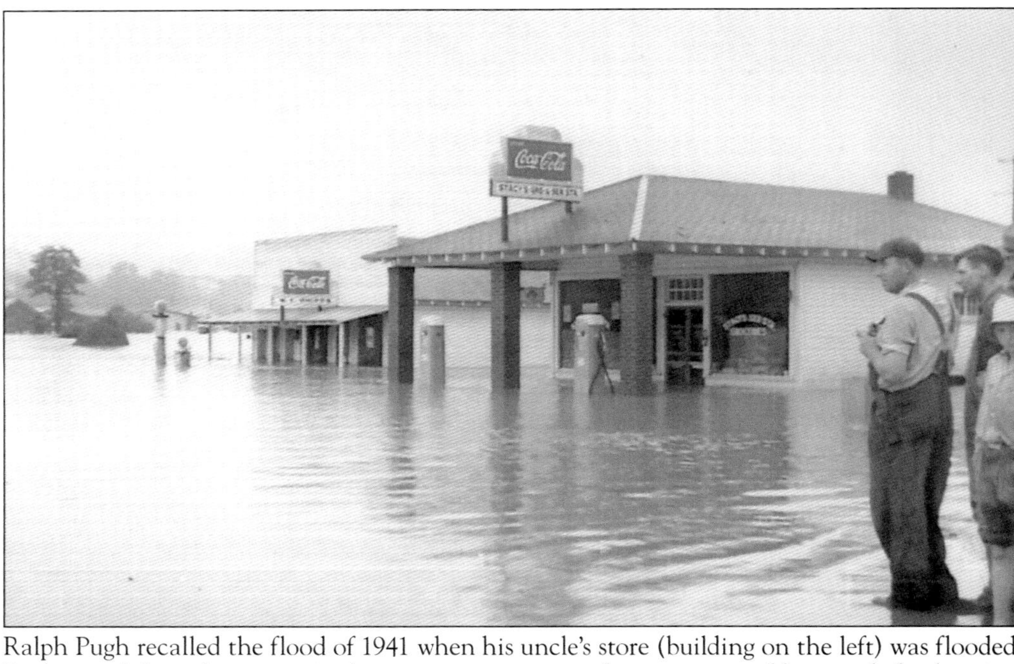

Ralph Pugh recalled the flood of 1941 when his uncle's store (building on the left) was flooded. Pugh stated that a barn or a similar structure was swept downstream and became lodged against the old Highway 58 bridge, creating a dam that backed the waters of the creek out "into the bottom." (JW.)

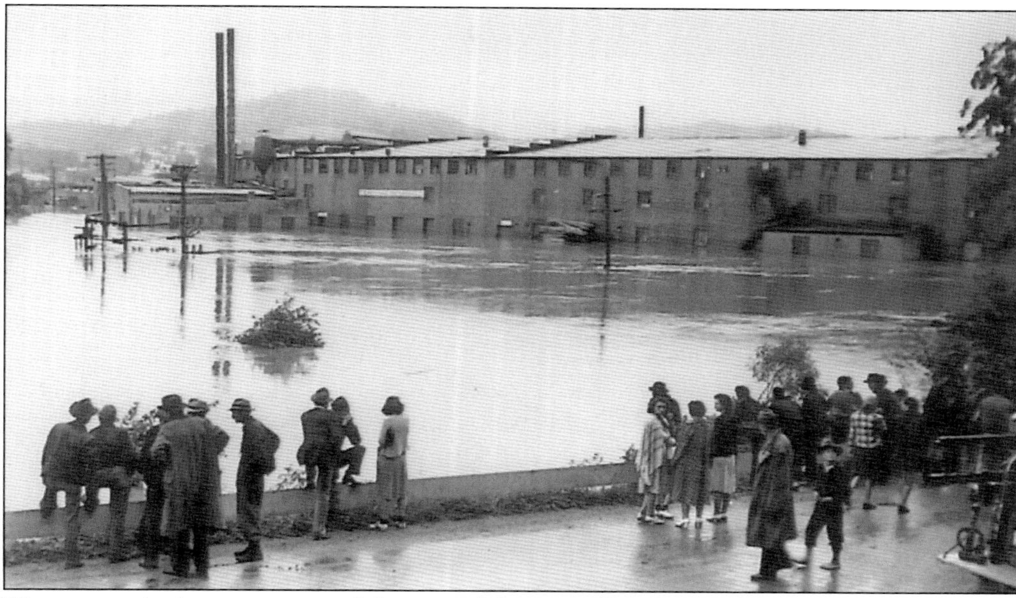

This view is looking west toward the rear of the partially submerged T. G. Vaughan Furniture Factory. The flood problems in Galax were finally resolved when civic leader Glenn Pless contacted the U.S. Army Corps of Engineers and requested that Chestnut Creek be straightened and that the banks be reinforced. (JW.)

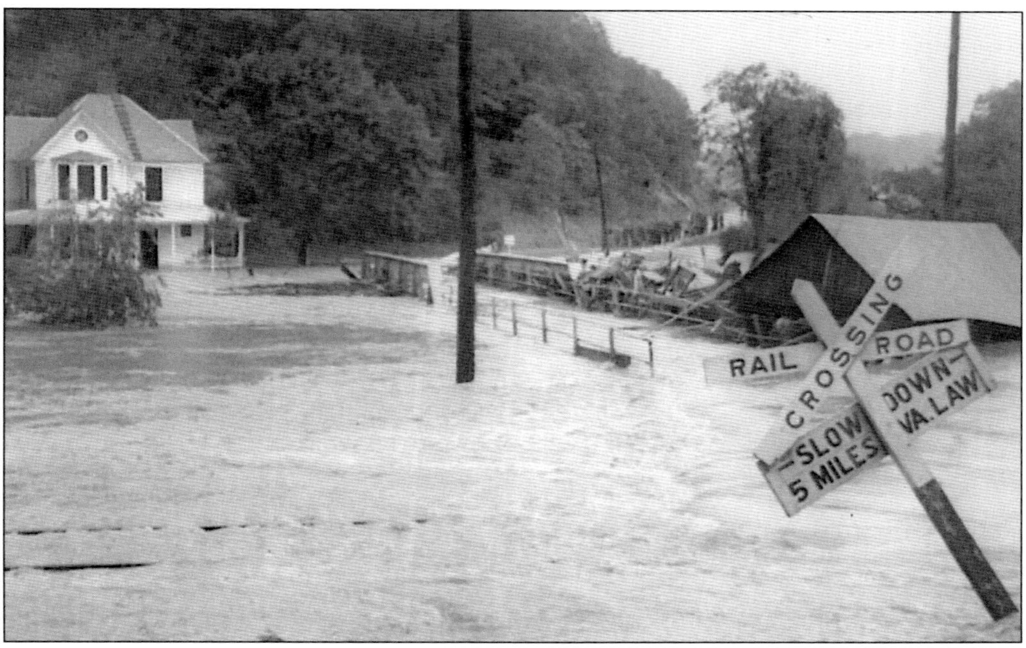

This view is looking east at the same location on Chestnut Creek. At left is the Robert Caldwell home, and behind the railroad crossing sign is the structure that was swept downstream and became lodged against the bridge, creating a dam. The flood caused millions of dollars in damages. (JW.)

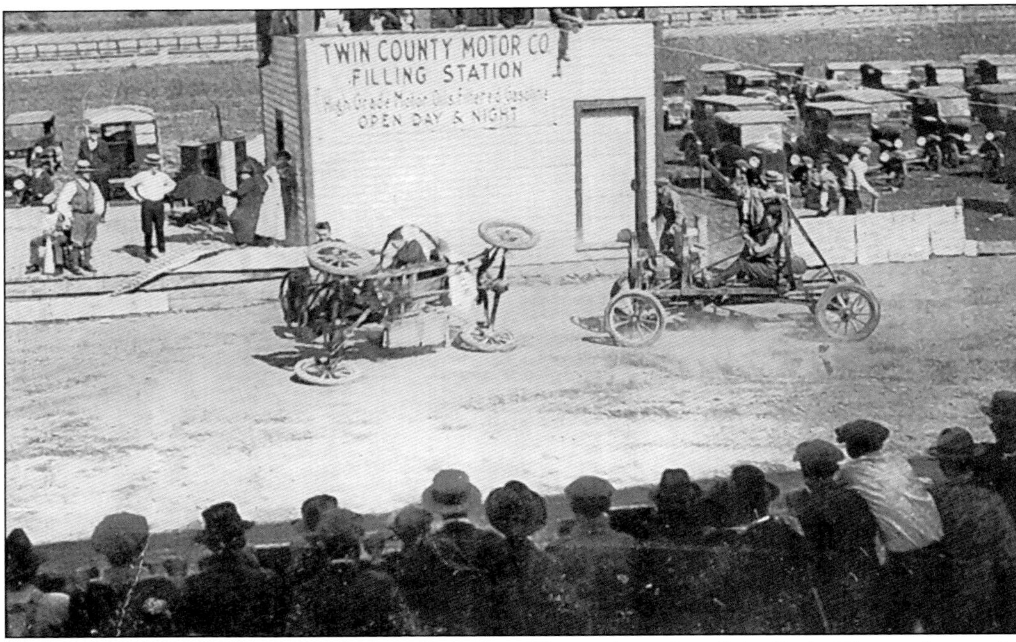

This is an undated photograph taken from the old grandstand in Felts Park. The park was the scene of a large variety of events in Galax. Car races, horse shows, fairs, football, baseball and softball games, and even May Day celebrations. It would later become the home of the Old Fiddlers Convention. (MM.)

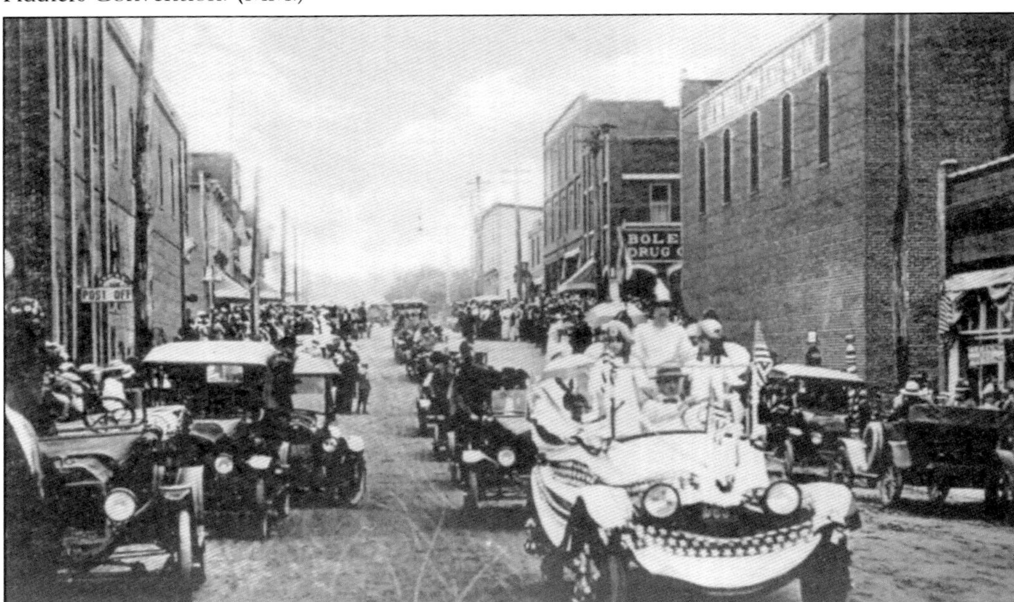

Everyone loves a parade, especially residents of Galax! This photograph, dated August 16, 1923, may be one of the last pictures taken before the town council approved the paving of the streets that year. Note that the post office is still located on the west side of South Main Street, and the familiar landmarks of the Bolen Drug Company and J. B. Waugh's store can been seen on the east side of the street. (GG.)

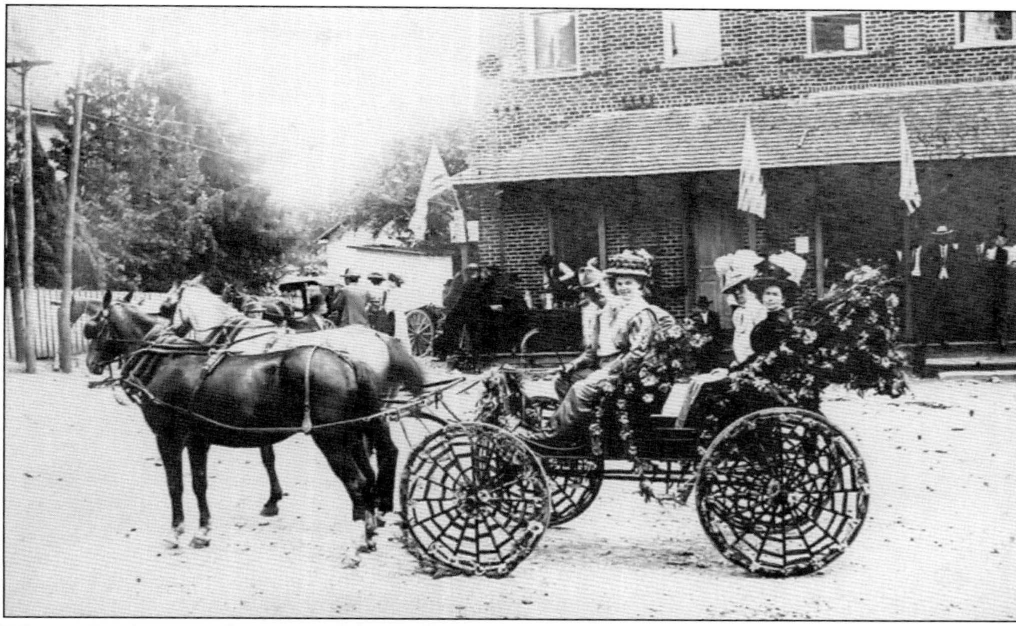

This early photograph is one of the authors' favorites. The carriage was definitely decorated by the ladies. Note the Ascot-style hats worn by the ladies. (MM.)

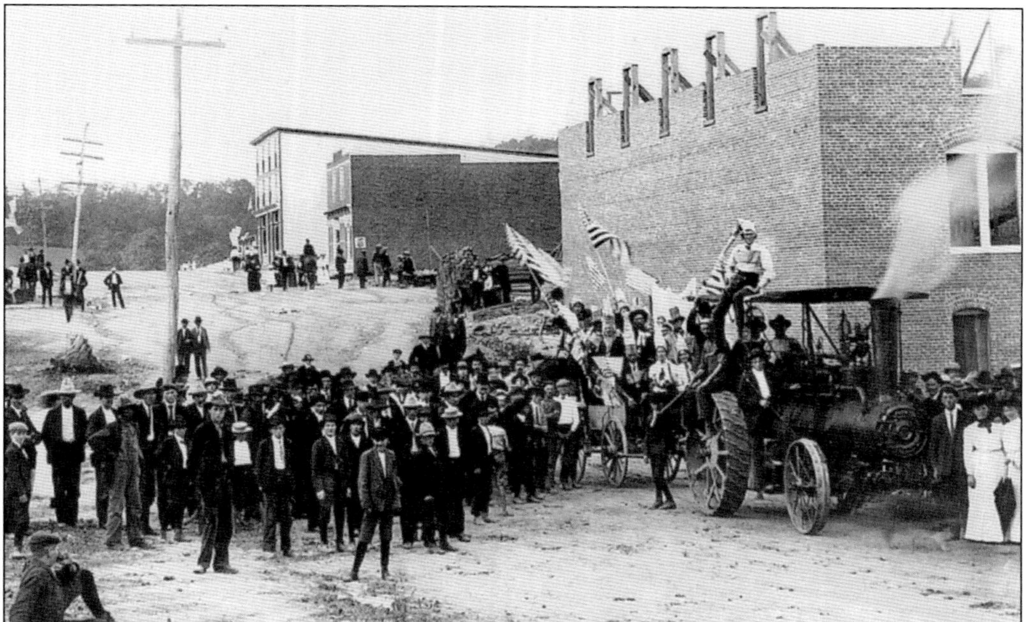

This is an early photograph of Main Street looking north. The J. B. Waugh building was under construction, and Dr. Bolen had not begun his building on the east side of Main and Grayson Streets. People are gathered around to see the Frick steam tractor, which had been brought from Wytheville for the first Twin County Fair held in Galax. Among those on the wagon behind the tractor are Clyde Nuckolls Couch, Myrtle Draper Sturdivant, Linnie Nuckolls Tongren, and Norman Williams. (GG.)

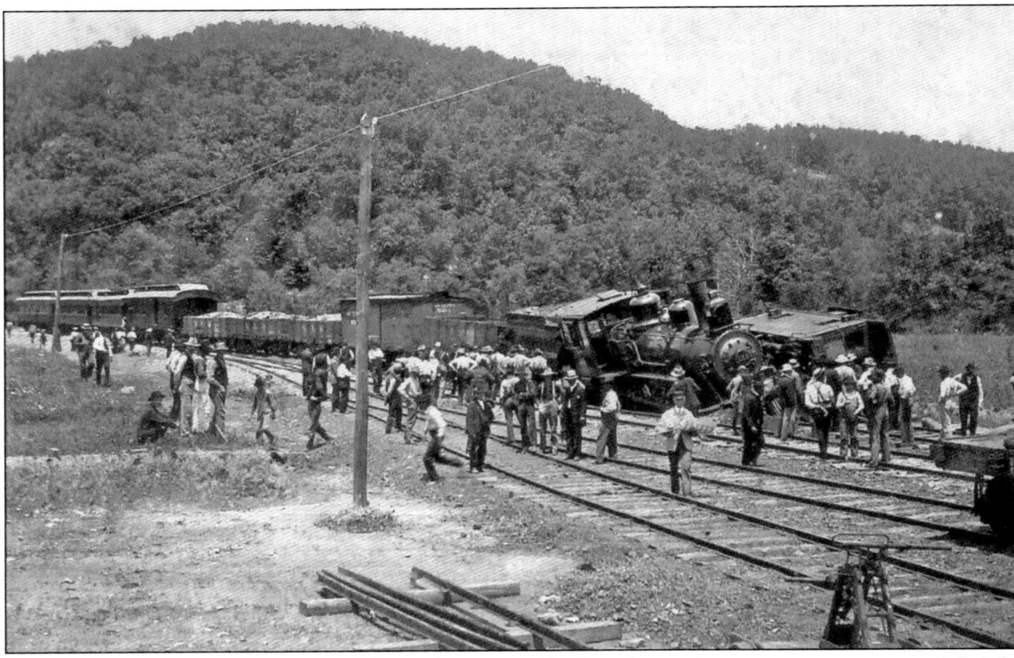

In midsummer of 1905, the Norfolk and Western Railway's combination passenger and freight train ran into the back of another freight train, which knocked the caboose off the main track just below the Galax Depot Station. (MM.)

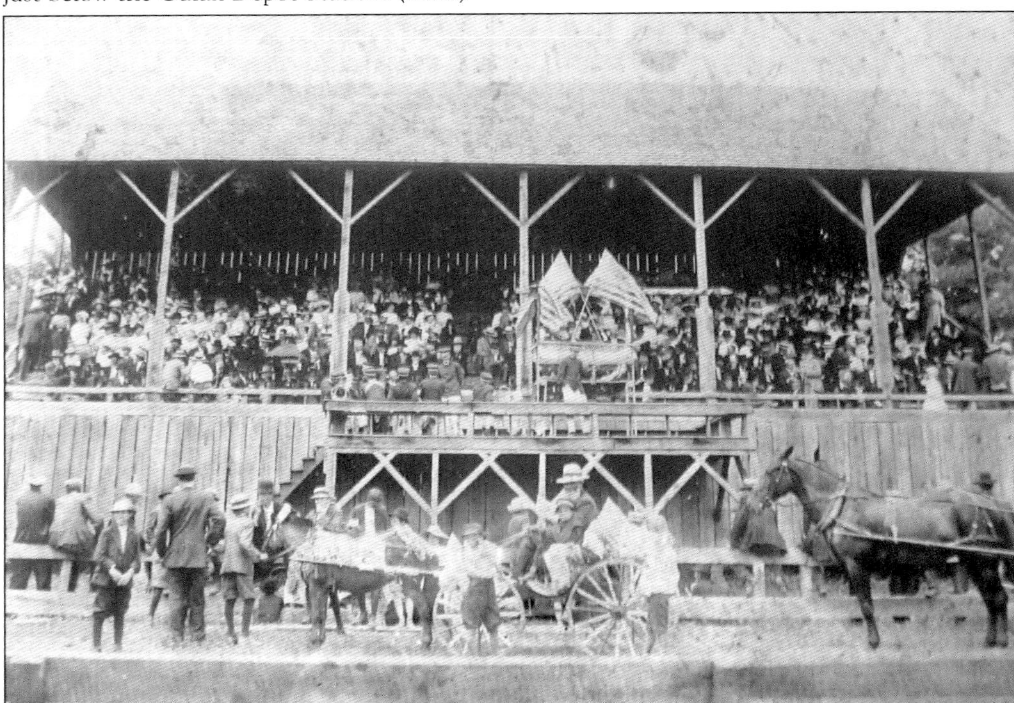

The event and date are unknown, but the grandstand at Felts Park was full of spectators when this photograph was taken. Note the band on the platform in front of the grandstand. (MM.)

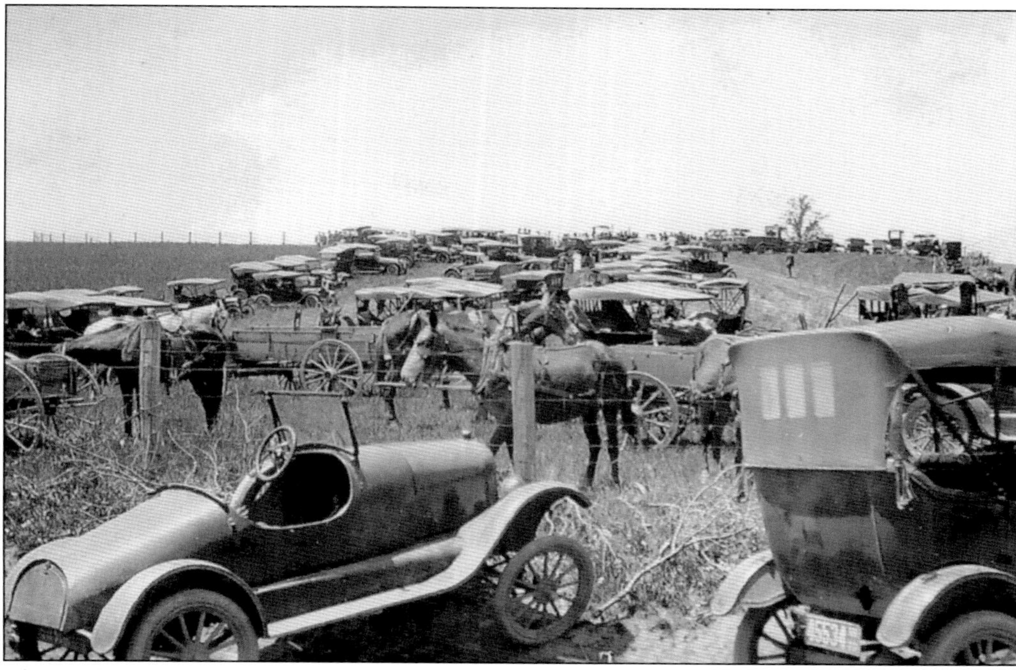

This undated photograph indicates that Galax did not always have a parking problem. People would come to town and stay a week when it was time for the Galax Fair. A car collector would love the little sports car in front! (MM.)

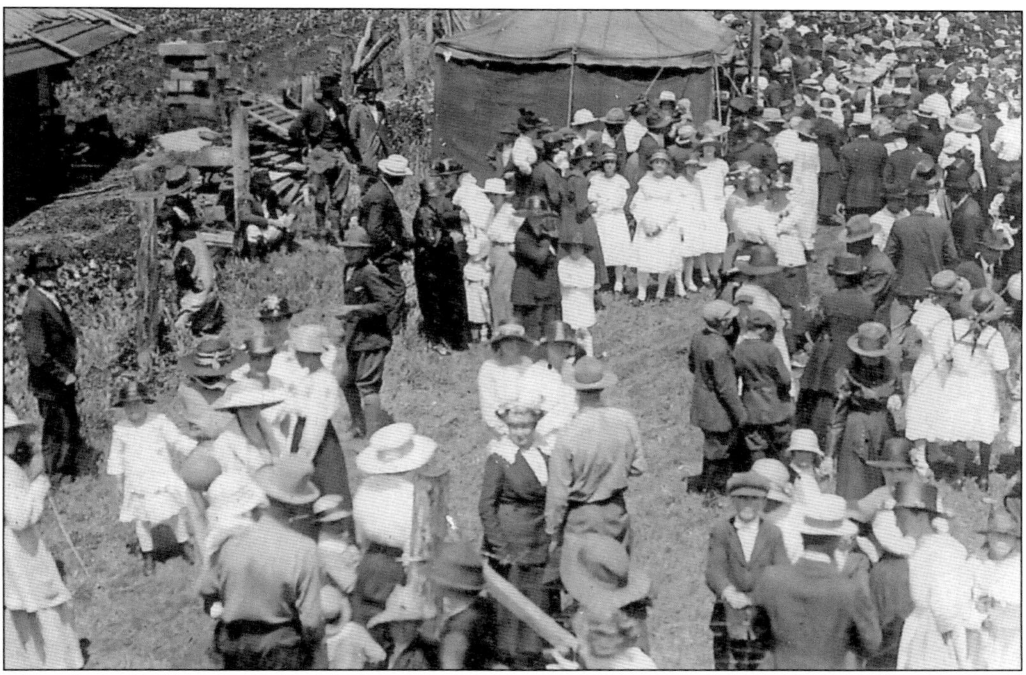

The Galax Fairs were always a popular social event during the early years in town. They provided an opportunity for everyone to visit with seldom-seen neighbors, as well as make new friends. Note the fine dresses and hats worn by the women. (MM.)

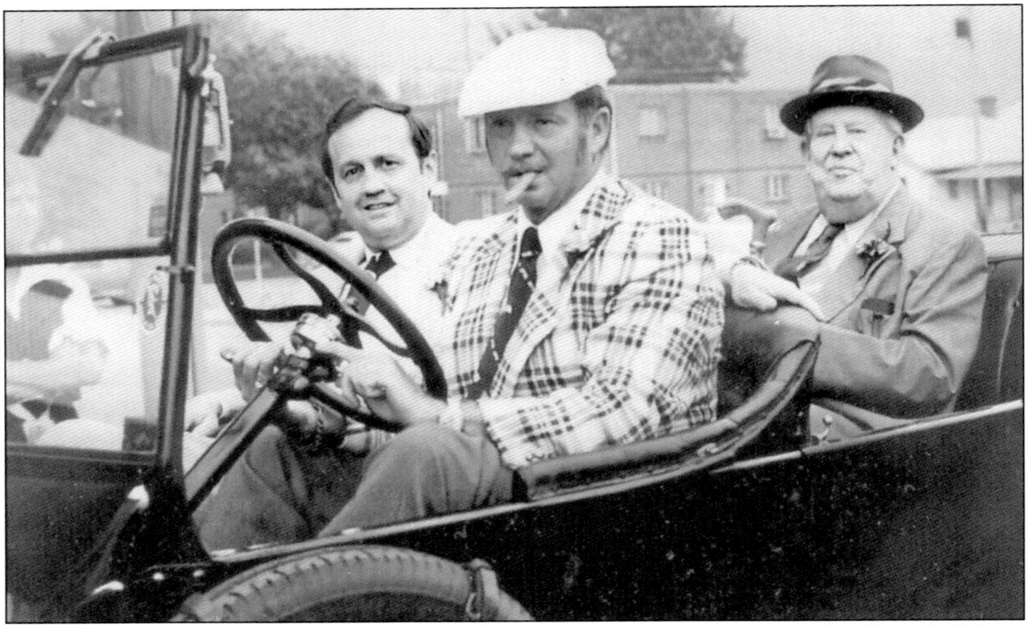

Gene T. McKnight provided transportation during the Golden Jubilee parade for (front left) John Dalton, a future governor of Virginia, and Sen. Floyd Landreth, one of the most well-known and respected citizens of Galax. Old-timers were delighted to be surrounded by people asking, "tell us about the early days!" (GPL.)

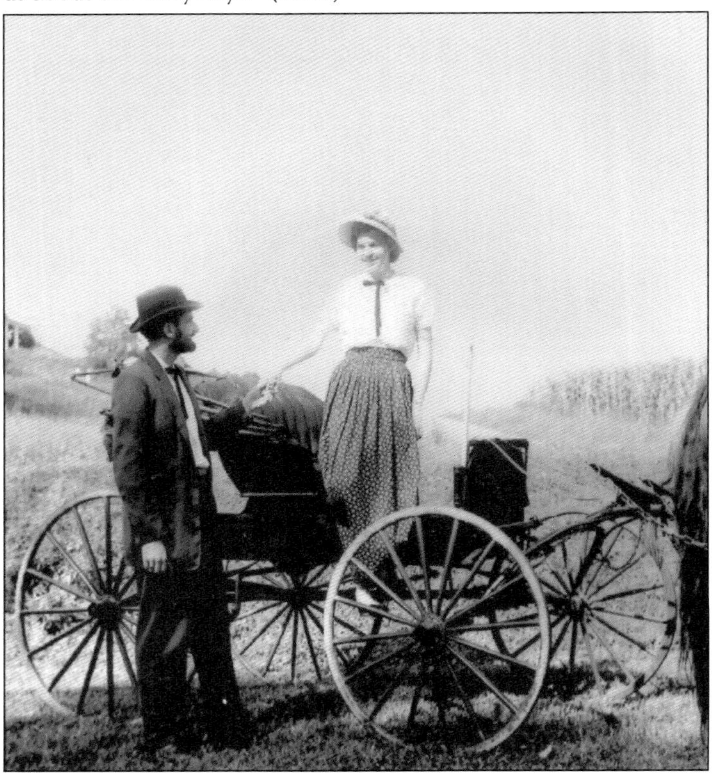

The entire town participated in the Golden Jubilee Celebration during the summer of 1956. Men grew beards and long sideburns, and ladies made outfits in the style of the early 1900s or raided their grandmothers' trunks. Treasured buggies were taken out of storage barns and given special treatment in preparation for the events. Olen and Norma Nuckolls Quesenberry take a ride in the buggy owned by Heath Nuckolls. (GG.)

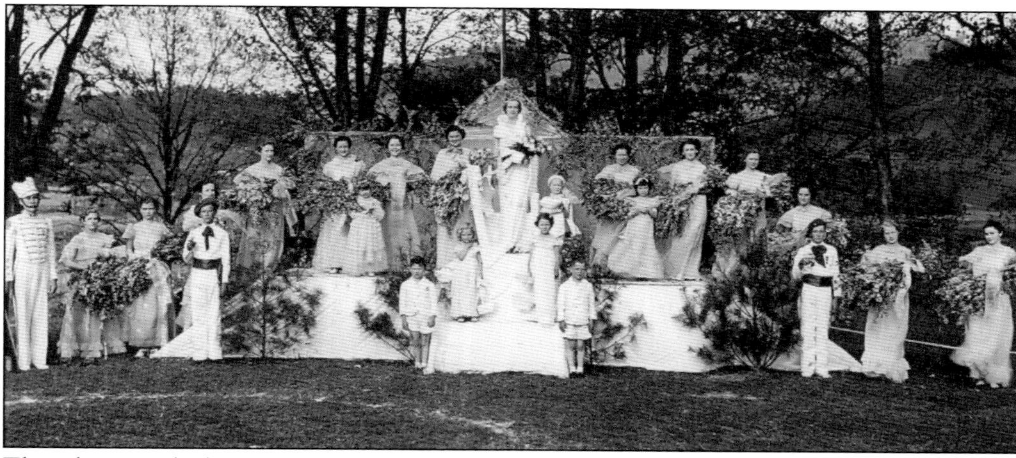

This photograph shows the Galax High School May Day festival, held in Felts Park in 1936. Pictured from left to right are Jack Williams (band major), June Kirby, Rose Thomas Smith, Joe Chappell, Nell Lawson, Rubye Combs Cockerham, unidentified, Vada Fields, unidentified, Louise Early Pollard (May Queen), Laura Todd Lemons, Irene Alderman, unidentified, Helen Hampton, Virgin Catron, Irene Lineberry, and Bonni Lyn Todd. The children are unidentified. (GG.)

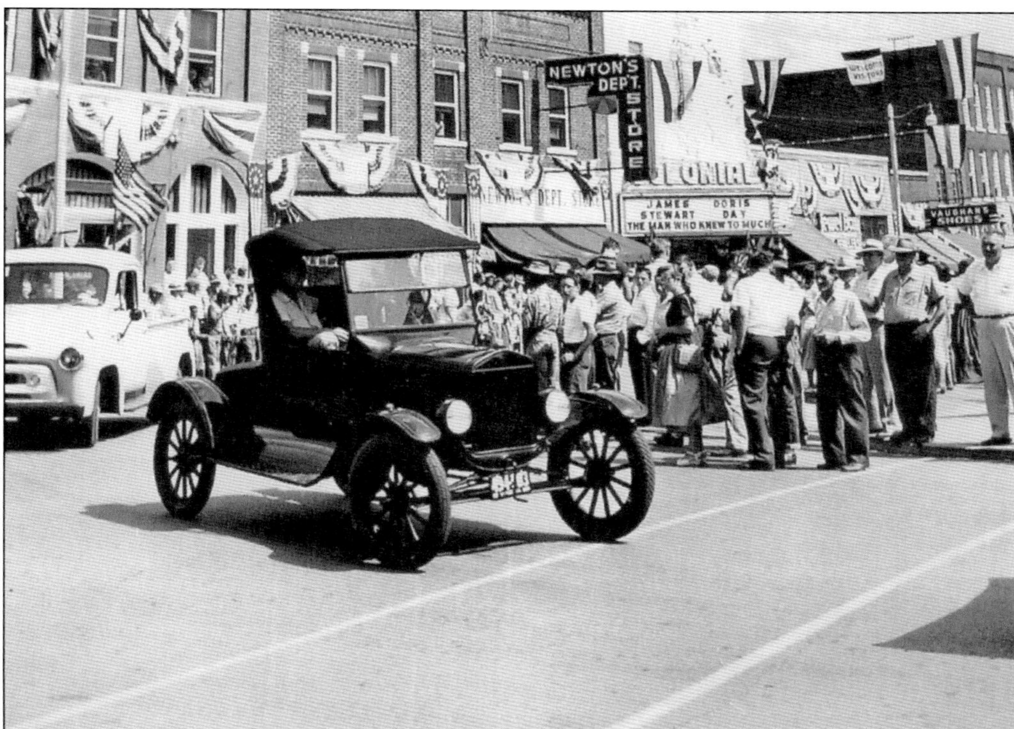

This car was lovingly restored and polished for the Golden Jubilee parade. The owner is unidentified. Men in town who joined the festivities by growing beards called themselves "brothers of the brush." A group of men, known as the "Keystone Kops," set up a mock jail on Main Street. They "arrested" any man of interest who had failed to grow a beard. The "inmates" were fined $1 before they could be released. (GPL.)

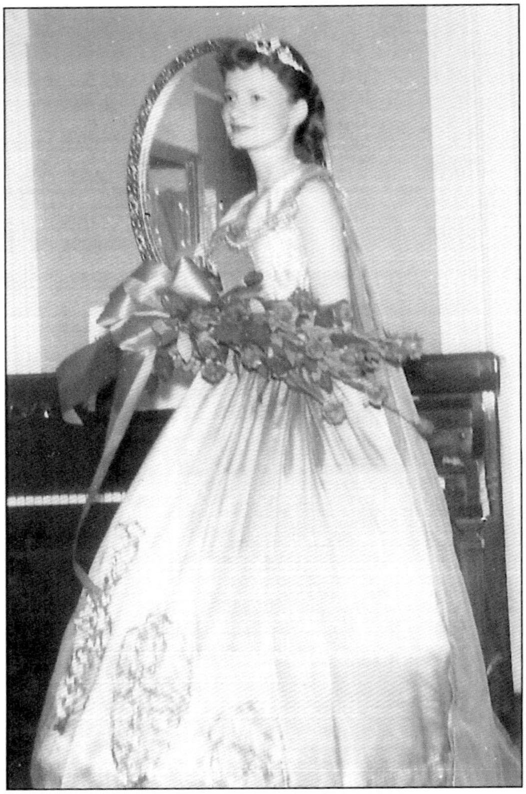

Judith Lucinda Nunn, daughter of Beatrice Messer Nunn, was chosen to reign over the festivities as queen of the Golden Jubilee celebration. She was a 16-year-old sophomore at Galax High School. Nunn grew up in the former home of Lelia Burt Nuckolls Waugh, one of the earliest residents in town. This photograph was taken shortly before she was to be crowned queen by the governor of Virginia. (Judy Alley.)

The 1956 models float in the Golden Jubilee parade featured beautiful young ladies who were seen by the thousands by those lined up to watch the Golden Jubilee parade on August 6, 1956. Standing on the Kiwanis float are, from left to right, Bonnie King, Kitty Green, Deanna Lou Hartsock, and Catherine Jenrette. (GG.)

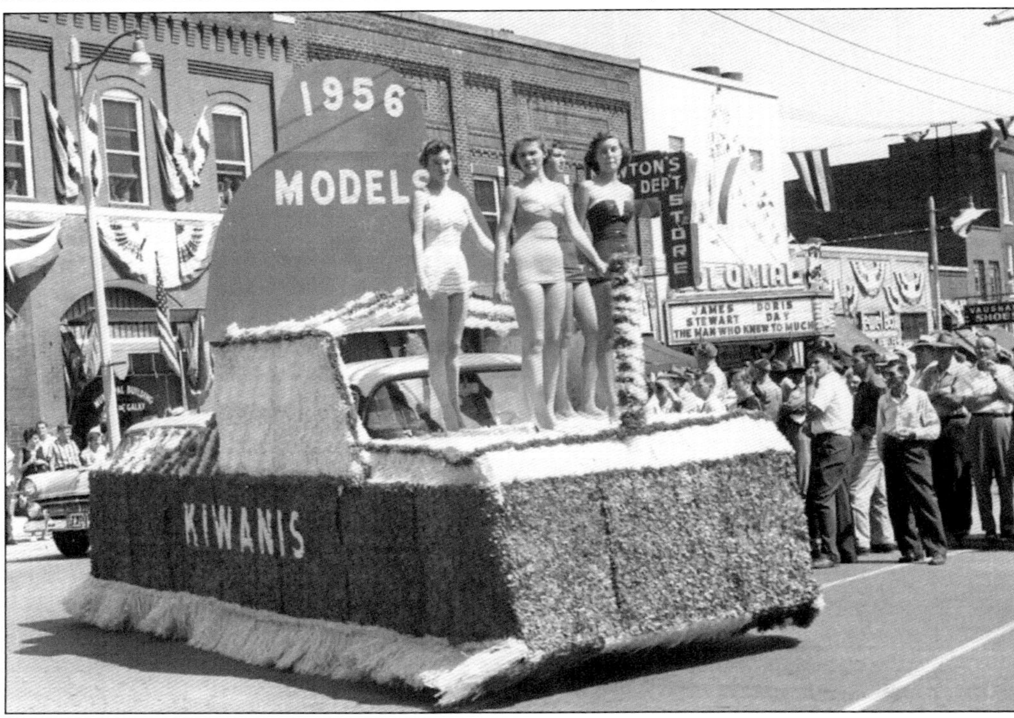

During the Galax Golden Jubilee, ladies, dressed in clothing similar to the styles worn by their grandmothers, were called "sisters of the swish." Jewel Amburn Melton (left) and Etoile Amburn Morton were definitely ready for a leisurely stroll down Main Street or to share afternoon tea with neighbors. (Jewel Melton.)

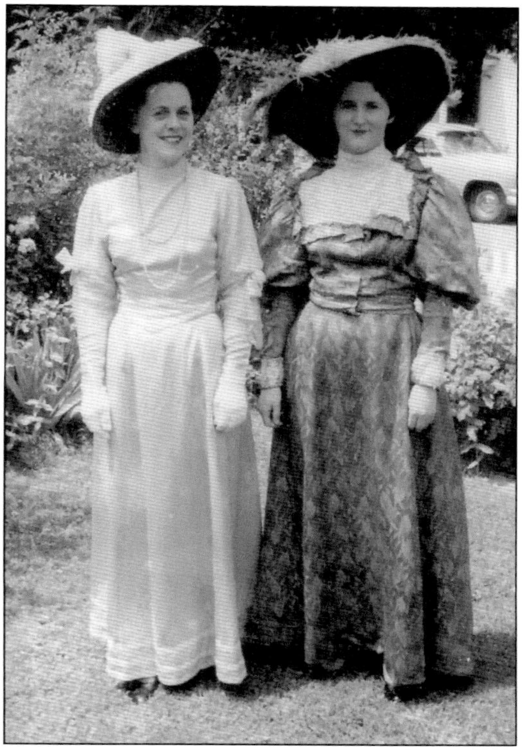

Below is a photograph of the Galax City Council taken in 1956. Note that three of the men are "brothers of the brush" for the Golden Jubilee celebration. Pictured from left to right are (first row) Clarence Alderman, McCamat Higgins (mayor), Mildred Cornett (treasurer), Conley Harris, Dan. B. Waugh, and Walter G. Andrews (city manager); (second row) H. Prince Burnett, Brad Dickens, Edd Matthews, and Henry Harris. (RL.)

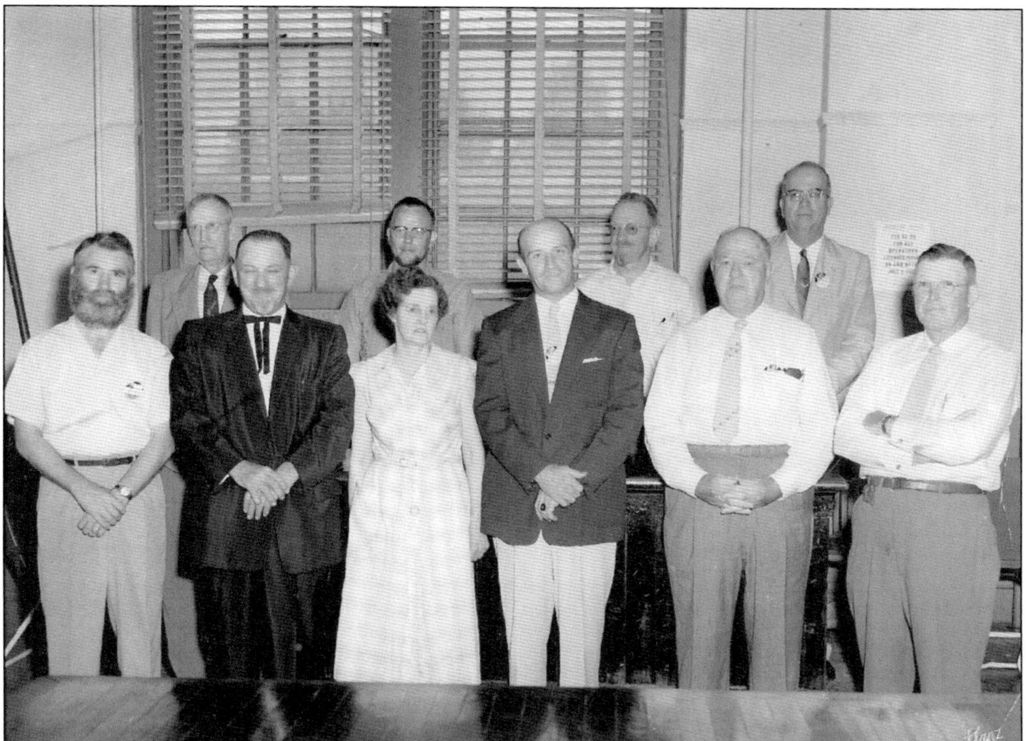

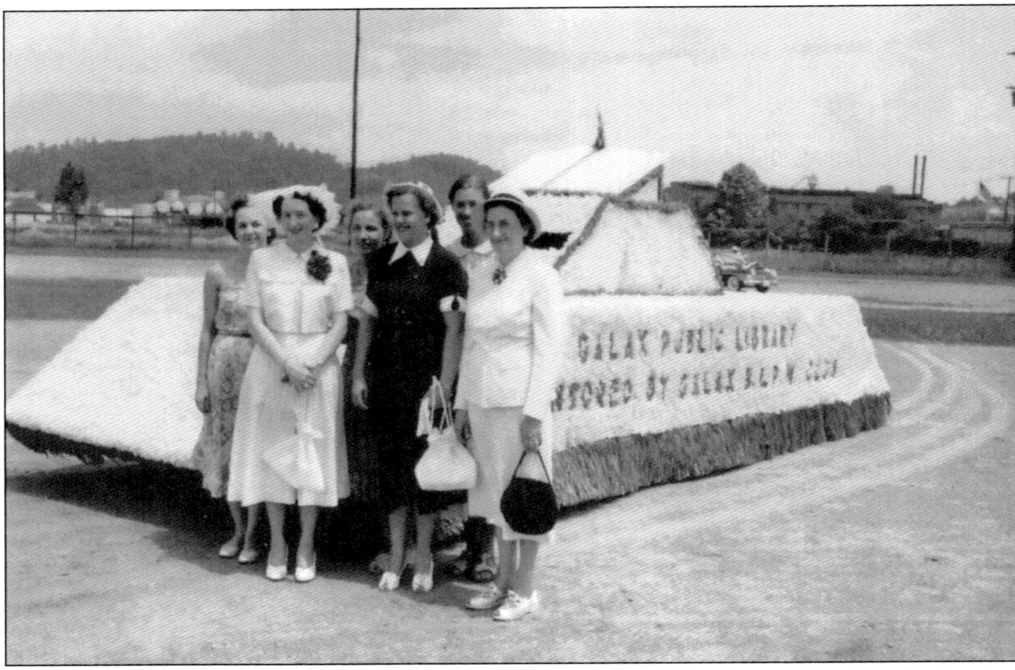

Members of the Galax Business and Professional Woman's Club sponsored a float for the Galax Public Library during the Golden Jubilee festivities. Pictured above are, from left to right, (first row) Muriel Bell, Carolyn Crockett, and Maude Gardner; (second row) Ruby Lindamood, Olida Cochran, and Kitty Halsey. (RL.)

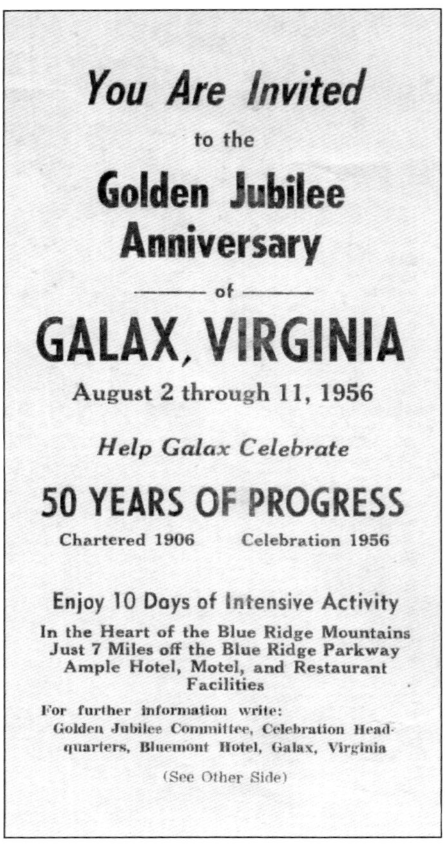

You Are Invited

to the

Golden Jubilee Anniversary

—— of ——

GALAX, VIRGINIA

August 2 through 11, 1956

Help Galax Celebrate

50 YEARS OF PROGRESS

Chartered 1906 Celebration 1956

Enjoy 10 Days of Intensive Activity

In the Heart of the Blue Ridge Mountains
Just 7 Miles off the Blue Ridge Parkway
Ample Hotel, Motel, and Restaurant Facilities

For further information write:
Golden Jubilee Committee, Celebration Headquarters, Bluemont Hotel, Galax, Virginia

(See Other Side)

The summer was filled with parades, family reunions, beard-growing contests, teas, a fashion show, and a historical pageant. Shops filled their windows with a rich display of old photographs and memorabilia. Owners of old cars made sure their vehicles gleamed in the sunlight, and "do you remember when?" was the topic of conversation. (JJN.)

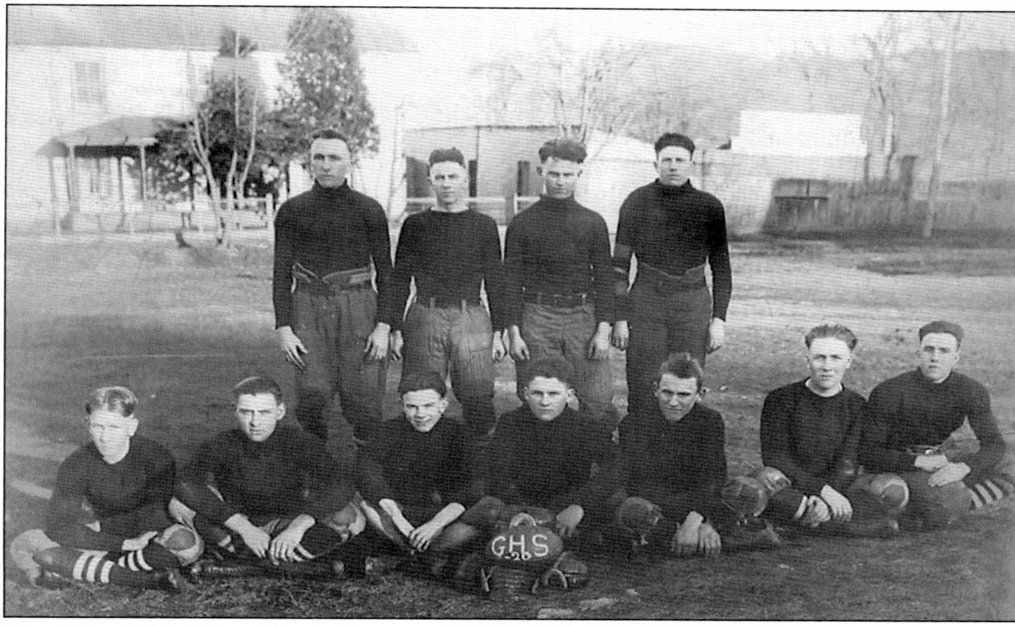

The Galax High School football team gathers for a photograph in 1920. One of the young men recalled that the team did not lose many games. Pictured from left to right are (first row) Fred Witherow, Howard Beamer, Vick Wright, Hurley Cox, Guy Hawks, Burr Lyons, and Raleigh Hampton; (second row) Cliff Kyle, John Reid Smith, Otto Hawks, and Danny Busic. (MM.)

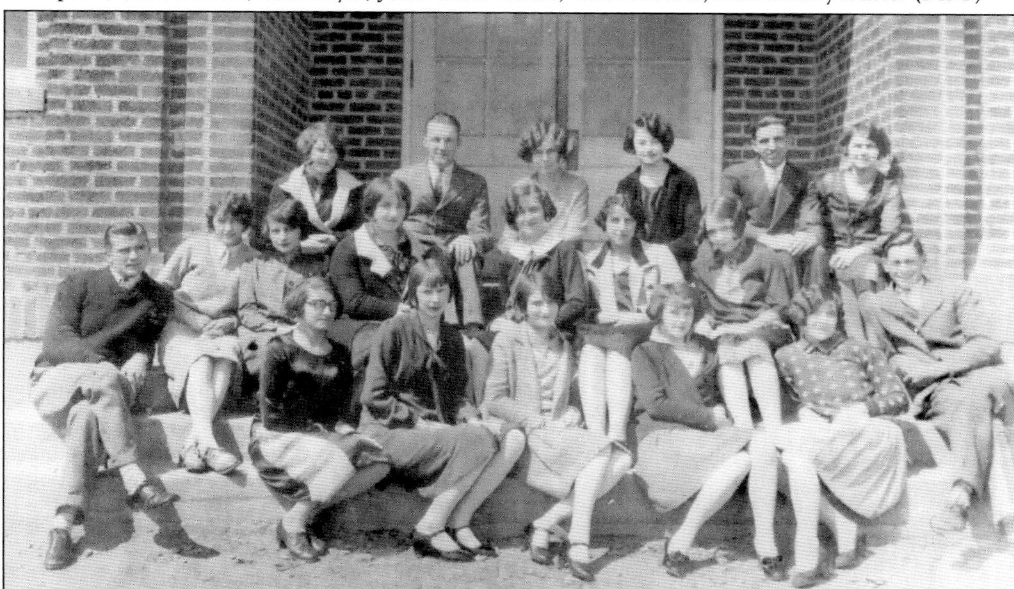

Members of the class of 1928 pose for a group photograph on the front steps of the school. The class members are, from left to right, (first row) Robert Caldwell, Fay Higgins, Dora Dobyns, Vivian Dalton, Ruth Busic, and Mary Ruth Bishop; (second row) Virginia McCarty, Bea Messer, Helen Jones, Virginia Witherow, Thelma Collier, Marguriete Phipps, and Willard Stoneman; (third row) Georgia Vaughan, Glenn Phipps, Madeline Cornett, Wavie Wilson, Sam Boyer, and Eilene Ward. (Judy Alley.)

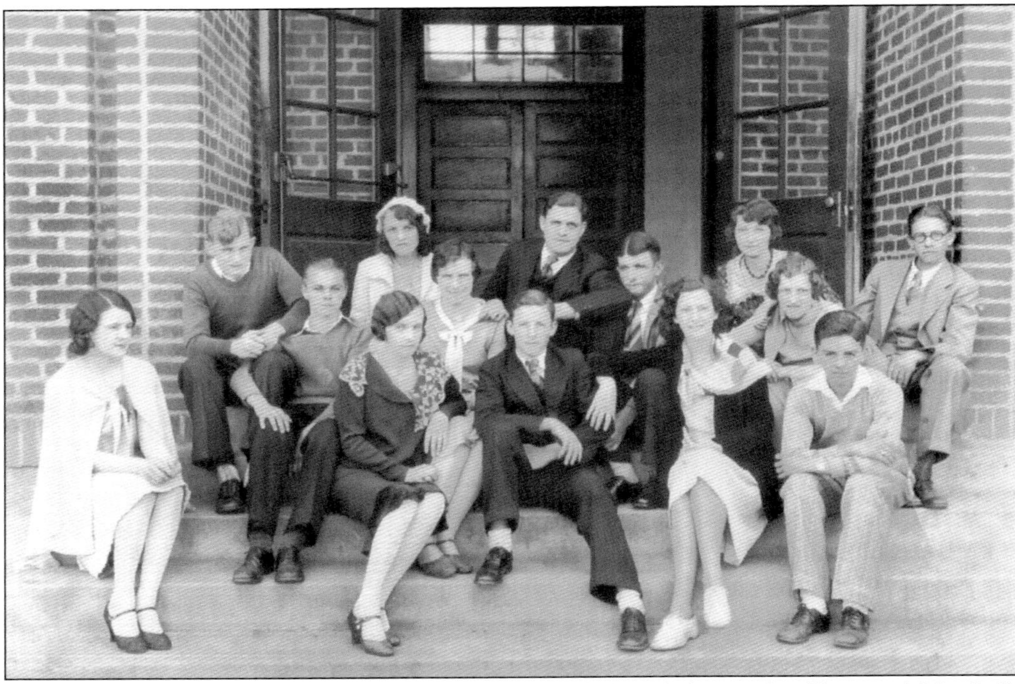

The Galax High School senior class of 1930 included, from left to right, (first row) Maribelle Godbey (teacher), Carrie Lineberry, J. K. Davis, Frances James, and Rom Hawks; (second row) Herman Hurst, Lacona Diamond, Clinton Osborne, and Dorothy Dobyns; (third row) James Hortenstine, Lee Porter, Reid Calloway, Euna Lee Martin, and E. S. Lundy. (GG.)

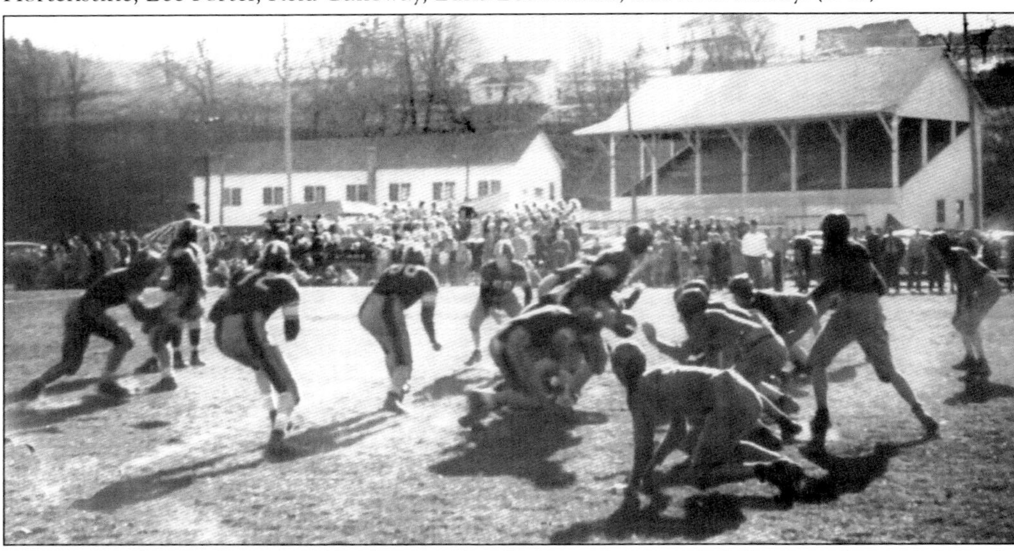

Galax played its archrival, Hillsville, on Thanksgiving Day in 1943, beating them 41-6. In the background is the old exhibit building and grandstand. Team members included Elwood Newman (cocaptain), Raymond Horn (cocaptain), Herbert Carelton, Bryon Lineberry, Bobby Davis, David Spraker, Edwin Cox, Joe Lundy, Rex Cullop, Hines Peddy, and Jimmy Ballard. Newman remembers that they were executing a "33-triple reverse to the right" play when this photograph was taken. (GG.)

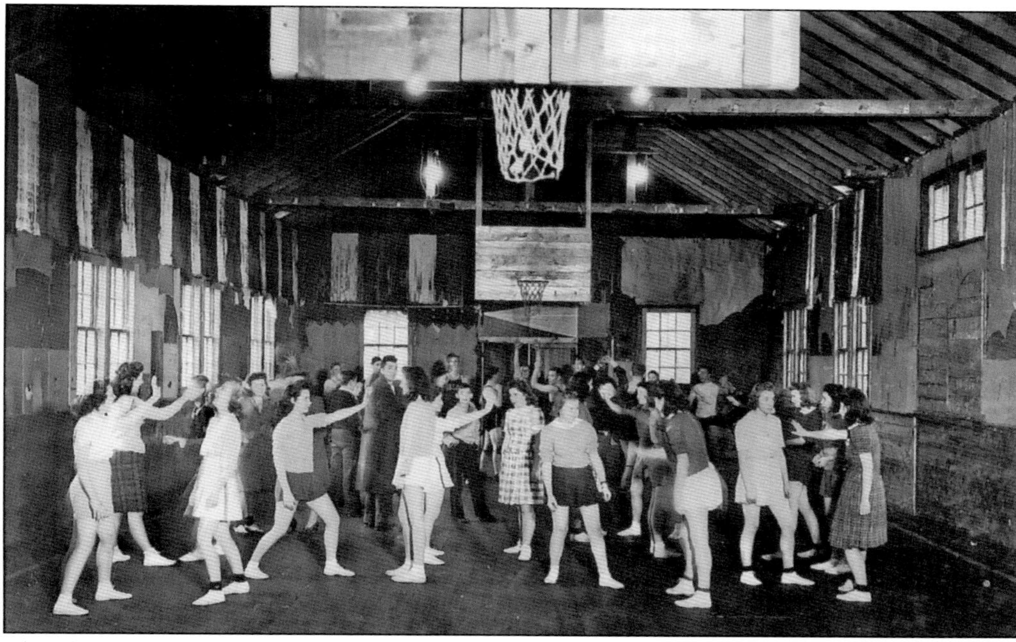

The old multipurpose exhibit building, located near the grandstand in the fairgrounds, was an excellent location for basketball practice and games. Among those pictured are, from left to right, (first row) Ruby Mabe Lindamood, Mary Leonard Norman, Anne Reeves, Dot Moore Matthews, Josephine Kirby Sutherland, Ruth Burnette Felts, and Beulah Rector Bobbitt; (second row) Pauline Reedy, Lois Brown Todd, Alice Jones Jenkins (manager), Jean Hampton Shaw, and Kathleen Moore Gentry. (RL.)

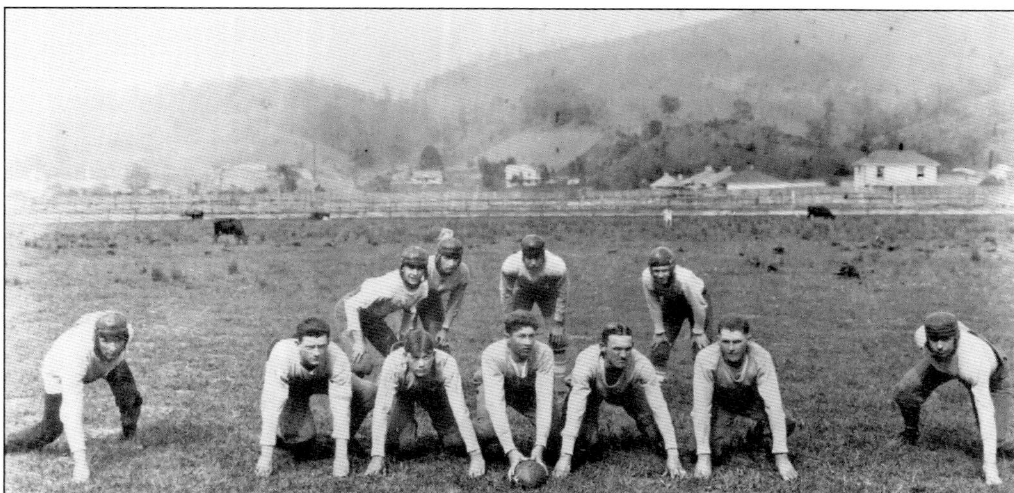

The Galax High School football team included, from left to right, (first row) John Bolen, Jack Matthews, Bergen Branscome, Earnest Cox, Guy Hawks, Hurley Cox, and Payne Gentry; (second row) Gray Anderson, J. C. Lindsey, Earl Nuckolls, and Olen Ward. What is impressive about these young men is what they did with their lives. The members became a judge, a doctor, several lawyers, and business, civic, and church leaders. They were all born between 1904 and 1906. (Barbara Eanes.)

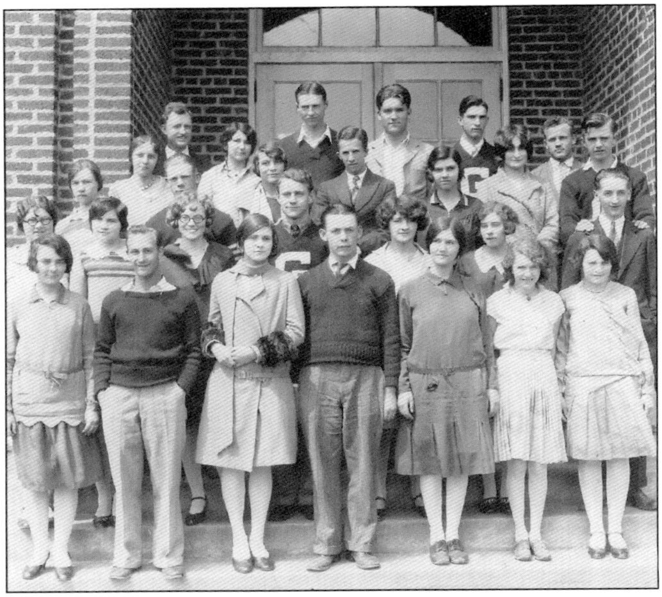

The class of 1929 stands on the steps of Galax High School. Pictured from left to right are (first row) Ethel Bartlett, Marler Kegley, Vera Ward, Dan Anderson, Hazel Hawkins, Alice Lee Robertson, and Dale Robinson; (second row) Dottie Patton, Hattie Cooley, Ruth Melton, Elane Whitley, Ruth Cox, Elva Fulks, and Elvin Sutphin; (third row) Ila Edwards, Claude Matthews, Marian Lundy, William James, Anna Austin, Nita Sue Cox, and Lewis Morris; (fourth row) Prof. Henry Stradley, Etoile Cox, Clay Cox, Ranzie Jones, Emmett Osborne, and Prof. Johnny Miller. (Barbara Eanes.)

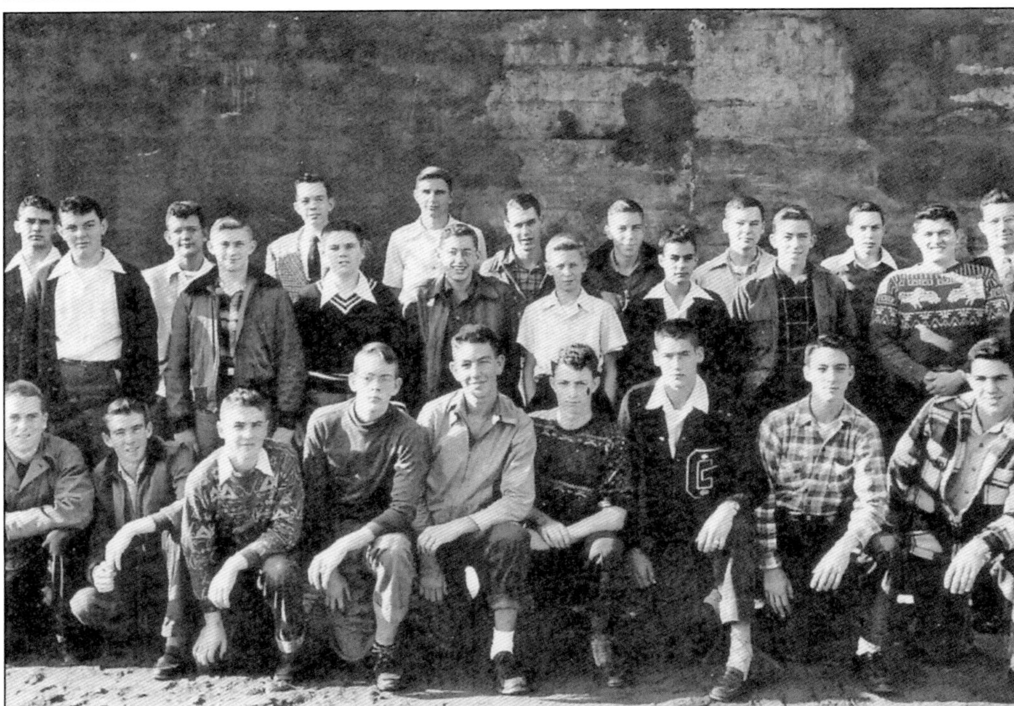

Galax High School's Hi-Y Club of 1949 includes, from left to right, (first row) Bill Mann, George Johnson, Glen Cock, Bob Gordon, Bob Hash, Bill Gentry, Parks Deaton, Bill Branscome, and Joe Lindsey; (second row) Ralph Morris, Sonny Todd, Bill Eddins, Jack Bolen, John Matthews, Jim Williams, Jim Bowie, and Billy Frank Todd; (third row) Bill Lineberry, Randolph Carico, Bunny Wampler, Chapman Davis, Pierce Kline, Ellison Wilson, Glen Foster, Robert Melton, and Walter Safrit (YMCA director.). (MM.)

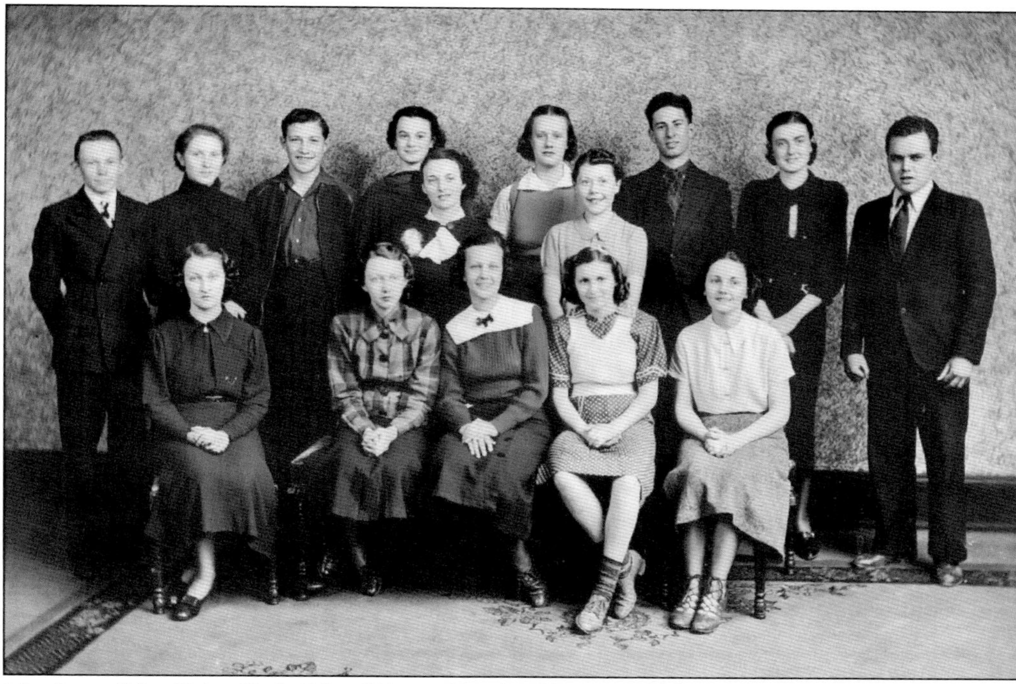

Members of the Galax High School Young Peoples Christian Club are, from left to right, (first row) Irene Alderman Pinner, two unidentified, Juliene Cox, and Winnie Nuckolls Messer; (second row) Worth Cox, unidentified, Joey Williams, Kathleen Wampler, Lucille Cox, Louise Early Pollard, V. Fields, J. Atkins, Helen S. Crockett, and Basil Rice. (GG.)

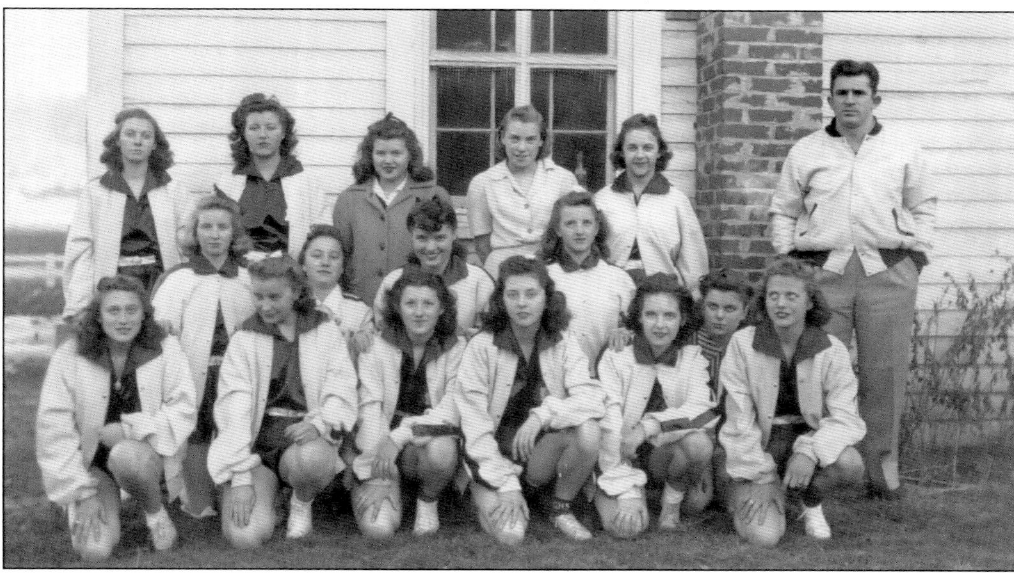

Members of the girls' basketball team pose with their coach, Jim Sessoms (standing, far right), in 1942. They are, from left to right, (first row) Alice Henderson, Josephine Kirby, Doris Brown, Jean Hampton, Ann Reeves, and Mary Leonard; (second row) Kathleen Moore, Kathryn Schrader, Ruth Burnette, Dorothy Moore, and Alice Jones; (third row) Celene Young, Pauline Reedy, Lois Todd (manager), Beulah Isom, and Ruby Lindamood. (RL.)

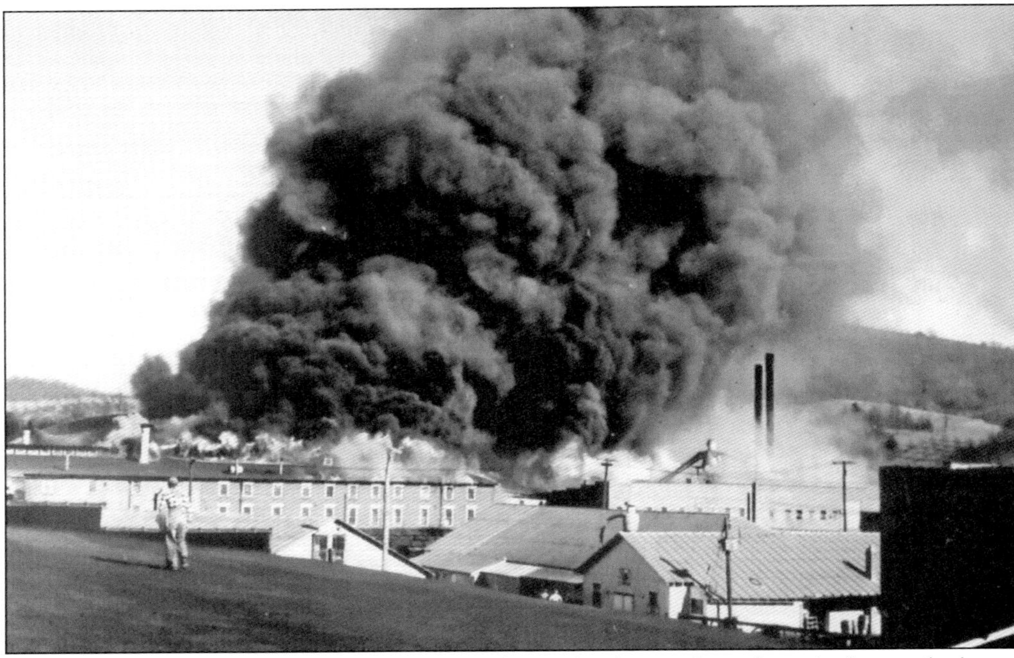

When the fire alarm pierced the serene atmosphere of Galax, it always brought fear to the hearts of the residents. The $1,250,000 fire that destroyed the Vaughan-Bassett Furniture Factory in 1951 was no exception. Firefighting equipment and men from seven towns bravely fought the fire for 24 hours to prevent it from spreading to the Galax Furniture and Webb Furniture factories. They used millions of gallons of water pumped from the city and Chestnut Creek. (Jack Pless.)

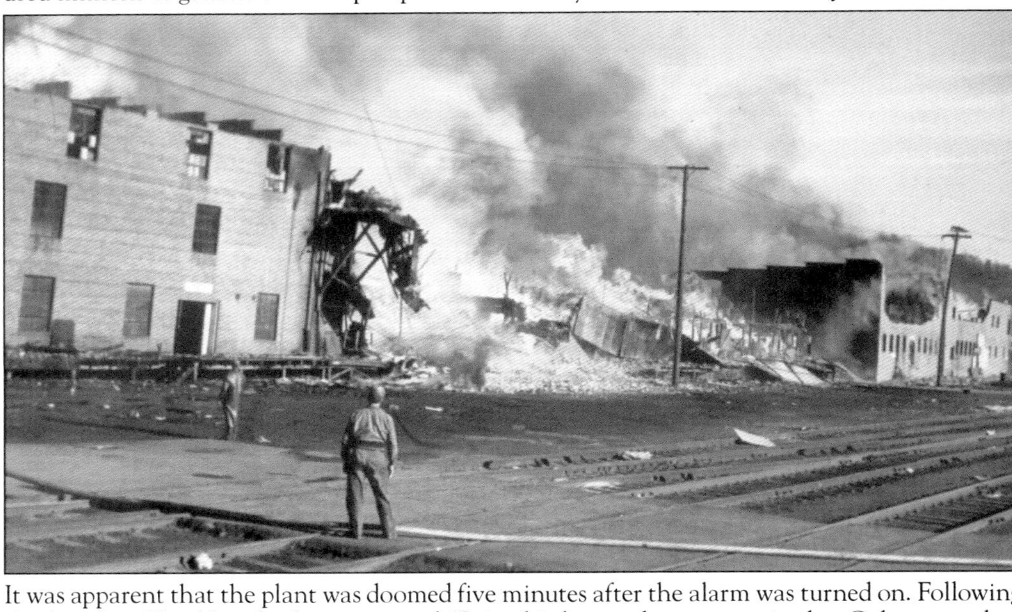

It was apparent that the plant was doomed five minutes after the alarm was turned on. Following the fire, Sen. Floyd Landreth commented, "It is a big loss to the community, but Galax never lays down when something like this happens. I have no doubt that we will be able to weather this storm just as we have others." Mayor R. C. Bowie commented, "It is the biggest loss Galax has ever suffered, but we must now think not of the loss, but the remedy for that loss." (Jack Pless.)

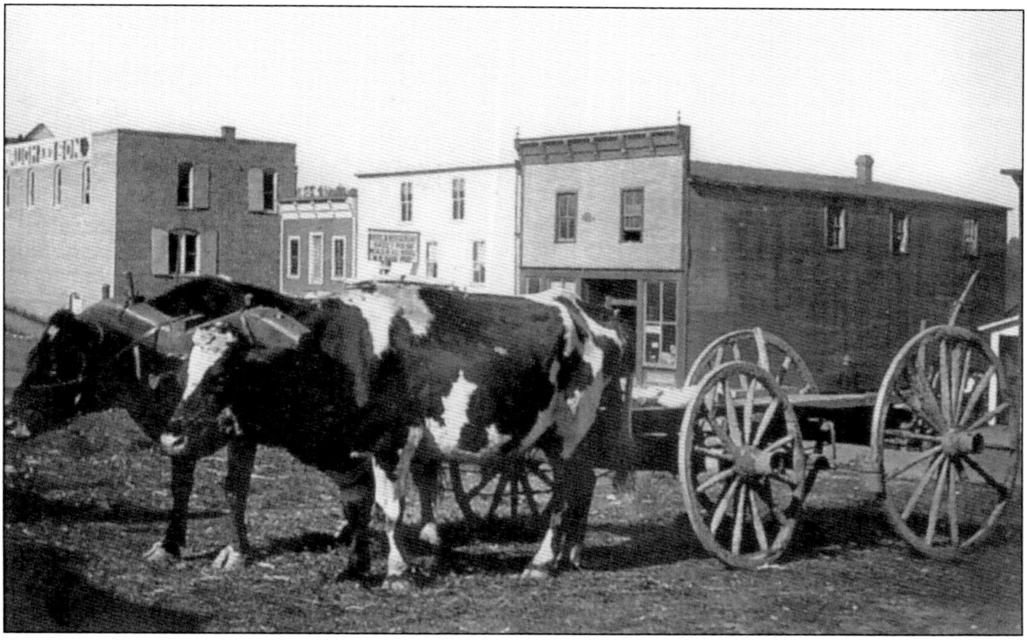

Two oxen (Bessie and her traveling friend Daisy) patiently wait for their owner near the intersection of Main and Oldtown Streets looking north. Waugh's can be seen in the background. Oxen and wagons were a necessity for people who had to bring products to the train depot or tree logs to the sawmills. (MM.)

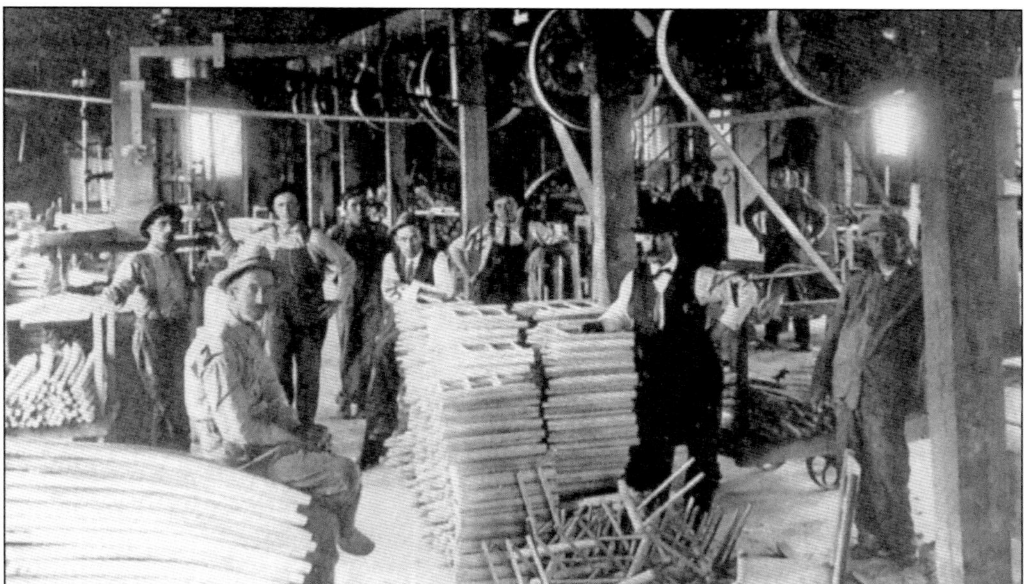

The Edwards Chair Company began manufacturing double cane seat chairs in the summer of 1913. Edwards hired some of employees of the Galax Furniture and Lumber Company when it was destroyed again by fire on December 9, 1913. Losing a manufacturing plant meant a severe loss of employment to the local residents, as well as a loss of business for local merchants and sawmill owners. (GG.)

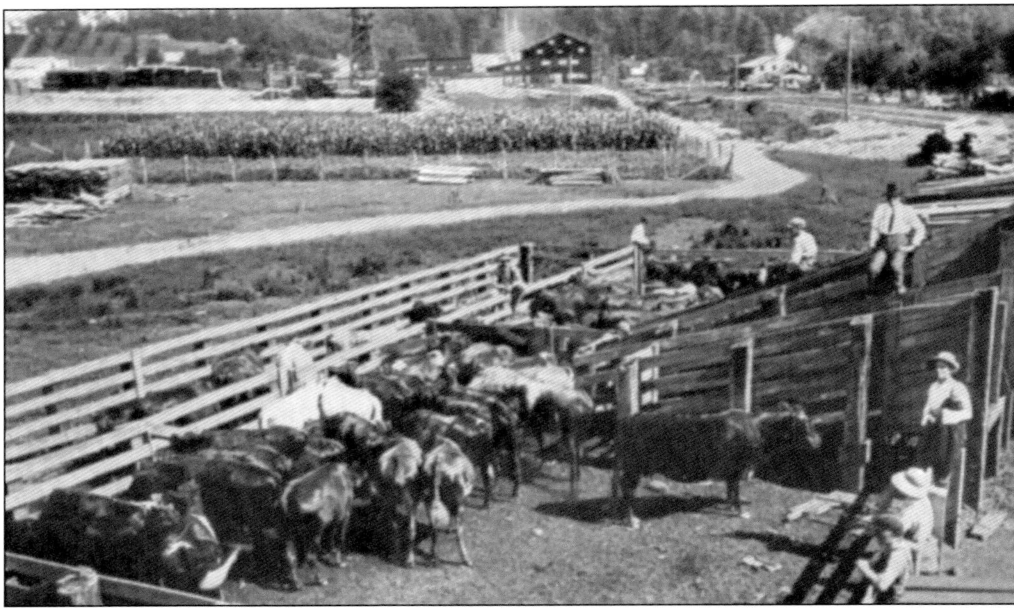

The railroad was the link between Galax and the outside world. Cattle, sheep, hogs, poultry, lumber, eggs, chestnuts, Galax leaves, feathers, chestnuts and chinquapins, and other products were shipped to markets. In 1905, a loaf of bread cost 3¢, and a gallon of milk sold for 9¢. This is a photograph of the stock pens near the depot. The Galax Furniture and Lumber Company can be seen in the background. (JJN.)

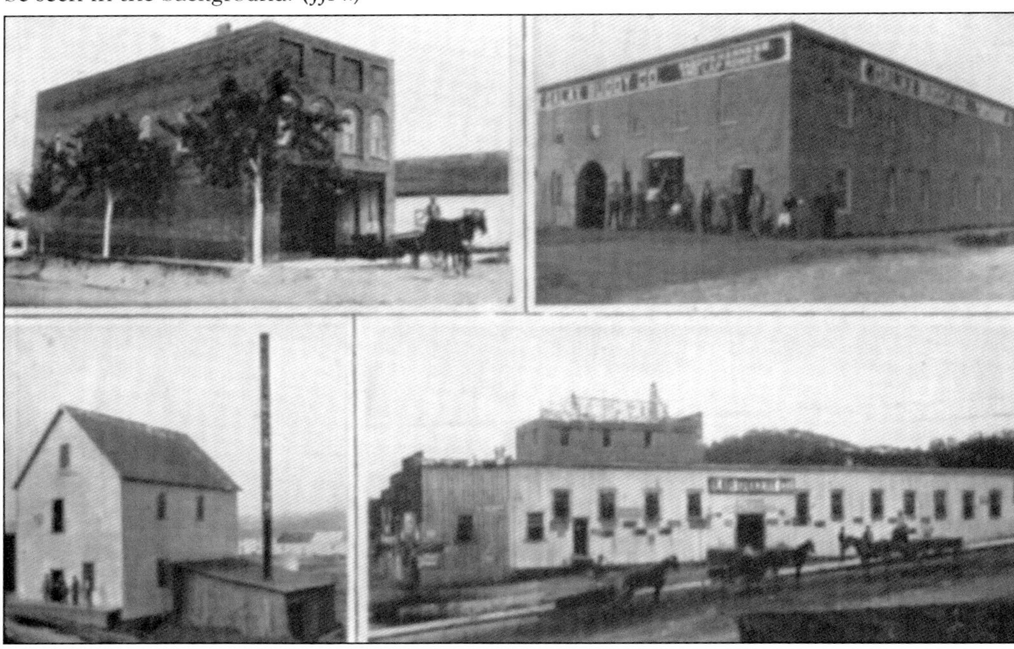

In 1914, the Galax Board of Trade published an advertising booklet about Galax describing it as the largest 10-year-old town in Virginia. It included the pictures of four businesses: (top) Nuckolls Springs Bottling Works and Galax Buggy Company and (bottom) J. O. Speas Mill and Blair Grocery Company. (JJN.)

The first Old Fiddlers Convention was held on April 12, 1935. The new Moose Lodge was seeking a way to raise much-needed funds. The decision was made to offer a string music program with cash prizes given to the winners. The Bog Trotters won first place as the most entertaining band with the song, "Who Broke the Lock on the Hen House Door?" Pictured from left to right are (first row) Crockett Ward and Dr. W. P. Davis; (second row) Alex Dunford, Fields Ward, and Wade Ward. (GG.)

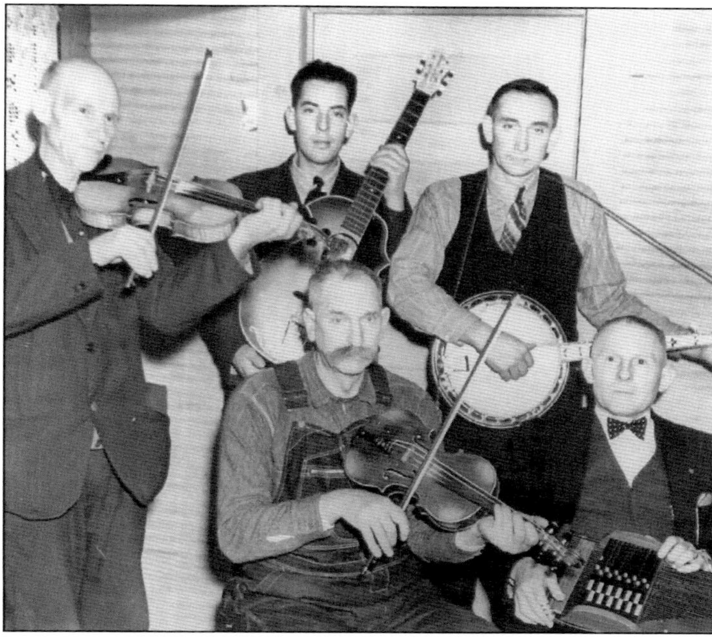

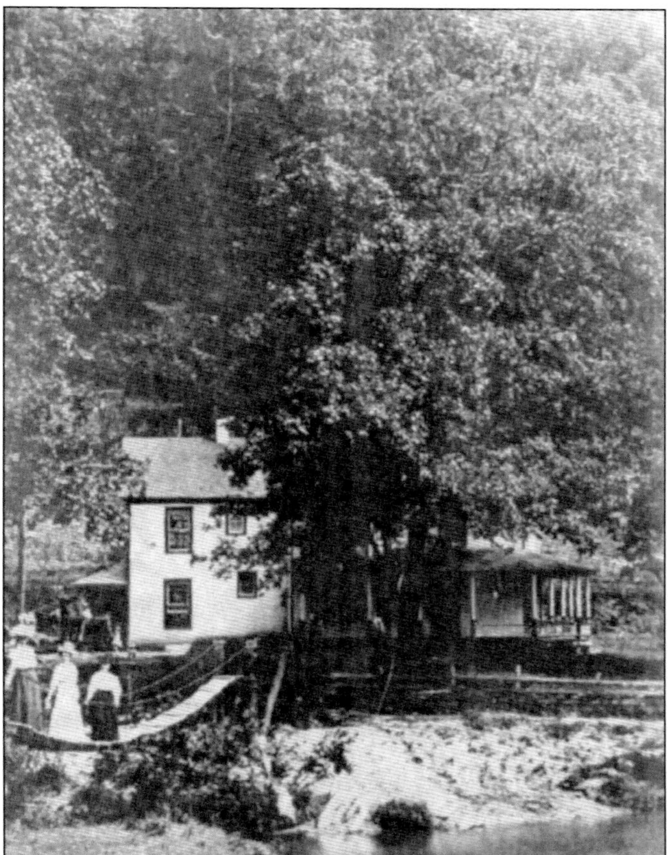

This is a photograph of the Robert Caldwell house on the east side of Chestnut Creek. Note the old swing bridge. One can almost hear the laughter of the unidentified ladies as they made their way across the bridge. (JJN.)

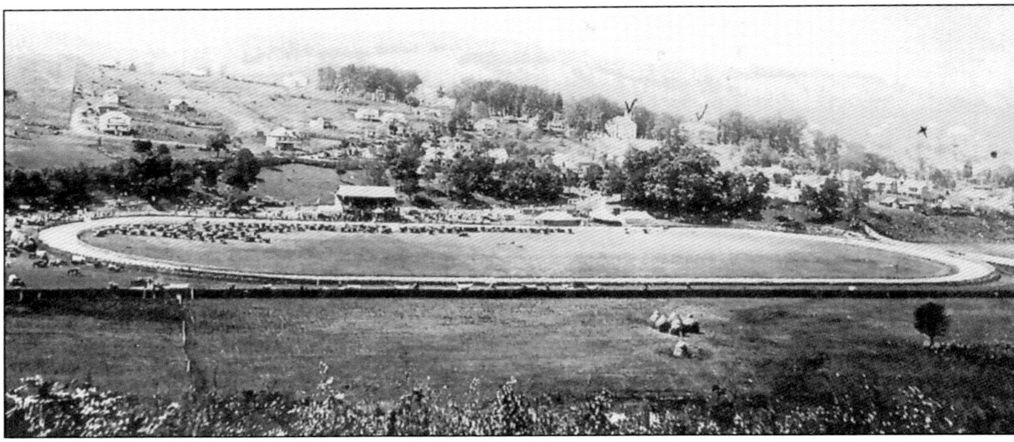

The first Galax Fair was held on September 19–21, 1908, in the new fairgrounds. Everyone in town went down to the train station to watch the fair equipment and wild animals being unloaded and moved to the fairgrounds. People traveled by buggies, wagons, and train to attend the event. Farmers had the opportunity to display and sell their crops and animals. Women displayed their needlework, baked goods, jams, and preserves. (Jewel Melton.)

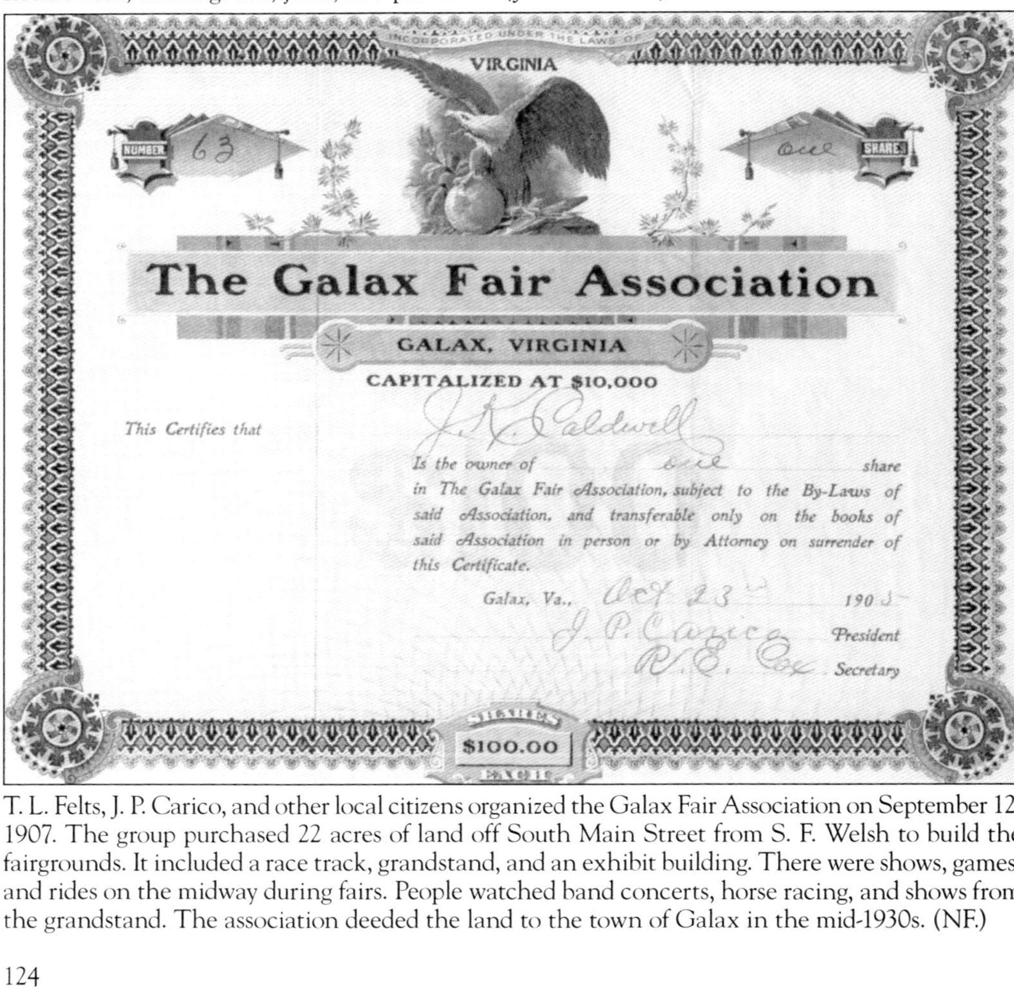

INCORPORATED UNDER THE LAWS OF VIRGINIA

NUMBER 63 — One SHARE

The Galax Fair Association

GALAX, VIRGINIA

CAPITALIZED AT $10,000

This Certifies that J. K. Caldwell *Is the owner of* one *share in The Galax Fair Association, subject to the By-Laws of said Association, and transferable only on the books of said Association in person or by Attorney on surrender of this Certificate.*

Galax, Va., Oct 23 *190*8

J. P. Carico *President*

R. E. Cox *Secretary*

SHARES $100.00 EACH

T. L. Felts, J. P. Carico, and other local citizens organized the Galax Fair Association on September 12, 1907. The group purchased 22 acres of land off South Main Street from S. F. Welsh to build the fairgrounds. It included a race track, grandstand, and an exhibit building. There were shows, games, and rides on the midway during fairs. People watched band concerts, horse racing, and shows from the grandstand. The association deeded the land to the town of Galax in the mid-1930s. (NF.)

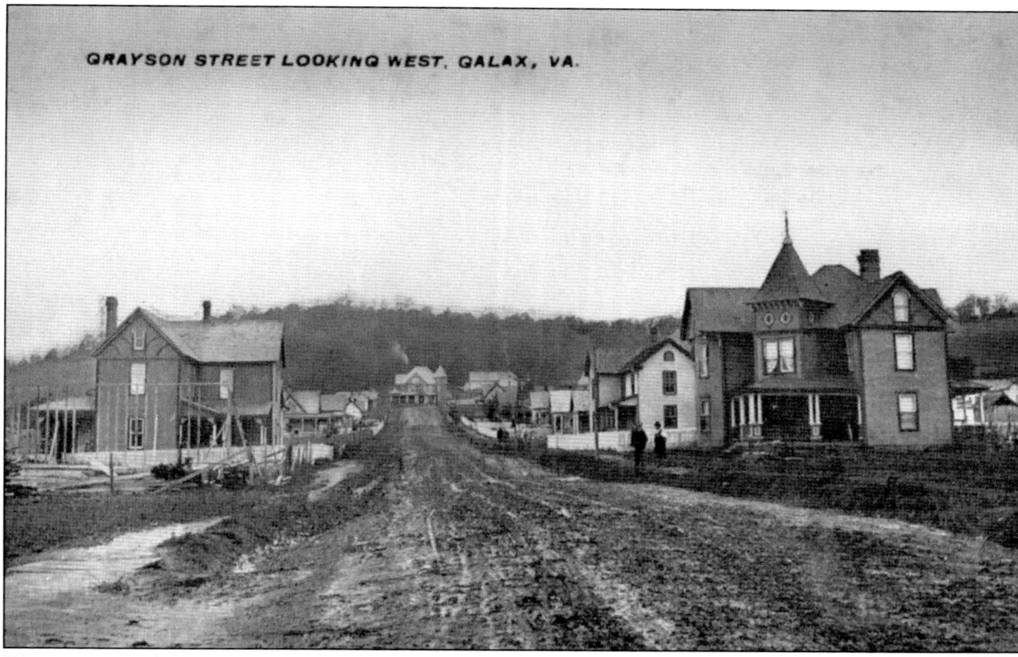

This is an early scene of Grayson Street looking west. The house at the right was the home of Mr. and Mrs. E. Laine Whitley. At the end of the street is the home of Dr. James Henry and Josephine Dufphey Witherow. Note the very muddy street. This was a major problem in Galax that was not addressed until 1923. (JJN.)

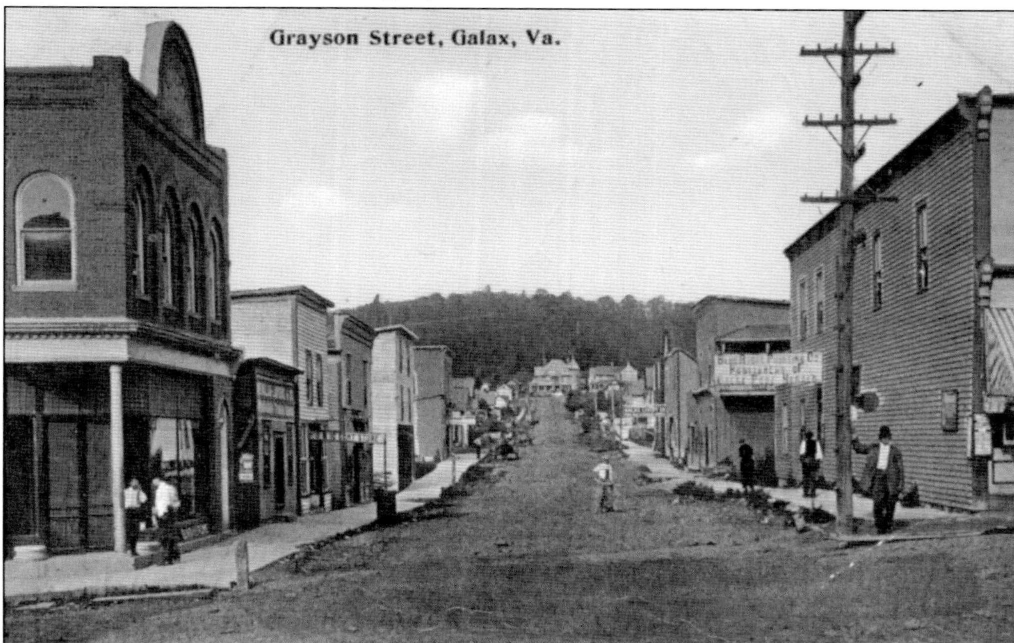

This postcard is dated April 21, 1913, and is the same view of Grayson Street looking west. The frame building on the right corner is Witherow's Drugstore. The J. C. Matthews Hardware Store is across the street on the south side of the intersection with Main Street. (JJN.)

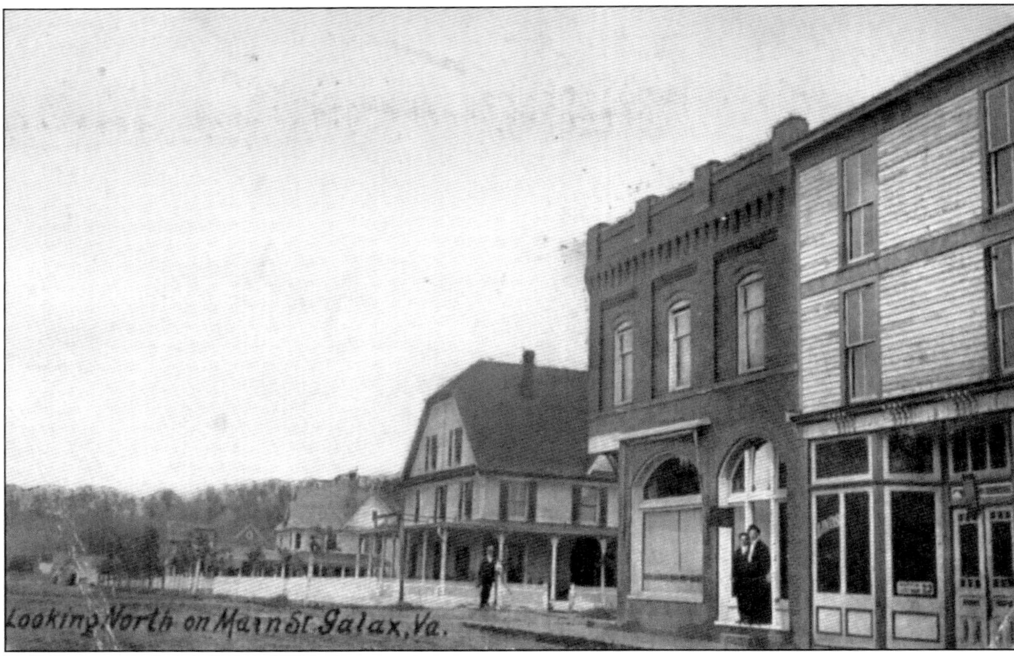

This is an old postcard, with the postmark of September 20, 1912, that was mailed with a 1¢ stamp. It provides an excellent view of the east side of North Main Street. The W. K. Early home is to the left of the Waugh Hotel, located on the northeast corner of Main and Center Street. The First National Bank was located on the southeast corner of Main and Center Street. Next door to the bank was the Curtis L. Lindsey store. (JJN.)

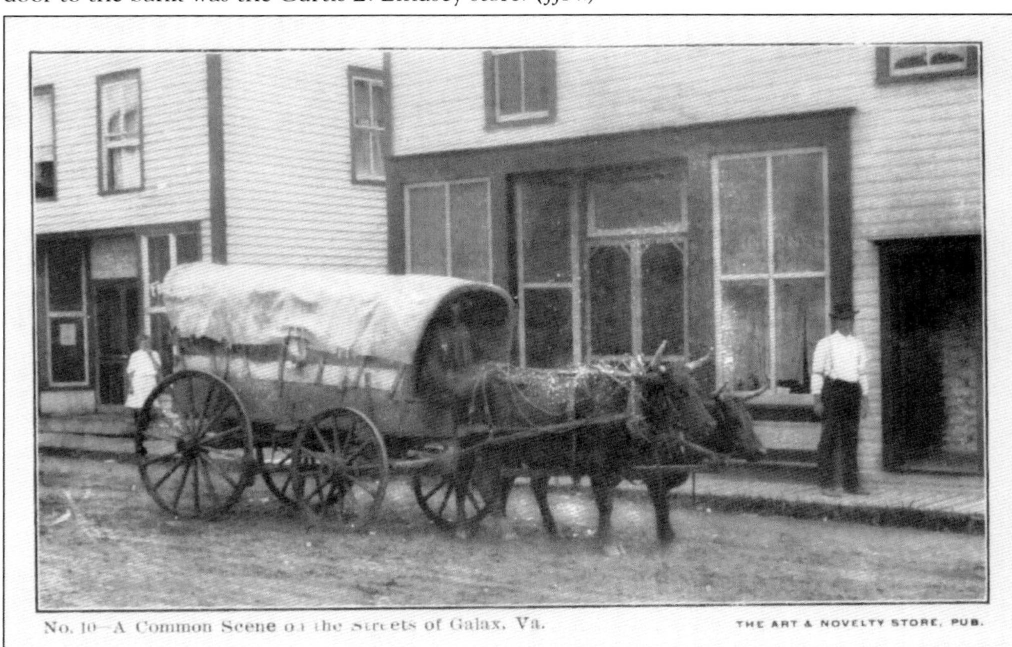

This photograph was taken before 1907. It shows an early street scene in Galax when covered wagons pulled by oxen were a common sight. The people in the picture are unidentified. (JJN.)

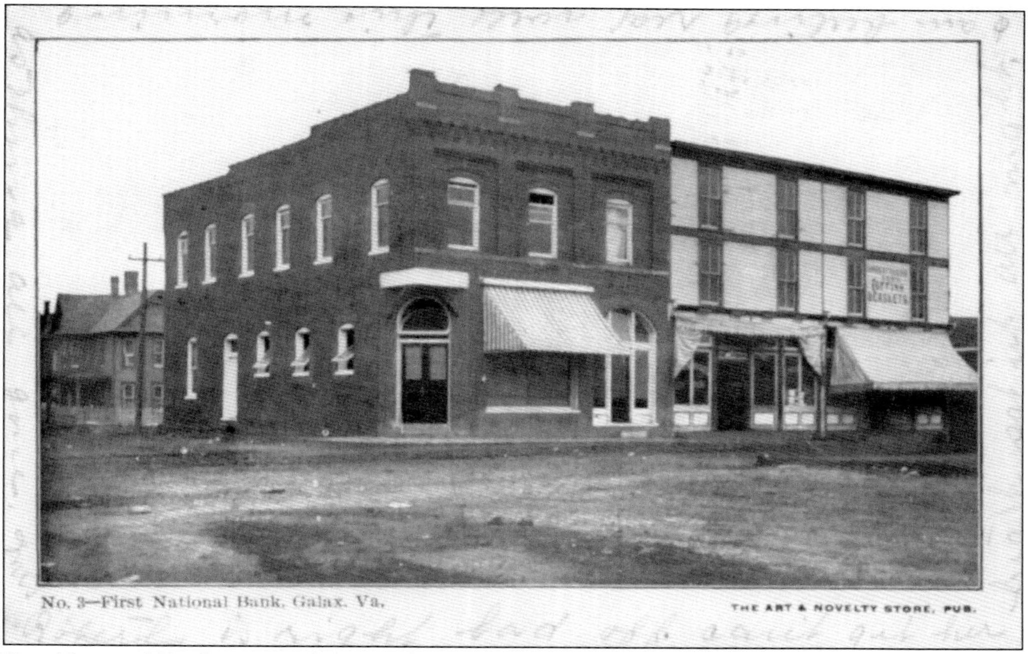

First National Bank occupied the southeast corner of Main and Center Streets until a new brick building was constructed on the northwest corner of Main and Grayson Streets. Construction of the new bank began in 1921. The Town of Galax purchased the original bank site and established town hall, a courtroom, council chambers, the police department, water services, and the fire department. (JJN.)

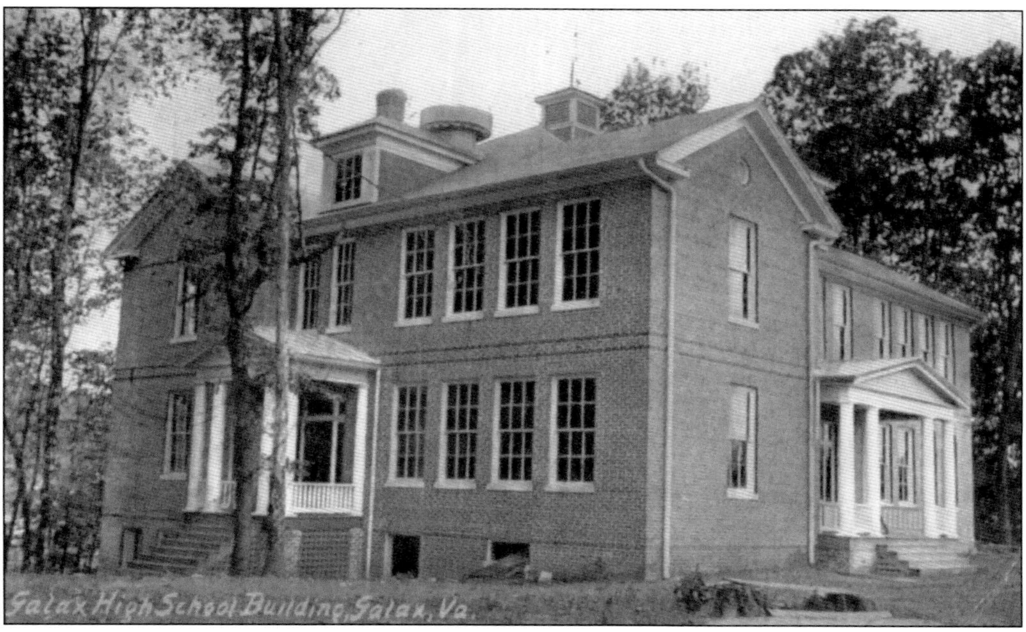

This postcard of Galax High School was mailed in September 1910 to a lady in Durham, North Carolina. The sender wrote that they had been attending the Galax Fair and having a fine time. What a perfect way to end the book. (JJN.)